# THE BOYS' CLUB

# MICHAEL WARNER

# THE BOYS' CLUB

hachette
AUSTRALIA

hachette
AUSTRALIA

Published in Australia and New Zealand in 2021
by Hachette Australia
(an imprint of Hachette Australia Pty Limited)
Level 17, 207 Kent Street, Sydney NSW 2000
www.hachette.com.au

10 9 8 7 6 5 4 3 2 1

 A catalogue record for this
book is available from the
NATIONAL
LIBRARY National Library of Australia
OF AUSTRALIA

ISBN: 978 0 7336 4494 8

Cover design by Luke Causby, Blue Cork
Front cover images: football courtesy iStock; Melbourne Cricket Ground courtesy Scott Barbour,
Getty Images; images of men standing courtesy Adobe Stock (9nong; curto; ArtFamily;
denisismagilov; ASDF; Steve Cukrov)
Typeset in Adobe Garamond Pro by Kirby Jones
Printed and bound in Australia by McPherson's Printing Group

*For Abby and Georgia,*
*who never got the chance*

# CONTENTS

# Author's note

JOURNALISM, SO THE SAYING GOES, IS A FRONT-ROW SEAT TO history. My grandfather, Denis Warner, was a newspaper man of international acclaim, covering conflicts across the globe; first as a commando in Syria during World War II and later as a war correspondent in the bloody theatres of the Pacific War, Korea, Malaya and Vietnam. The Melbourne *Herald*'s chairman, Sir Keith Murdoch, dispatched him to Asia in August 1945 with the simple instruction to 'tell us how it is'. It was a directive that would last a lifetime.

My own career at the same newspaper, which merged with the *Sun News-Pictorial* in 1990, pales embarrassingly into insignificance, but after a decade covering general news, state rounds, crime and gaming I was offered my own assignment: reporting on the politics of the nation's biggest sport, the AFL.

I love Australian Rules but the AFL machine I encountered concerned me. The national competition is controlled by a ruthlessly entitled Melbourne-based executive, given close to

1

free rein by a commission that long ago lost its oversight or will to intervene.

A lack of transparency and accountability in decision-making, jobs for the boys, bullying and a string of blatantly compromised 'integrity' investigations have become hallmarks of the AFL administration since the rise of Andrew Demetriou and his successor, Gillon McLachlan.

Deals are done and outcomes reached in almost every instance with brand protection (or defence of their own positions) the priorities. That's how you end up with scandals, cover-ups and farces like the Melbourne tanking affair, the West Coast Eagles illicit drugs crisis, the Essendon doping saga and the Talia brothers leaking case. The seeds of these episodes were not sown by the AFL but they festered and deepened as a result of AFL manipulation aimed at achieving a preferred outcome.

The accumulation of these decisions and behaviours presents a disturbing picture. They are not one-off events but a structured pattern of behaviour.

Nobody says there isn't a place for deal-making in dispute resolution, but when settlements are reached in legal proceedings the judge doesn't do the deal, the parties do. In the Essendon saga, the parties did a deal with the judge, jury and executioner. There is no independence or due process in the AFL's procedures. Worse, decisions are often made out of personal animus, because they can be.

I found that out for myself at the height of the Essendon debacle; first when Demetriou pressured then News Limited boss Kim Williams to sack me or stand me down from reporting on football, and later that same year when the AFL denied me accreditation to the 2013 finals.

I declare this up front, but I'm not on my own. This was standard operating procedure for an organisation that had learnt long before to punish those who questioned its authority.

The administration of the AFL can and should be better.

The purpose of this book is to shine a light on almost two decades of questionable conduct; a system in need of reform. The AFL's cosy relationships with governments, politicians, regulators and sections of the media must also change.

Many industry figures agreed to talk on the record about their views on the AFL. Some didn't have issues with the administration's conduct. Others did. A number of people involved in football also assisted me but declined to be identified, fearing retribution to themselves or their club. That alone speaks volumes. I have chosen to publish some of their comments to give context where appropriate.

To borrow a phrase from Sir Keith, I want to tell it how it is.

# Prologue

'Only when the tide goes out do you discover who's been swimming naked.'
Warren Buffett

GILLON MCLACHLAN, CHIEF EXECUTIVE OFFICER OF THE Australian Football League, weaved his way through the outbound customs and security lines at Melbourne Airport.

He was hard to miss.

Just shy of six foot five with dark foppish hair, McLachlan, the blue blood master deal-maker, was jetting off to Los Angeles on a week-long reconnaissance of America's best and boldest sporting stadiums.

It was the beginning of March 2020 and McLachlan's mission, accompanied by two senior AFL staff members, was to gather concepts for the redevelopment of the league's fully owned private football ground in Melbourne's Docklands business district.

A law graduate and unbending negotiator, McLachlan had played it beautifully, convincing the Victorian Labor government to foot the $225 million stadium rebuild bill as part of a deal to stage the AFL Grand Final at the Melbourne Cricket Ground (MCG) until 2057.

It was a classic AFL manoeuvre. Bag the elephant and get someone else to pay for it.

Life was good for the 47-year-old AFL boss about to embark on his sixth full season in the big swivel chair of Australia's richest and most powerful sport, boasting a national workforce of almost eight hundred.

A day earlier, in his office on the second floor of AFL House, the league's sprawling two-storey Melbourne headquarters, McLachlan expressed confidence in the AFL's ability to withstand the economic impact of the coronavirus crisis that had begun sweeping the world.

'Exposure for us is limited,' McLachlan declared in an interview with one of a handful of senior football journalists ushered into league headquarters for a private twenty-minute, season-eve audience with the game's supreme ruler. 'Things may change. Because we're a domestic game and, at the moment, the coronavirus has implications for those with supply chain or international links and that's not where we're at.

'So as we sit here today, without looking too far into the future, our economic exposure is limited. We look to the federal government and the relevant interested bodies for advice and, you know, until that changes, that's where we're at.'[1]

But, of course, things did change.

Rapidly. And catastrophically.

A short time later, back in Melbourne from his US trip, McLachlan conceded that the league would be forced to stage matches in front of empty grandstands if the COVID-19 outbreak worsened in Australia.

Just days after that, following an emergency telephone hook-up of AFL commissioners, he announced the home-and-away season had been cut from twenty-three rounds to seventeen rounds and the length of matches would be slashed. They were desperate moves for an increasingly desperate situation, all aimed at cramming multiple matches into the back end of the year if weeks and months were lost. And they would be.

Just after 4.30 p.m. on Sunday 22 March, before the year's opening round of games staged in depressingly empty stadiums had even been completed, an ashen-faced McLachlan fronted a press conference in the bowels of the same Docklands stadium he was preparing to renovate and announced he was suspending the 2020 season.

In the blink of an eye, the AFL's once impenetrable, $1 billion-a-year empire was on the brink of financial ruin.

The COVID-19 pandemic unleashed a trail of destruction on the world. The AFL was far from alone in suffering a crippling, almost instant loss of revenues. But the sudden shutdown of the eighteen-team national competition exposed an uncomfortable truth about Australia's biggest-spending, tax-exempt, sporting corporation. For all its chutzpah and market domination, when the music stopped the mighty AFL was unable to sustain itself. Not even for a single week.

An organisation that had pocketed billions of dollars in TV and sponsorship revenues across a two-decade golden run had plundered almost all of it on the expressway to supremacy.

'This has been a nuclear bomb going off for the AFL,' Collingwood president Eddie McGuire declared. 'The Channel 7 money, the Foxtel money, stopped this week. It's finished, it's all over ... The bottom line is footy could lose over $500 million this year. That's on our best day. And we could still go under.'[2]

The morning after the season was postponed 80 per cent of the AFL industry workforce was stood down without pay, propped up on government-funded JobKeeper subsidies. Many would never return.

It would be eighty-two days before footy returned and when it did it was a sad, diminished version of itself played in front of ghostly empty grandstands before the game's Victorian heartland was abandoned completely for the staging of matches with socially distanced crowds in Queensland, South Australia and Western Australia.

Stripped naked, the AFL was eating the same humble pie it had served up cold to countless adversaries over a twenty-year reign of arrogance.

But McLachlan was no stranger to a crisis. He'd helped steer the competition through scandal and upheaval before and would plot another way out of hell. Those who have faced off against him describe an unnerving, calculating opponent who avoids face-to-face confrontation where he can, unlike his predecessor, Andrew Demetriou, whose preferred approach was a sledgehammer to the head.

'I'm trying to be your friend, but this is how it is,' explained one casualty of McLachlan's method. 'He doesn't get angry or raise his voice, but it isn't really a negotiation either. He gives you the impression he's being reasonable, but he's not. It's accept what we are offering or else.'

Only this time, McLachlan didn't have all the answers. No amount of government lobbying or backroom manoeuvring could stop the coronavirus tidal wave.

Attempts to convince the governments of Western Australia, South Australia and Tasmania to hand the AFL special exemptions to stage matches outside strict quarantine regulations were rebuffed. If not for a Queensland premier keen on a win in an election year, the season may not have been completed.

Within weeks of the shutdown in March, the impenetrable walls of AFL House were being scaled by club bosses and a players' union demanding the league throw open its books and conform to full financial transparency for the first time in a generation.

Unable to meet its contractual obligations to broadcast partners Channel 7 and Foxtel, the game's lucrative TV rights deals were drastically downsized and an emergency $600 million line of credit was secured from the banks, which ultimately wasn't needed as the league found a way to pull the season from the fire.

In late October, in the days leading up to the historic night grand final played between Richmond and Geelong at the Gabba in Brisbane – the first premiership decider ever staged outside the competition's Victorian heartland – two separate incidents told the tale of what the game had endured and the remedy it so desperately needed.

Former AFL boss Demetriou had joined the board of Crown Resorts as an independent director at the invitation of its billionaire owner James Packer just six months after vacating the league's top post. In Sydney on Tuesday, 13 October 2020, Demetriou appeared at a public inquiry probing Crown Resorts' fitness to hold a New South Wales casino licence because of its failure to police money laundering and its relationship with junket operators linked to Chinese criminals.

Demetriou's train-wreck testimony descended into farce when he was caught red-handed reading from notes about a definition of 'culture' he admitted he had downloaded 'off the net'.[3] His notes also contained a description of the duties of an independent director, of which he clearly needed to be reminded.

An email tendered under evidence from Demetriou to Packer had also exposed the ex-league supremo's concerns that the board's focus on legal compliance was coming at the expense of profits.[4] 'We exist to win; I asked management and the board to come back in the new year and turn our minds to strategies and to grow revenue,' Demetriou told Packer. 'I remain committed to serving the best interests of Crown and, most importantly, you.'

Such brazen behaviour and conduct had been tolerated – and even lauded – during his reign at the top of the AFL. But now he was beyond the protection of the sycophantic Melbourne bubble he had stood over for more than a decade and he was eviscerated for his performance in the witness box.

Coincidentally, the very next day, 14 October 2020, Sydney Swans chairman Andrew Pridham spoke up in a meeting between club bosses and the game's powerful ruling body, the AFL Commission, and suggested it was time for a sweeping structural review of the entire competition. Within weeks, Pridham had secured the support of multiple club bosses.

The jig was almost up.

A virus had exposed the country's most bloated and secretive sporting bureaucracy and done what no person had come remotely close to achieving.

COVID-19 had derailed the boys' club.

But for how long?

# CHAPTER 1

# Cape Schanck

THE EXCHANGE THAT LED THE AUSTRALIAN FOOTBALL League down the road of no return took place in a conference room of the Cape Schanck Resort on the Mornington Peninsula, an hour and fifteen minutes drive to the south of Melbourne, in the winter of 2000.

On the final morning of the AFL planning and strategy workshop, the league's freshly appointed general manager of football operations, Andrew Demetriou, bluntly asked the man who had just hired him, AFL Commission chairman Ron Evans, to consider a seismic change.

It was time, Demetriou urged his boss, for the commission – the game's powerful ruling body since 1984 – to step back and cede greater control to the AFL executive team.

'Wayne Jackson was the CEO but it was Andrew who brought it up,' an official present at the Cape Schanck retreat recalled. 'He felt the executive were being under-utilised and should take the lead in making decisions and driving the future strategy of the AFL.'

Evans, the wealthy managing director of the Spotless Services catering empire, was the sole commissioner to make the trip down the peninsula. He listened intently and agreed to take the proposal back to his fellow commissioners.

For almost two decades, the heavy-lifting and key negotiation of matters affecting Australia's biggest sport – the introduction of new clubs, television broadcast rights and major stadium deals – had been led by formidable hands-on commissioners like Graeme Samuel, Peter Scanlon and Ross Oakley.

But within weeks, Demetriou got the answer that he wanted.

Greater authority and strategic responsibility would be handed to Jackson's executive team, including 39-year-old Demetriou, the league's fierce and ambitious administrator, who would become chief executive officer less than three years later.

'They released the shackles and let us go,' the official said.

There would be no turning back.

\*\*\*

A second-generation Australian from the wrong side of the Yarra River, Andrew Demetriou's rise to the top of the nation's most powerful sporting code was achieved against all odds.

The youngest of four sons to Greek Cypriot immigrants who ran a fish and chip shop in Bell Street, Coburg, Demetriou attended the rough and tumble Newlands High School, next-door to Pentridge Prison, in Melbourne's inner-north.

It was less than ten kilometres away, but may as well have been a million miles, from the privileged private schools of the city's leafy east that would feed the top ranks of his administration.

Maybe that's what drove him?

'The joke amongst the students was that the prison wardens in the towers used to point their guns at us,' a school friend of Demetriou told me. 'No one busted a door down to get in there. There were a lot of kids from low-income working-class families. Every week there was always some sort of fight arranged after school down at Coburg Lake Reserve, it was that kind of school.'

Demetriou completed his HSC in 1978 – one of less than twenty from his year level to do so. He played footy for Pascoe Vale and studied at La Trobe University. And in his climb to the top of the AFL bureaucracy, he made some friends and some enemies. A lot of people who have met him on the course of his career don't like the man.

'It was in his DNA to be an arsehole,' the school mate said. 'Even back then he felt his shit smelt like roses. He was always looking for an angle or opportunity to benefit himself. He could never be told, you could never challenge him and he always thought he knew better than you.

'He was an okay footballer, but an even better cricketer. He bowled fast and had a magnificent, fluid action, it was like poetry. One of the best I've ever seen.'

But Australian Rules won out and Demetriou got his chance at North Melbourne, where he would play 103 games and another three at Hawthorn between 1981 and 1988.

'When he came in for a contract negotiation, Andrew was always looking for Keith Greig's salary or Malcolm Blight's salary – and, of course, he never got it,' veteran Kangaroos administrator Ron Joseph recalled. 'But he was never backward in coming forward. He used to be very critical of Cable [North Melbourne champion Barry Cable] in a very condescending sort of a way, which used to give me the shits.[1]

'Cabes was a down to earth, simple sort of a bloke, and sometimes he'd get his English wrong and Demetriou was the first one to be sniggering in the locker room with the players,' he explained. 'Barry had a way of pronouncing Wednesday, which was "Wen-des-day" – it was a habit he grew up with as a kid in country WA, and he never corrected it. It stayed with him because he never had any need to change it, but Demetriou used to titter behind his back with other players of his ilk about it. I would hear it and I always read it in a nasty vindictive way. I used to hate it.'

Teammate Grant Thomas played with Demetriou for two seasons in 1983 and 1984 after shifting to North Melbourne from St Kilda. The pair butted heads from the start.

'Demetriou was this brash, arrogant, supremely confident bloke who took the piss out of some of the younger guys who I felt couldn't defend themselves, even though he was relatively young himself,' Thomas said.[2]

'I had him pegged, so any time I heard him giving it to one of the younger guys in the locker room, I'd stick it to him – and he hated it,' Thomas claimed. 'He'd say, "Why are you having a go at me?" And I'd just say, "Listen – any time you have a go at one of my teammates, who are usually more vulnerable and younger, I'm going to have a go at you. So stop having a go at them and I'll stop having a go at you – how about that for a deal?"

'That's when I said that they built the fence at Arden Street to keep him on the ground,' he added, in a dig at Demetriou's on-field bravery. 'I wasn't by any means the toughest or hardest player going around in that day, and I can assure you Andrew wasn't either, but the disparity between his verbal strength and physical strength on the footy field was a bridge too far.'

Thomas recalled Demetriou, a lover of horse racing, being heavily involved in the players' regular punting syndicates.

Most players worked jobs in the semi-professional era, and for a while Demetriou taught politics and legal studies at Melbourne's Trinity Grammar, where Ron Joseph had been a student in the 1950s and early 1960s.

The school's headmaster, Don Marles, called the North Melbourne stalwart for a character reference prior to employing Demetriou in 1984. 'I told him, "We're not friends, but I'm not going to tell you not to employ him,"' Joseph said. 'Don called me some time later, and angrily said, "I've just let your mate Andrew Demetriou go for gambling with a student."'

A sentence buried away in *The Age* newspaper in May 2003, after Demetriou announced himself as a candidate in the race to replace the retiring Wayne Jackson as AFL CEO, said: 'The only professional black mark during his career at North was when he departed Trinity Grammar school – where he taught legal studies during the '80s – after an incident in which Demetriou and one of his 16-year-old students together placed money on a horse.'[3]

Demetriou cut his losses and ventured into the false-teeth distribution business in 1987. 'We used to drive to Sydney and, because it would save money, sell out of the boot of the car,' he later said of his company's fledgling days. But the dentures game soon turned lucrative.

'The colour has to last,' Demetriou told the *Australian Financial Review* of the winning falsies formula in 1996. 'Teeth get mixed with saliva, water, food, and they still have to be the same colour five years later ...'[4]

'In Australia, we require whiter teeth. In Europe, they want darker teeth, more yellow, to go with the darker complexion. In Asia, they want small teeth.'

But then the Asian financial crisis hit, the export market dried up and Demetriou got crunched, borrowing a small amount of money from his Western Australian business partner, the future West Coast Eagles chairman Dalton Gooding, to help make ends meet.

Demetriou's big professional break came in 1998 when he emerged as a surprise choice as chief executive of the AFL Players' Association (AFLPA), thanks to the backing of a loose group that included players (and future coaches) Alastair Clarkson and John Longmire; and top player agent Ricky Nixon.

Nixon recalled receiving a phone call about Demetriou from one of his biggest clients, Hawthorn superstar Jason Dunstall. 'Dunstall rang me and said could I see Demetriou because he was hoping to get involved in football,' Nixon said. 'I met Demetriou literally an hour later at a hotel in Collingwood. I was very impressed. He seemed like a very switched-on bloke. I rang a couple of my players and convinced them that Demetriou was the right man for the job.'[5]

Essendon star James Hird, a member of the players' union's executive, was one of those contacted by Nixon, who urged him to meet with Demetriou and support his bid for an interview. 'John Longmire and myself met with him and then recommended to the people who were doing the interviews that they should interview him,' Hird recalled. 'It wasn't that he should get the job, but more that he had a football background, was very commercial and had been successful in business. That's what we were told anyway. Ricky Nixon was very much integral in putting him up.'[6]

The irony of Hird helping Demetriou break into football administration would surface spectacularly more than two decades later.

Another Demetriou advocate was lawyer and influential North Melbourne and West Coast Eagles powerbroker John Adams, the son of legendary Roos administrator Jack Adams.

Brendan Schwab – son of the late AFL commissioner Alan Schwab – who had founded Professional Footballers Australia (the Australian soccer players' union) in 1993, had been the raging favourite to win the AFLPA job until Demetriou and his backers swooped.

Demetriou immediately restructured the AFL players' union, achieving 100 per cent membership for the first time, and negotiated a generous collective bargaining agreement between the league and its 672 players, which saw the minimum wage increase to $35,000 and $1750 per senior game.

'In all fairness, that deal was better than we'd ever had before,' Hird told me years after the Essendon supplements saga.

Media star Eddie McGuire, who had secured the Collingwood presidency in October 1998, offered Demetriou the Magpies chief executive job over lunch at a Richmond café in 1999, but Demetriou had eyes on a bigger prize.

He had impressed commission chairman Evans and fellow league commissioner Bill Kelty, the Australian Council of Trade Unions secretary, and was installed as the AFL's football operations chief in June 2000, soon after the departure of Ian Collins and barely two years into his tenure at the AFLPA.

'His appointment was heavily pushed by Kelty,' commissioner of the day Terry O'Connor recalled.[7] Kelty had quietly told Demetriou that the football operations role was really just an 'apprenticeship' to the big job.

And he was right.

On 30 July 2003 – at the age of forty-two – Andrew Demetriou, the scrapper from Newlands High, became the most powerful man in Australian sport: chief executive officer of the AFL.

It was a genuine rags-to-riches rise.

'I don't imagine there will ever be a scandal attached to Andrew. He's a straight arrow,' friend, historian and prime ministerial speechwriter Don Watson declared at the time.[8]

How wrong he was.

\*\*\*

On the face of it, the AFL Demetriou shaped would become a beacon for professional sport: eighteen clubs across five states fuelled by boundless commercial riches and community passion.

'Andrew remains, to me, the best visceral negotiator I have ever seen,' one veteran club boss said. 'Where some leaders will spend hours thinking about what they are going to say, he just went into a room and imposed his personality. The stadium deals he secured with government backing, and with almost no money from the AFL itself, were extraordinary.'

Only three other sporting competitions around the world – the National Football League (NFL) in the USA, Germany's Bundesliga and the English Premier League – boast bigger average crowds than the AFL.

As foundation commissioner Peter Scanlon said: 'The competition is in great shape. It's got to be the envy of any other comparable sporting code in Australia. It's just so far ahead of anyone else.'[9]

But something else was at play.

Unlike its rival sporting codes – cricket, soccer and rugby league – the AFL was its own world governing body, unelected and answerable to no one.

A culture of arrogance, a sense of entitlement and the absence of accountability contaminated the AFL administration.

Lucrative contracts were dished out to industry mates without transparent tendering processes and the league's much-vaunted commitment to 'integrity' would take a back seat when more valuable commercial interests were at stake.

Transparency and due process were discarded, replaced by horse trading, intimidation and heavily negotiated backroom deals.

Anybody or anything that stood in the path of the modern AFL was steamrolled or sacrificed to protect the empire.

Legal professionals encountering the AFL's 'justice' system for the first time expressed astonishment at the brazen conduct and behaviour of the league's most senior officials. James Hird's solicitor, Steven Amendola, bluntly described the AFL as a 'bunch of cashed-up bogans', who believed they could behave in any way they wanted.[10]

The AFL's *raison d'être* had been to champion the interests of the clubs, its players and the fans, but somewhere along the line was recast to prioritise its own self-interests. The ruling body was unrecognisable from the one the twelve Victorian Football League (VFL) clubs envisaged when they endorsed the appointment of a new independent commission to take charge of the game's administrative affairs 'on a trial basis' on 7 November 1984.

The Masters of the Universe had taken over, and a once-potent commission laden with prominent football figures and business luminaries was relegated to honorary status, stacked with manageable interstate commissioners with little football IQ.

Ron Evans' death, in March 2007, opened the way for businessman and ex-Carlton ruckman Mike Fitzpatrick to take the wheel and embolden the new culture. He agreed with Demetriou's philosophy that it was the executive that should take the lead.

'During the Ross Oakley–Wayne Jackson era, AFL commissioners were hands-on in the day-to-day operations of the league,' retired commissioner Graeme Samuel explained.[11] 'All that changed under Demetriou, and the commission reverted to a board of directors role. In theory it's okay, but you've also got to then have a chair that's just keeping in control of things, and I was never terribly sure that Mike was sufficiently engaged.'

Former Victorian premier and Hawthorn president Jeff Kennett was more direct. 'Mike was a fairly suave fellow and very focused on what he wanted to achieve and Andrew was worse,' he said. 'I mean, I get on well with Andrew but he can be a thug, and he was a thug, very domineering and very insistent.'[12]

The emergence of a rising star executive from South Australia called Gillon McLachlan, Demetriou's long-time henchman and ultimate successor, completed footy's Gang of Three.

When Demetriou walked at the height of the Essendon drugs inferno in March 2014, it was McLachlan, anointed by his boss and appointed by Fitzpatrick, who would step in, carry on and ensure an external applicant wouldn't get the chance to take a peep under the rug.

They all take credit for the growth of the game but in truth the hardest yards in establishing a national competition had been ploughed during the Oakley era, and armies of rusted-on, tribal fans across the southern states all but guarantee success, despite the steady erosion of football's charm.

'The successors I don't think realise what has been delivered to them on a plate,' former West Coast Eagles and

Sydney Swans chairman Richard Colless said. 'If you look at the natural advantages that the game has got – there are any number of people who could do the job. It's not like there are only eight or nine chosen ones.'[13]

The debacle of the $250 million Gold Coast Suns expansion club was proof of that, bearing the fingerprints of Demetriou, Fitzpatrick and McLachlan. 'They've got the greatest product in the world, without any competition – it's impossible to fuck up – so how they ever mucked up what they did with the Gold Coast Suns is simply extraordinary,' one club boss said.

Muddying the waters for football fans seeking to make sense of it all is a band of senior club figures, journalists, broadcasters, lawyers and player agents with their own snouts buried deep in the AFL trough. A symbiotic relationship exists between many of the game's key stakeholders. They rely on each other and protect each other. The old school ties that bind are everywhere, some carefully hand-picked, others strongly recommended.

Good people turn a blind eye. Few speak out, few rock the boat, and when they do, they're attacked, blackballed or ostracised. Rewards for playing ball and keeping it all in-house are rich. Take your medicine. Suck it up. Don't become an enemy of the state.

\*\*\*

So how exactly did an organisation morph, in less than a generation, from a fledgling state administrative sporting body to a full-blown football dictatorship, controlled by a closed circle of powerful executives, industry mates and loyal enablers?

Scores of past and present administrators, staff, volunteers and, of course, the players who put on the show can be proud of their work and sacrifice in helping to build a thriving national competition.

The bulk of the football media – writers, broadcasters, photographers and camera operators – play a crucial role in covering and celebrating the Australian game. Footy at its core is magnificent.

But there have been too many instances of compromised AFL investigations, cover-ups, lies, leaks and character assassinations since the early 2000s for it all to be a coincidence.

There are too many people out there with stories to tell about threats, bullying and intimidation. Many have assisted in the writing of this book.

This is the inside story of the deals and behaviours that have shaped Australia's biggest sport.

## CHAPTER 2

# Rivers of gold

THE BOARDROOM OF THE AUSTRALIAN FOOTBALL LEAGUE sits at the far end of the second level of the competition's two-storey headquarters overlooking Victoria Harbour and Bolte Bridge in Melbourne's busy Docklands business district.

Dark leather chairs surround a large rectangular table in the centre of the room where the suits behind Australia's biggest sport meet each month to chart the course of supremacy.

Gold-framed portraits of long-gone Victorian Football League administrators like Charles Brownlow, William C. McClelland and Sir Kenneth Luke peer down from the walls, a reminder of footy's simpler times.

A door at the rear of the boardroom leads directly to the office of the chief executive officer. Here, in the quiet executive wing of AFL House, the game's overlord, his personal assistant and his deputy have access to a small private kitchen and their own private bathrooms. On days of crisis, and there have been plenty of those, it has served as a welcome retreat from the raging inferno outside.

At the turn of the century, just seventy-six people worked for the AFL in far humbler digs on the southern side of the MCG in East Melbourne, but by the mid-2000s, under the stewardship of Andrew Demetriou, the AFL had come to see itself as a major Australian corporation. Accomplishment was measured through key performance indicators, or KPIs – crowds, ratings and revenues – and the mega bucks were rolling in.

In 2003, AFL revenues were disclosed at $170.9 million and attendances at stadiums across the country at 5.87 million. A decade later, it had grown to $446.5 million with attendances at 6.36 million, and by 2019, revenues topped $794 million and attendances reached 7.5 million.

Between 2017 and 2019, the league banked combined profits of almost $150 million and by early 2020 – before the coronavirus crisis – it was reporting net assets of $240 million and a reserve fund of almost $60 million.

The advance of the empire was fuelled by an explosion in TV rights cash.

Once worth as little as $200,000, the AFL broadcast rights fetched about $3 million a season in 1986, $17 million in 1993, $100 million in 2001, $250 million in 2011 and a mammoth $416 million in 2017 thanks to a monster $2.5 billion, six-year deal split between Fox Sports and Channel 7.

Sponsorship deals also soared with a car manufacturer pumping $17 million a year into the AFL's coffers alone. A supermarket chain paid another $3 million as part of a deal to advertise its logo in the centre circle of all AFL grounds.

Under the design of the league's socialist system where the stronger clubs are curtailed and the weaker clubs propped up, the rivers of gold that flowed into AFL headquarters were distributed at the discretion of the commission, meaning most clubs had become reliant, over time, on head office for survival.

It was from here, as the keeper of the purse and controller of the economics, that the AFL's all-conquering power over its clubs and subordinates was born.

'In truth, I think they enjoy having clubs on the poverty line; it feeds the dictatorship,' one club boss said. 'Do you want your money or not?'

By early 2020, before the league began slashing jobs because of the impact of COVID-19, staff numbers within the league's bureaucracy had exploded to a staggering 795 – almost as many workers as the eighteen-team competition had players.

The AFL machine was divided into multiple departments – not unlike government ministries – with rank-and-file workers reporting to a senior executive in charge of each portfolio. Members of the executive team grew to a dozen, each paid hefty six- and sometimes seven-figure salaries, beefed up by a generous annual bonus system introduced by Demetriou.

Documents annually filed with the Australian Securities and Investments Commission (ASIC) revealed the AFL's twelve executives were paid a combined $10.73 million – including bonuses of $3.56 million in 2018 – equating to an average salary package of $894,000. But the exact size of their individual salaries (other than the CEO's wage until 2017) has never been publicly disclosed.

In his first year at the helm of the AFL, Demetriou took home $560,000, but by 2012, his salary, including bonuses, hit $2.2 million. In 2014, his final year in charge – despite his contentious handling of the Essendon drugs debacle – his salary topped a colossal $3.8 million.

Skyrocketing salaries within the AFL's top ranks became an annual source of embarrassment when financial papers were lodged with ASIC.

So the AFL made the issue go away.

In early 2018, AFL Commission chairman Richard Goyder enforced a policy change that stipulated the wages of Demetriou's successor, Gillon McLachlan, would no longer be aired publicly.[1]

Only one of the eighteen club presidents dared question it.

'There is no accountability, in real terms, at the AFL,' the sole dissenter, Hawthorn president and former Victorian premier Jeff Kennett, declared. 'They don't have to report to anyone. They report to themselves.'[2]

Ex-commissioner and retired Western Australian Anti-Corruption Commission head Terry O'Connor, QC, said the amounts being paid to the senior executives was 'absurd'. 'In my view Ross Oakley [AFL CEO from 1986 to 1996] did the really hard yards in getting the AFL competition established and his successors have had all the benefit of that work – and Ross was paid nothing like the amounts they are getting today,' O'Connor told me before his death in early 2020. 'And in so far as their bonuses depend on crowd numbers, it must be remembered that crowd numbers can be influenced by fixturing. Paying bonuses for what they do is just so over the top because the game basically sells itself.'[3]

But money, it seems, is no object.

In 2011, the Hawthorn board discussed – and immediately rejected – what it considered to be a $10 million 'bribe' from the AFL (to be paid over five years) to tear up the club's contract to play four 'home' matches a season in Tasmania, thus leaving the Apple Isle free for North Melbourne to occupy.[4]

This wasn't the only thing the AFL was happy to splurge on.

Such is the secrecy surrounding AFL expenditure, even club presidents are denied access to details surrounding wages, departmental costs and personal expenses splashed out by the league's top brass. Business class flights, fine dining and rooms at the best hotels are all ploughed through the AFL corporate credit card in the name of being the 'keeper of the code'.

Long-time Sydney Swans boss Richard Colless said it never sat well with him when AFL staff, some he said he would never have employed, would get on a plane and slump into a business class seat, while 'the people running the businesses that actually added the value were sitting down the back because they didn't have the money'.

Explained Colless, 'It was just a bloody bad look.'[5]

It wasn't until mid-2019, after concerns were flagged about exorbitant waste at head office, that business class flights on trips of less than two hours were finally reined in.

But a rule allowing AFL executives and commissioners to stay in swank five-star hotels, while rank-and-file staff had to settle for lesser digs still rankled many. One high-rolling AFL executive, who resided interstate, insisted on regular business class commutes flying Qantas, instead of the league's preferred carrier Virgin, and stayed at Melbourne's five-star Crown Towers in Southbank over the slightly less salubrious Sofitel in Collins Street that was deemed good enough for interstate commissioners to use. The league later rented the executive a CBD apartment. 'That is symbolic of a culture that hasn't progressed,' a senior league figure told me. 'They drive the cultural wedge between the haves and the have-nots. There is a sense of entitlement at the top of the AFL that is absolutely insidious. They eat, drink and pay themselves a ridiculous amount of money relative to their staff.'

Preferential treatment for the executives stepped up a notch in 2017 when a special wardrobe allowance was introduced, allowing female execs to purchase high-end designer shoes and dresses to be worn at league events.

'Given they are on huge six-figure salaries and receive enormous annual bonuses, it's hard to see why they would need money for a dress more than all the other women in the business who spend thousands of dollars a year to look the part,' one staffer said. 'But it's all about lining the pockets of the executives and everyone else just needs to feel honoured they are allowed to be in their presence.'

The excessive remuneration scheme let loose at AFL House meant at one point the highest paid executive in the game earned almost four times as much as the best paid player. Delegations from US sporting codes expressed astonishment at the disparity when meeting the AFL players' union during a visit in 2011. The average player still earns about $400,000.

Pay negotiations between the AFL and the game's stars turned ugly in 2011 and again in 2017 as the league point-blank refused the union's demand for a fixed 27 per cent share of the game's revenues.

Demetriou, who in a previous life had acted for the players as head of the AFL Players' Association, described the demand as 'a lazy way of doing business', staring them down in 2011 before his successor, McLachlan, relented six years later.

\*\*\*

Key to the AFL's financial might is its curious status as a tax-exempt not-for-profit organisation. Outdated taxation laws going back to the early 1950s exempt not-for-profit entities established 'for the encouragement of sport' from coughing up. Effectively, the AFL is treated the same way as a charity and pays no income tax. But unlike a charity it is not subject to regulatory oversight by the Charities and Not-for-profits Commission.

It would take a brave government to challenge the tax-free status of the AFL or NRL, but the free kick is hard to justify given the exorbitant executive wages and billions of dollars in government funding dished out for sporting stadiums and community programs.

'My understanding is that at some point the AFL sought a private ruling from the commissioner of tax that they were eligible for income tax exemption,' University of Melbourne taxation specialist Professor Ann O'Connell explained. 'I would argue that even if, say twenty years ago, they were primarily – "for the encouragement of sport" – that is no longer the case. To come within the exemption, the encouragement of sport must be the main purpose and any other purposes such as providing social facilities for members or engaging in commercial activities may only be incidental or ancillary. It could be argued that, given the size of the commercial activities, the making of profit is now the predominant purpose of the AFL.'[6]

The AFL is a company limited by guarantee under the *Corporations Act* and, in theory, it is the 'appointees' from each of the eighteen clubs that control the league and vote for the directors, or in this case the commissioners.

The reality is far different, but for the purpose of avoiding tax, it's a lucrative arrangement.

According to Professor O'Connell, 'The notion of "not-for-profit" means that the entity must not make distributions to members. In fact, that is just what the AFL does – it distributes most of its revenue to the clubs. In addition, being a not-for-profit means there is a principle of "no private benefit". The most common example of private benefit is excessive remuneration of officers and employees. Unfortunately, we do not know what Gillon McLachlan and others are paid.

'Although the AFL is not obliged by the *Corporations Act* to provide a remuneration report as part of its annual financial report, an entity that receives significant public funding and tax concessions should be held to a higher standard of accountability,' she said.

For the cherry on top, the AFL's dubious 'charity' status also makes it eligible for a reduced rate of Fringe Benefits Tax (FBT).

'This means that benefits such as cars and credit cards can be given to AFL executives and employees and the AFL only pays half the rate of FBT of other employers,' Professor O'Connell said. 'This exemption from tax in other jurisdictions is not usually extended to professional sporting bodies. For example, in the United Kingdom only a "community or amateur sporting association" is exempt from corporation tax. But will a federal government do anything about it? I very much doubt it.'

\*\*\*

The grand old town of Melbourne is footy's epicentre and cornerstone of the cartel.

Nine of the league's eighteen teams are located within a thirty-kilometre radius of the CBD. A tenth team is based in Geelong, less than an hour's drive to the west.

Australian Rules is like a religion in Victoria. Days of the winter week are spent counting down until a chosen tribe returns to weekend battle. In between, team selections and football issues are endlessly dissected by newspapers, radio stations and top-rating TV shows. Almost 700,000 Victorians are paid-up members of an AFL club; about one in ten of every man, woman and child.

Footy is the great social leveller, a conversation starter for Melburnians of all walks of life. Fans, rich and poor, can talk about their beloved game in the street, around the water cooler at work or in the local pub until the cows come home.

To serve on the board of an AFL club, or in the higher echelon of the commission, is to wear a badge of honour. Bankers, business leaders, lawyers, politicians and media stars clamour to be appointed. Most are driven by a genuine love of the game and have helped transform their clubs into accomplished professional organisations in their own right.

In times gone by it was the clubs who chose the AFL commissioners. In theory, commission members are still selected by a nominations committee, which includes club presidents, but in reality, they have been hand-picked from within – like-minded men, and a few women, who play by the rules and stay the course.

Long-time North Melbourne director Peter de Rauch recalled attending a meeting of club bosses at The Australian Club in William Street, Melbourne, in August 1999 as a proxy for Kangaroos president Ron Casey. The clubs had gathered to nominate a preferred candidate to fill a commission vacancy only to be told that the AFL had already appointed retired Hawthorn defender Chris Langford.

'Bang. That was it,' de Rauch said. 'From then onwards the clubs had no say in who gets on, they just appointed their mates. That's when it became a boys' club.[7]

'Everything started off okay because they said we were all stakeholders and could vote on the commissioners, which we did a few times, but then it all changed.'

Colless said the stripping of the clubs' right to appoint commissioners 'just happened by osmosis'. 'It was a gradual thing,' he said. 'Almost under the cover of darkness the nominations committee became two members of the commission and two hand-picked club presidents.'

Captains of industry in their own right, commissioners can become intoxicated by the power when their feet slide under the boardroom table at AFL House.

Top silk David Galbally, QC, recalled a hearing before the commission in late 2012 into blatant salary cap cheating by the Adelaide Crows. Galbally was representing star forward Kurt Tippett who was guaranteed payments of $200,000 outside of his contract in a secret arrangement masterminded by Crows chief executive Steven Trigg and agreed by his manager, Peter Blucher.

The hearing was closed and the Tippett camp pushed unsuccessfully for it to be open 'in the hope the truth would be revealed'.

'The commission were very anti-Tippett and very sympathetic to Trigg, who was a favoured administrator,' Galbally said. 'They gave Trigg a terrific hearing and that is what annoyed me. It was very, very clear that he had a much better relationship with the AFL than we had. It was aimed at getting Tippett and Peter Blucher.'

Galbally complained to Linda Dessau (an AFL commissioner who would become Governor of Victoria) about what he considered to be the one-sided way in which the proceeding was being conducted. 'She just sort of looked at me and said, "Mr Galbally, we don't speak like that."

'I was convinced that they'd already made their minds up – absolutely convinced,' Galbally said.

'The AFL Commission are very difficult to deal with because they are parochial to the sport. It's as though they regard Australian Rules football as their own and everyone else in the country is subservient to them.

'Those who sit to hear cases on the commission are privy to all sorts of chitchat and opinions. It's really all done in the interests of the AFL. I've always held a view that they should appoint an independent body that sits outside the AFL to deal with these things.'[8]

Trigg was fined and suspended but was later strongly endorsed by McLachlan to fill the vacant chief executive position at Carlton.

'It was the worst hearing I've ever had – absolutely appalling,' Galbally said.

The power afforded to commissioners is paraded on the last Saturday of every September when a conga line of Australia's business and political elite are wined and dined at the VIP grand final lunch in the MCG's Olympic Room. Seating is pored over scientifically. The closer to the head table you are, the more power you wield.

'It brings you great cachet and influence to be on the commission,' one football figure said.

An ex-AFL official said they believed the majority of commissioners 'enjoyed the life associated with being on the commission'. 'The power that comes with it, the almost deification of those roles in Melbourne is sycophantic,' they said. 'I was blown away by how people treated you very differently because of the role you held, not the person that you are.'

Peter V'landys, the Australian Rugby League Commission chairman and New South Wales horse racing tzar, said 'the extreme superiority complex some in the AFL have' caught him by surprise after the 2020 coronavirus crisis forced the shutdown of both codes.

'When we announced that we were going to recommence [the NRL season] on 28 May the most criticism came from elements of the AFL,' V'landys said. 'We were labelled irresponsible, arrogant, amongst a barrage of unrelenting, disparaging remarks. It was obvious they believed if it was not their initiative or proposal that it would fail. Consequently, after all the diatribe, they followed us two weeks later.

'Ironically, our pleb audacity probably saved them tens of millions of dollars as our ambitious start set the wheels in motion, even though they will never admit it.'[9]

The late John Cain, Victorian premier for three terms and a long-time member of the MCG Trust, said the state had never known an entity with as much power as the AFL.

'There's nothing like it, that I know of,' Cain told me in the weeks before his death in December 2019. 'I can't think of any other organisation that rivals it and, as an observer on the outside, it's become more the case.

'They choose their own successors, that's always a danger, in any field of endeavour, because you tend to choose people who will perpetuate what you've done.'[10]

Footy's eighteen clubs have retained powers under the AFL constitution to remove commissioners if the majority vote in favour of it, but the clubs have become so dependent on financial handouts that such a move is now unlikely.

The AFL's control of the clubs quietly stepped up a gear on 27 March 2014 when the Adelaide Crows and cross-town rival Port Adelaide bought back their AFL licences from the South Australian National Football League (SANFL) for a combined $18 million. In the case of Adelaide, the AFL covered the Crows' costs of about $11.3 million to be repaid over fifteen years, ending in October 2028. In return, the AFL assumed the right to appoint seven of the club's nine directors under the terms of a revised Adelaide Football Club constitution.

'And if you control the board, you control the club,' South Australian lawyer Greg Griffin explained. In essence, Griffin said, the Crows' 80,000 paid-up members now have little say in the direction of their club.

'Neither club should ever have allowed that to happen. It took away their autonomy,' Griffin said. 'I mean can you imagine Carlton or Collingwood agreeing that its board members be selected by the AFL?'[11]

The AFL also retains the power to nominate directors for the Sydney Swans, Port Adelaide, Gold Coast Suns and Greater Western Sydney.

Only one commissioner, Western Australian Terry O'Connor, QC, has ever been voted out (in 2001 over a dispute with Melbourne club bosses who wrongly accused him of wanting to get rid of Victorian clubs), although a group of club presidents considered a plan to parachute ex-Channel 9 boss and former league legal adviser Jeff Browne onto the commission in 2014. Clubs were angered that year when chairman Mike Fitzpatrick reinstated Langford, who had retired from the commission, with little consultation.

'This smacks of people guarding their positions. It's absolutely self-serving,' retired Swans chairman Richard Colless said at the time. 'It just seems like a captain's pick – it's like the Prince Philip knighthood.'[12]

In 2013, commissioner Chris Lynch (one of three Rio Tinto directors serving on the AFL Commission in that period) relocated to London to become the mining giant's chief financial officer. He offered his resignation but was kept on the commission for another year to the further bemusement of clubs.

Commissioners today – almost all of them coming from non-football backgrounds – are largely kept at arm's-length from the AFL's day-to-day operations. The majority, including the commission chairman Richard Goyder, live outside Victoria.

Real power was ceded long ago to the ranks of the executive.

'The commission is really only there to rubber stamp decisions these days – and not much gets knocked back anymore,' a senior AFL staffer said.

\*\*\*

The ministries that make up the AFL machine include the office of the CEO, football operations, broadcasting, commercial operations, game development, legal and integrity, corporate affairs, finance and administration, diversity and social inclusion, growth, digital and audiences, strategy, and human resources.

An organisational chart leaked during the 2020 coronavirus crisis revealed there were eight in-house lawyers, forty-two staff in the finance division and twenty-six in strategy. Another 104 were employed at AFL NSW, eighty-eight in Queensland, forty in the Northern Territory and twenty-nine in Tasmania. There was even an office in Shanghai.

The powerful integrity and investigations unit alone had swelled to fifteen full-time staff, four medical consultants and nine casual security officers.

Six former Victoria Police officers, including an ex-homicide squad detective, were hired to bolster the division responsible for policing gambling, doping, illicit drug use, ground security, the salary cap and player behaviours and associations.

The AFL integrity unit – the biggest in Australian team sport – resembles a private police squad.

A federal submission in 2017 revealed it had the power to access premises 'occupied by or in control of a club', seize 'all documents, records or articles or things in the possession or control of a person relevant to an inquiry or investigation', sanction any person contravening AFL rules 'in any manner they in their absolute discretion think fit' and stand down 'any person subject to an inquiry or investigation from participating in or in connection with the AFL competition'.[13]

Those who have faced interrogation at the hands of the league's private police department tell tales of threats, bullying, cover-ups and intimidation.

And for all integrity investigations, the AFL is the investigator, prosecutor, judge, jury and executioner.

'It does everything. It initiates the investigation, it prosecutes you, it convicts and sentences you,' lawyer Steven Amendola, who represented James Hird, said. 'It completely lacks independence.'[14]

Protecting the brand at all costs and retaliating first rather than listening became the mentality of the system and its leadership. Clubs or industry figures who dared challenge decisions or the AFL's authority were punished or blackballed. The same rules applied to journalists. The fox was guarding the henhouse.

In the AFL's governance structure the chief executive officer is included as a member of the commission to which they report and which is ultimately responsible for his hiring and firing.

'It's not uncommon for CEOs to sit on boards, but well-governed organisations have strict conflict of interest policies that they apply,' one critic observed. 'That's certainly not been the case at the Australian Football League.'

The problem would be exposed in 2013 when Demetriou declared that he was 'privy to information that goes beyond what has been reported' on the Essendon drugs investigation while being part of the commission that enforced the penalties against the club and club officials for breaching AFL rules.

Within this prism of entitlement thrived a culture of arrogance and intimidation; and chauvinism.

One senior female staffer found out the hard way when an angry member of Demetriou's executive flung an object that struck her in the head during a meeting. The woman, former Victoria Police officer Sue Clark, later resigned and told Demetriou in her exit interview that he was running a boys' club.[15]

Demetriou bragged openly about the discussion over a couple of beers on a bus trip with a group of senior (male) club figures during a fact-finding trip to New York in July 2013. According to a passenger on the bus, Demetriou leaned back, 'beer in hand' and said words to the effect: 'I told her, "Of course I run a boys' club, it's a boys' game; if it was netball, I'd run a girls' club."'

A string of other disheartened women have walked away from the organisation across the years frustrated by the 'blokey culture' and lack of opportunity afforded to female workers; a notable exception being the late Jill Lindsay, a tough and respected football department figure who died aged sixty-one in 2011.

Despite the bus comment and other incidents under his watch, several league staffers said they believed Demetriou was genuine in his championing of women. In 2005, Sam Mostyn, a former policy adviser to prime minister Paul Keating, became the AFL's first female commissioner.

One insider said: 'Andrew was a brilliant visionary leader and very much his own man. There was a sense he had deeply held views when it came to things like diversity and furthering the cause of women but, for whatever reason, lots of his executives were the opposite. They were mostly cut from the same cloth – white alpha males who went to private schools and shared the same conservative view of the world. Championing diversity wasn't on their agenda. They were too preoccupied with furthering their own ambitions and jostling for position.

'For all its talk about diversity there still isn't enough at head office. There have been a number of women who've gone into senior roles at the AFL and come out the other side very bruised by the experience,' the insider explained. 'It's a very clubby environment and sometimes the loudest voice prevails. That is not untypical of the corporate world but too often bad behaviour went unchecked. Meetings could be very combative and often hostile to those not experienced in that culture. Many good people got chewed up and spat out simply because they struggled in that environment. The politics inside the AFL is as intense as you'll see anywhere, politics included.'

A female staffer who left because of a barrage of bullying that had driven her to the edge of a breakdown told me the AFL was 'the most toxic place I have ever worked in my life … I was screamed at, sworn at, abused and publicly humiliated,' she said. 'They promote a strong mental health workplace, but in truth the behaviour is disgusting.'

In 2014, a mid-level male office worker, subjected to years of bullying and torment by senior executive Andrew Catterall, received a secret $200,000 payout signed off by Demetriou after the lawyers were called in. The settlement included additional costs for 'medical expenses' for the victim's ongoing 'psychological problems'. Incredibly, the AFL helped Catterall study at a prestigious international business school before penning a glowing reference after he applied for a top job at a rival sport without reference to his conduct.[16]

Leaked internal surveys of AFL staff have revealed an alarming number hold a poor opinion of the performance of their bosses.

But before hitting the exits, some departing AFL staff are asked to sign non-disclosure confidentiality agreements offering a few weeks extra pay but preventing them from ever discussing their experiences at league headquarters.

Another league executive with a well-earned reputation for sleaziness was dubbed the 'King of Tinder' by female employees and was counselled for parading photographs around the office of women he planned to meet on the dating app. He was also cautioned for 'unhinged' drunken behaviour in the company of league and club leaders, including commissioner Linda Dessau, at a function for the reopening of the Adelaide Oval in 2014.

In another appalling incident, a senior male staffer walked up to the work station of a newly employed female worker, looked her up and down and remarked, 'Good appointment,' within earshot of others before wandering off.

A damning report in July 2017 describing a 'toxic culture' at AFL House revealed some men in the office had created a 'Top 10' list of female employees they wanted to sleep with. 'The *Sunday Herald Sun* has confirmed a woman was told of her ranking on the wish list of males at AFL House,' the report said. She was told: 'You're number five on the list.'[17]

The report followed the sacking of two married male executives, Simon Lethlean and Richard Simkiss, caught having 'inappropriate sexual relationships' with younger female office workers. While the league trumpeted publicly that the two men had to go, behind closed doors an emotional McLachlan astounded staff by threatening to hunt down the whistleblowers who had leaked to the media about the office romances.[18]

A former female executive from a top Victorian-based club said women were still 'very under-represented' in senior executive roles in the industry. 'I will point you to the original senior women in management program where they picked the twelve or fourteen most talented women that they saw for progression in the AFL system, and I reckon there are only two left,' she said.

'I enjoyed my time in the AFL, I learnt a lot and so I don't necessarily want to bag it, my only question is why don't women seem to be able to progress?

'When you refer to the AFL as a boys' club, there are even some really good men who are excluded from it, so I don't like to refer to it as a boys' club because there are so many great men that haven't progressed either, that really deserved to progress, because they might not be in the inner sanctum.

'And if you look across professional sports, to be honest, women aren't represented at senior levels, so it is hard to say that the AFL alone aren't doing a great job in that space. But they're not retaining women – and I think that is the question that has to be asked: why are women leaving? And why are they judged differently on performance? I just don't think we are judged against the same criteria.'

The AFL considers itself a leader in gender equity, but since the formation of the commission in 1984, just five women have been appointed to serve alongside twenty-seven men around the league's board table.

It was AFL club Richmond that smashed the glass ceiling in 2016, appointing commercial lawyer Peggy O'Neal as the game's first female club president.

Female executives at AFL House have been few and far between; just four have ever made the grade outside the human resources portfolio. Yet, in February 2019, the AFL bizarrely gained recognition as an employer that 'values gender equity ... for having 40 per cent women on its executive, improved numbers of women at all levels and ongoing sexual harassment awareness training'. The calculator must have been broken because women have never made up 40 per cent of the AFL executive.

The league's seasoned spin doctors explained it away by saying their general manager of strategy, Walter Lee, a member of the executive on all of its official listings, did not report directly to McLachlan. Not surprisingly, the AFL fell off the 'leading gender equity workplace' list the following year.

Victorian businesswoman and philanthropist Susan Alberti told me she would never forget the attitude displayed by Demetriou when a group of female club board members were summoned to AFL House for a meeting in 2011. The group had expressed concern about the league's handling of revelations that St Kilda footballers had been engaging in sexual encounters with a teenage schoolgirl.

The story exploded when it emerged top AFL player agent Ricky Nixon was also accused of inappropriate dealings with the girl.

The group of female board members had accused the AFL of being 'wimpish' in its response to the scandal and questioned the meaning of the league's respect and responsibility policy.

Demetriou didn't like it and told them so over cut sandwiches.

'I felt like I had left the school principal's office,' Alberti reflected. 'My opinion on the matter was worthless in his eyes. How dare I have an opinion. I am only a woman.'[19]

More often than not, the behaviours at AFL House are tolerated by members of the commission, or they simply have no idea it's happening.

\*\*\*

A disproportionate number of white alpha males, usually hailing from prestigious Melbourne private schools or A-grade amateur football clubs, have filled the league's top posts. 'If you go to a Uni Blues–Old Xaverians game on a Saturday arvo you'll see more AFL executives than you would at the MCG on Anzac Day,' one ex-league executive quipped of the clique that runs the game.

Concerns were raised in 2018 when a plum AFL job was handed to the brother of senior AFL executive Travis Auld instead of being advertised. 'Surely if you are going to appoint a bloke's brother you've got to run a process,' one club chief complained.[20]

'Typically, when you deal with the AFL, you deal with people who don't have overly impressive backgrounds, because more often than not they are there because of who they know and not on merit,' another industry figure explained. 'It's rare to meet someone new at AFL House who isn't already known within the place. And when dealing with these people, they invariably take the position that they are doing you a favour, even though they are asking you to do something for them. They think it's a privilege for you to deal with them.'

In an incident that wouldn't have been out of place at the New York broking house Stratton Oakmont, depicted in the Hollywood hit movie *The Wolf of Wall Street*, league executive Darren Birch once swam across Victoria Harbour in front of AFL House, with dozens of hollering staff lined up along the causeway, after he lost a bet to McLachlan.

McLachlan recounted the story during an internal staff speech in October 2020. 'He was working for me and I always thought he was sandbagging his targets and so we put an aggressive target out and he said, "I'll get that,"' McLachlan said. 'And the bet was, if he got it, I had to swim from the NAB building across to Central Pier, across that filthy harbour – and if he missed it, he had to swim.

'Now, history says that for one of the few times Darren missed the target and I remember hundreds of people lined up as Darren risked all sorts of diseases. He swam across that filthy harbour with his teeth out and a swimming cap and goggles on.

'That was how it's been. We get stuff done and if we don't we honour our deals, and it's all done with good fun.'[21]

Representatives of one major AFL sponsor were left stunned during a contract renegotiation when a senior AFL executive became so incensed at being asked to explain the rationale behind some projected AFL growth figures that he stormed out of the meeting.

'The sponsor and the remaining AFL staff sat there speechless,' a witness said.

So sensitive was the AFL to scrutiny, that at one point it attempted to ban consultancy company Gemba from taking part in negotiations relating to a client's sponsorship renewal. 'They soon realised that this may be illegal and broadened it to all client agencies before eventually dropping the policy,' a football figure said. 'The sponsor had never experienced anything like it.'

The hubris spilled over during a round of TV rights negotiations when an order came from above to search AFL headquarters for bugs. A team of surveillance experts trawled through the building in search of covert listening devices and suspicious signals.

'It was Andrew Demetriou's idea,' a senior league figure said. The then-AFL chief executive wanted to be certain his lucrative negotiations with would-be broadcast partners weren't being compromised by industrial espionage.

'You just can't be [too careful],' Demetriou later said. 'The information that we hold is very commercially sensitive … we go through the proper risk management and we have all our phones and our headquarters swept, of course we do.'[22]

Nothing was ever found, of course, but it gave an insight into the psyche of the men roaming the corridors of power.

'It says a lot about the mindset of an organisation when they think it's necessary to sweep their offices for illegal bugging devices,' an AFL stakeholder said. 'It makes you wonder if they are judging people by their own standards. I mean, seriously, did they really think it was possible that Channel 7 or Network 9 had approved somebody to break into their offices at night and plant these devices? It's delusional, even as important as Demetriou thought his broadcast negotiations were.'

But by the time Demetriou handed in his badge, the AFL was the envy of Australian sport, entrenched in the five major states, generating revenues and newspaper column inches that rival codes could only dream about.

The secret formula, apart from the appeal of a game embedded deep into the cultures of Victoria, South Australia, Western Australia and Tasmania since the late 1800s, was rampant capitalism at head office and a strictly controlled socialist framework at club level.

Stronger teams were curtailed by the salary cap, a national draft and unequal annual cash distributions designed to bridge the gap between the richer and poorer clubs.

In 2018, the Gold Coast Suns, the league's seventeenth club, received $25 million in funding, struggling St Kilda got $20.6 million and wealthy clubs like Hawthorn and Collingwood were allocated less than $11 million.

The AFL even bankrolls the salaries of the game's 850 players under tripartite contract agreements between head office, the clubs and the men who put on the show.

The AFL's goal was to engineer a system similar to the NFL in the United States where teams were said to be so evenly matched they could beat any other team on 'any given Sunday'.

But what also emerged was a system of dependence and fortified barriers to proper scrutiny.

Criticism was either ignored or punished until the complainant was brought to heel or simply banished from the game.

To understand the twenty-first century AFL you have to rewind to the late 1970s and early 1980s when footy was still a tribal game, played on muddy suburban grounds, and the professional age was in its infancy.

From there, the origins of a commission system that would be overrun by a boys' club can be found.

# CHAPTER 3

# Sefton

IN DECEMBER 1974, AT THE AGE OF TWENTY-THREE, DAVID Galbally, a hot shot young Melbourne lawyer, won a seat on the board of the Collingwood Football Club as part of a three-man ticket that rolled president Tom Sherrin, the great nephew of Thomas William Sherrin – a.k.a. T.W. Sherrin, the famed manufacturer of the oval-shaped leather footballs still used in AFL matches today. Galbally's uncle, Jack, and his father, Frank, were also long-time Magpies board members during the halcyon days of the VFL.

In 1979, Galbally Jr played a key role in Collingwood's signing of legendary four-time Richmond premiership coach Tommy Hafey, a deal ingeniously sealed when he couriered an expensive mink jacket to Hafey's wife, Maureen.

It was a volatile time for Victorian football, with the majority of clubs insolvent or on the brink of financial ruin. By the early 1980s, crowds and membership numbers were falling and increased player movement began, accompanied by a rampant rise in transfer fees and wages, meaning costs were easily outpacing the money rolling in. The cash-strapped South Melbourne Swans were in the worst shape and boldly relocated to Sydney for the 1982 season.

Management of the competition rested with the VFL board of directors, made up of one representative from each of the league's twelve clubs, but self-interest always drove the agenda and decision-making had become paralysed.

'Jack Hamilton, the VFL general manager, came and spoke to us about forming a commission,' Galbally recalled of the move that would transform Australian Rules. 'One of the biggest problems the competition faced was that when issues came up to the VFL board of directors to deal with, everything was done on a parochial basis: "Will it suit Collingwood? What's the downside for Collingwood? Is it going to benefit Carlton? Well, we won't do it if it's going to benefit Carlton." It needed to change and the powers that be recognised that. The game was bigger than the clubs.'[1]

In 1983, Supreme Court Justice William Crockett handed down a decision in a restraint of trade case involving South Melbourne and St Kilda player Silvio Foschini in which he described the VFL as a 'confederation of sworn enemies'.[2]

Football was ripe for change and the threat of a Kerry Packer–style breakaway competition like World Series Cricket loomed large.

At a secret meeting of club bosses held at Mount Macedon in September 1984, Carlton president John Elliott pitched a detailed plan for a breakaway competition – to be led by an independent board – involving the best VFL teams and some top state league teams from Adelaide and Perth. Blues general manager Ian Collins had worked on the project in secret for months, preparing a detailed dossier.

Stalwart North Melbourne secretary Ron Joseph was among those who attended the Mount Macedon meeting held at Sefton estate, an hour's drive out of Melbourne. 'We all arrived and the next thing you know there were blokes walking around in black bow ties and cummerbunds, serving up silver trays of entrees and cocktails and Christ only knows what else,' Joseph recalled. 'There was a four-course feed and then John Elliott stood up and made his pitch about what we were doing there. There was a lot of unrest and a lot of clubs who were struggling financially.'[3]

Footy's move towards a national competition was imminent, the only question was how?

'As tough as I knew it was going to be for North to be a survivor, we always supported the fact that football just had to go national,' Joseph said.

The Sefton meeting was conducted without the knowledge of VFL president Allen Aylett and the league's general manager Jack Hamilton.

Aylett, a star North Melbourne player across the 1950s and 1960s (who also played eleven games of first-class cricket) had become Kangaroos chairman in 1971 and helped mastermind the club's historic first premiership in 1975. He took charge of the VFL in 1977 and was among the first to understand the need for reform and national expansion.

In a paper presented to his board in early 1983, Aylett called for 'a system of independent commissions, appointed by the VFL board to assume responsibility for making final strategic decisions in those key areas where clubs' emotion would be present'.[4]

But Elliott moved faster than the VFL with the secret Sefton pitch.

Melbourne Football Club boss Dick Seddon was the Demons delegate at the Mount Macedon gathering. A top commercial lawyer, Seddon agreed to walk away from his successful legal career in July 1980 to become Melbourne's CEO and executive director.

'John Elliott was a very powerful figure both commercially and politically,' Seddon said.[5] 'On the way home Ron Joseph and I were able to persuade Ian Collins that we should inform Allen Aylett and Jack Hamilton of the Elliott breakaway concept, because it is always preferable to achieve reform from within.

'We met with Aylett and Hamilton the following day, who were initially shocked and hostile that this had gone on behind their backs, but soon came on board with the realisation that urgent action was required to save the league,' he said. 'This was the catalyst for the creation of the commission, which was seen as the panacea of all the problems.'

A sticking point for the VFL's ambitions was an entity known as the National Football League (NFL). Originally called the Australian National Football Council, the NFL had been the official governing body for Australian Rules football since 1906.

Made up of delegates from the VFL, SANFL, West Australian Football League (WAFL) and Tasmanian Football League, the NFL was the 'keeper of the code' and owner of the laws of the game.

It was responsible for organising State of Origin matches and carnivals, and supervising the transfers and clearances of players between the top state competitions.

In 1972, the premiership-winning teams from the VFL, SANFL, WAFL and Tasmanian State Premiership faced off in an end-of-season Championship of Australia tournament in

South Australia where North Adelaide beat Carlton by a point in the grand final.

Four years later, the NFL replaced the championship with an even bolder mid-week tournament known as the NFL Night Series, which ran in conjunction with the state competitions' regular seasons. Played mostly at Adelaide's Norwood Oval on Tuesday nights, the series pitted the top VFL, SANFL and WAFL clubs in round robin matches televised live and in colour on Channel 9.

Sensing the moment, Aylett withdrew the VFL clubs for the 1977 tournament and set up a rival night series, staging a mid-week competition under new light towers installed at Waverley Park, in Melbourne's outer east.

By 1980, the VFL version had wooed the SANFL and WAFL clubs and killed off the NFL competition.

Victoria's control over Australian Rules was tightening.

\*\*\*

Years of debate, pitches and strategic reports culminated in the birth of the independent VFL Commission in December 1984.

A special VFL subcommittee chaired by North Melbourne president Bob Ansett was formed to select footy's first five commissioners. Jack Hamilton was installed as chief commissioner, and was joined by four part-timers: merchant banker Graeme Samuel, Elders IXL executive Peter Scanlon, National Country Party MP Peter Nixon and Dick Seddon.

Samuel knew almost nothing about football but had impressed trucking magnate and St Kilda powerbroker Lindsay Fox with a report he had prepared exploring the financial state of the Saints. 'Lindsay rang me one Sunday and said to me in his inimitable way, "Do you want to be a VFL commissioner?"

and I said, "Oh yeah." And he said, "Good, I'm nominating you." Bang – that was it,' Samuel said. 'The next morning I walked in to see my colleagues at the Macquarie Bank and said, "Who are the teams in the VFL?"'[6]

Watching his first ever match, Samuel mistakenly believed the game was over when the players and umpires headed for the sheds at the half-time break.

Samuel and Scanlon were selected for their business brains, Nixon for his political clout and Seddon as a highly respected football figure.

The theory of the first commission was sound, but the early execution poor.

For fear of relinquishing too much control, it was decided the VFL board of directors would continue to operate and maintain substantial powers, limiting the commission's effectiveness and ability to spend.

A strategic report commissioned by the league in 1985, known as the 'Blue Report', is regarded by many as a key step in the VFL's ultimate takeover of Australian Rules football. It laid out a vision for interstate expansion, mergers, a national draft and ground rationalisation.

'That was fundamental – where we really set the direction to expand the competition from Victoria,' Samuel said. 'The crown jewels were the Victorian clubs but you had to recognise that you had to go national.'

Seddon, however, disputes the report's significance. 'In a sense, it was supposed to be a justification for the continuance of the commission,' he said.

'It contained a lot of motherhood stuff, like ground rationalisation, the need to improve facilities, reduction of clubs in Melbourne and the need for expanded markets, which had been discussed ad infinitum at the VFL and was old hat to the footy people, but was of course new to the new non-footy commissioners.

'Some of its findings were regrettably misguided, such as their recommendations on mergers, relocations and forms of private ownership. The Blue Report was massively overrated.'

Seddon insisted the single biggest reform that set the VFL on the path to salvation came before the commission was even formed: the introduction of the salary cap.

Conceived in 1983 and trialled the following year under the VFL presidency of Aylett, the salary cap – limiting the amount of money clubs could spend on player wages – was fully enforced by the start of the 1985 season.

The seeds for the idea were planted during an information-gathering trip that Seddon, Hamilton and Hawthorn president Ron Cook took touring the USA in June 1983 to visit the major sporting leagues on behalf of the VFL.

In New York they met with the four commissioners of the National Football League, National Basketball Association, Major League Baseball and National Hockey League. David Stern, the then-deputy of the NBA, was the one who enlightened them about the benefits of a salary cap. It was a lightbulb moment for Australian Rules.

'We brought the salary cap concept back and sold it to the directors of the VFL and the twelve clubs, which was a remarkable feat, because in those days it was difficult to get the clubs to agree on anything,' Seddon said. 'This was a major, immediately effective reform, because it stopped all the nonsense of excessive payments and threats of Supreme Court challenges if transfers of poached players were blocked. The introduction of the salary cap stabilised the competition and allowed the clubs to recover from their insolvencies. It created a level playing field again and gave weaker clubs a chance.'

The second major reform came with the introduction of licence agreements between the league and the clubs. These agreements would impose contractual obligations on the clubs to adhere to the rules. Seddon knew the wealthy Nordstrom family in the USA, who had successfully bid for the expansion franchise of the Seattle Seahawks in the NFL, and obtained a copy of their licence agreement. He modified it to suit the VFL's unique circumstances and presented it at the first meeting of the commission.

'To my surprise it received a lukewarm reception from Samuel, Scanlon and Nixon,' Seddon said. 'This transfer of power from the clubs to the VFL was against the corporate philosophies of Samuel and Scanlon. Scanlon's initial view of the VFL would be heavily influenced by his boss John Elliott, and they believed in allowing free market forces to determine outcomes. They were against regulatory interference which they believed distorted the natural marketplace and produced weaker outcomes.'

Seddon continued: 'Instead of permitting the VFL as the central administrator to impose order on the competition to achieve viable results, Scanlon's preference was for a laissez-faire system where control of the competition went the opposite way from the VFL to the clubs allowing them more freedom of action. This philosophy may be okay in business but it is the wrong approach in the closed competition context in the VFL. The VFL competition needs the checks and balances to encourage a level playing field. If unchecked, the stronger clubs would get stronger and the weaker clubs would become weaker until they eventually disappeared.

'According to Scanlon's philosophy, this would be the right result. Survival of the fittest. The problem is we would not be left with a viable competition.'

Seddon got his way and the salary cap and franchise agreement systems got off and running. In December 1985, the twelve VFL clubs agreed to sign the licence agreements.

'Everyone said the creation of the commission saved the game, but ... once these two reforms were in place, there was no compelling need for a commission,' Seddon said. 'The VFL could have successfully operated with a vastly empowered general manager oversighted by the VFL board.'

The third reform to change the game was the introduction of a national draft in the late 1980s, giving clubs equal access to the best young talent in the land. 'The commission cannot claim credit for the salary cap ... however it can claim credit for the implementation of the franchising of clubs and the introduction of drafting,' Seddon said. 'These are its two major successes in the early years. It made a mess of almost everything else.'

Jack Hamilton struggled with the VFL's top job and announced his decision to retire as chief commissioner in March 1986. He stayed on until season's end to allow a thorough search for his replacement.

In such tumultuous times it was a crucial appointment and the man the majority of the clubs wanted in the chair was Hamilton's deputy, Alan Schwab.

Seddon didn't know it, but two of his fellow commissioners, Scanlon and Samuel, had used a search firm to come up with another name: Ross Oakley.

A former St Kilda player and insurance industry executive, Oakley had missed the Saints' historic 1966 premiership triumph because of a knee injury suffered in the semi-final.

The VFL board nominated Tony Capes (president of Footscray), Ron Cook (president of Hawthorn), Albert Mantello (North Melbourne VFL director) and the five commissioners as the selection committee.

'As Hamilton and Nixon were absent, this made six of us, who met at Scanlon's office to discuss the appointment,' Seddon said. 'That's when Scanlon and Samuel sprang Ross Oakley's name. Capes, Cook and Mantello all favoured Schwab. Scanlon and Samuel incorrectly assumed I favoured Schwab also, so rather than let it go to a vote where Schwab may get up, Scanlon proposed a joint appointment with Schwab in charge of football and Ross Oakley in charge of everything else.

'Of course it was never going to work,' he said. 'Schwab resented missing out on the appointment, white-anted Ross, was non-cooperative and leaked to the media. Ross, to his credit, bent over backwards to accommodate Schwab but it was always an uneasy relationship.'

Oakley went to work beefing up the VFL's commercial operations, marketing and sponsorships, but conceded his relationship with Schwab was strained. 'There was a lot of pressure for Schwaby to be the chief because I wasn't seen as a football person,' Oakley said.[7]

The dawn of a new national competition came in 1987 through the creation of the West Coast Eagles in Perth and the Brisbane Bears at Carrara Stadium on the Gold Coast.

Again, the theory was good, but the execution poor.

'We decided to admit a team from WA. Richard Colless got wind of this and formed a public company to buy the first licence for a fee which I think was for four million dollars,' Seddon said. 'But instead of assisting the new franchise to get on its feet, like they do in the USA with concessions and the like, the commission actually made it difficult for them. We punished them with poaching fines when they tried to get some of their players back from Victoria. The public company became bankrupt, and the West Coast Eagles were only saved by the WAFL taking over the licence.'

On the 'Bad News Bears', Seddon recalled: 'A bid was received from the TV actor Paul Cronin for a licence of a team to play on the Gold Coast at Carrara. Cronin was later joined in his bid by Christopher Skase, a high-flyer who also owned Channel 7 at the time, and this had appeal for some of our commissioners. There was another more considered bid but the commission recommended the Cronin–Skase consortium at Carrara, which was an unmitigated disaster.'

Seddon said the commission also got it wrong in allowing Dr Geoffrey Edelsten to take private ownership of the struggling Sydney Swans.

But the commission model recovered from its early missteps and, under the guidance of Oakley, and with the strategic strength of Scanlon and Samuel, the national competition began to find its feet.

In 1990, the year Collingwood broke through to win its first premiership in thirty-two years, the VFL changed its name to the Australian Football League, adopting a red, blue and white logo modelled on the Union Jack flag.

Fitzroy, the most cash-strapped of the Victorian clubs, did not survive and merged with the Bears at the end of 1996, while three new teams – the Adelaide Crows (1991), Fremantle Dockers (1995) and Port Adelaide Power (1997) – were added to a then sixteen-team competition.

Fitzroy's demise was a football tragedy, a wound that for many will never heal. For some it was the point at which they became disenchanted with the direction of the game.

'Although mergers may be good in business, they are not good in the context of the VFL because of the tribal nature of clubs,' Seddon said. 'Instead of rendering assistance to Fitzroy, as would happen today, the commission went out of its way to make life difficult for Fitzroy so it could finally force a weakened club into a takeover situation by the Brisbane Bears to create the Brisbane Lions.'

Footscray, later renamed the Western Bulldogs, as well as Hawthorn, Melbourne, North Melbourne and St Kilda were all linked to potential mergers throughout the 1980s and 1990s but drew on the passions of their supporter bases to remain afloat.

Another casualty was the Victorian Football Association (VFA), the state's secondary senior competition featuring iconic clubs such as Port Melbourne, Williamstown and Coburg.

The VFA thrived in the 1970s and early 1980s thanks to the staging of matches on Sunday afternoons (a move later adopted by Aylett in the VFL) but soon succumbed to the AFL onslaught, becoming a feeder competition for Victorian-based AFL teams.

As the years rolled on, struggling country leagues across the land would also accuse the AFL of turning its back on the grassroots game. Australian Rules in Tasmania, a proud football state that has produced four Hall of Fame Legends, would slip into a damning decline under the watch of the Melbourne suits.

In mid-1992, the AFL Commission, which still required explicit club approval for major decisions such as mergers, relocations, rule changes and capital works, commissioned another independent review of the game's administrative structure. A report compiled by businessman David Crawford called for a larger, more powerful commission, the installation of a chairman and a chief executive officer and the abolition of the board of directors.

It was the turning point for the game's administration.

'Until then there were just too many constraints imposed on the commission ... but the Crawford report suddenly allowed us to do things,' Samuel said. 'It was absolutely fundamental.'

But Peter Gordon, the man who led the campaign that saved Footscray from an AFL-enforced merger in 1989, remembers the Crawford report quite differently. 'It started out with everyone's support and with the best of intentions. But whatever it started out as, it became a strategy to dramatically increase the power of the AFL Commission and to decrease the power and independence of clubs at a time when key commissioners were fixated on further developing the national competition by reducing the number of Melbourne clubs.

'In the end, they only got Fitzroy, but if you had given truth serum to half of those commissioners in 1993–95 and said, "How many clubs do you *really* want to get rid of?" they would have said three, and the Bulldogs were one of them.

'Crawford was a hard-nosed economic rationalist. He was probably the most credentialled accounting expert in Australia and he approached the task with a laser focus on the optimal economic model. But you can't look at footy only through that prism. The obligation that you've got when you are a leader in the football industry is to make sure it's economically strong but also to be a keeper of the code and the clubs, and to honour football's culture and traditions.'[8]

Gordon recalled a meeting between club and AFL chiefs at the MCG in 1994 when Samuel stunned those in the room by proposing a merger between the Brisbane Bears and Sydney Swans. He put forward that the club would be known as the East Coast Bears, alternating its games between Sydney and Brisbane.

'Sydney is a good example of a club that is over 140 years old. What was the East Coast Bears going to do to that history and tradition?' Gordon asked. 'We all listened in shock. I remember Collingwood president Allan McAlister leaning in to me and saying, "He's got to be fucking kidding." And Allan didn't swear much!

'We lost a lot more when we lost Fitzroy than just one of eleven Victorian clubs. It tore at the fabric of the game, eroded confidence and caused misery for no good reason to a whole lot of people.'

As a result of the Crawford report, Oakley, whom long-time league lawyer Jeff Browne declared 'the person I believe had the most influence in changing how football operated', became the first AFL chief executive officer and Hawthorn coaching legend John Kennedy Sr the first AFL Commission chairman.[9]

Schwab was taken off the commission and moved to Sydney to assist the Swans before being found dead in a Sydney hotel in June 1993. It was the game's second sad loss after Hamilton was killed in a car accident in 1988.

The commission was expanded to eight members and Schwab was replaced by Carlton general manager Ian Collins in the key role of general manager of football operations.

The AFL national competition stabilised and then flourished.

The Oakley era, while tumultuous, saw a transformation of commercial revenues, attendances, club memberships and TV ratings. Samuel, a master negotiator and boardroom strategist, was in the thick of everything. 'No individual has contributed more to the strategic direction of the game during the last two decades, indeed arguably during the long history of Australian football,' Oakley would later say of Samuel.[10]

The $500 million TV rights deal struck by the AFL with Channel 9, Channel 10, Foxtel and Telstra in early 2001 – again driven mostly by Samuel – set Australian football on the road to invincibility.

'The early iteration of the AFL Commission is where the greatest respect and greatest acknowledgement should be paid – and that is Oakley, who was executive chairman and then CEO, and it's Samuel and Scanlon and others,' veteran administrator Richard Colless said. 'They were men on a mission and Graeme was the one who consistently took a bullet for the AFL. It didn't concern him that people abused him and criticised him. In the background was [league lawyer] Jeff Browne and a little bit after that [commissioners] Colin Carter and Terry O'Connor. Every meaningful document was drafted in that era. All of the heavy-lifting was done. The whole media rights thing and the break with the tradition of giving it to Channel 7 and actually putting it to market was driven by Samuel. I was there and I saw it.'[11]

Oakley retired in 1996, replaced by AFL commissioner and South Australian businessman Wayne Jackson, while Kennedy served as chairman for four years before being replaced by Ron Evans in 1998.

Evans, a former Essendon player and president between 1988 and 1992, understood first-hand the struggles of running a football club, but he also set the tone for what would become acceptable corporate behaviour by AFL bosses courtesy of his position as managing director of catering company Spotless Services.

In November 1991, while still president of the Bombers and a director at Spotless, Evans came under attack from Essendon members, including past chairman Allan Hird, for advocating that the team's home games shift from the club's spiritual home of Windy Hill to the MCG, where Spotless held the catering rights.

Evans' eyes had been opened to the lucrative 'cash business' benefits of catering at football stadiums in the early 1980s while serving on the Dons committee when the O'Brien Catering company operated the Windy Hill food and beverage stalls.

Spotless, originally a dry cleaning company, bought out O'Brien Catering in 1985 and assumed control of the catering contracts at the MCG, Waverley Park, Kardinia Park, Princes Park, Windy Hill, the Western Oval and the SCG.

Evans became the managing director of Spotless in 1992 before joining the AFL Commission in March 1993 – the same year the company bought out a small Western Australian company, Mustard Catering, which held the catering rights at Perth's Subiaco Oval.

Within two years, Subiaco, where the West Coast Eagles played half of its home matches in a sharing arrangement with the cross-town WACA ground, would undergo a major redevelopment (part funded by the AFL) and become the permanent home venue for the Eagles and the state's second AFL team, the Fremantle Dockers.

Catering revenues at Subiaco were estimated to have climbed from about $1.5 million in 1993 to more than $7 million in 2001.[12]

'It was a complete inside job,' a senior Spotless insider said of the Mustard acquisition. 'Ron got the heads-up about Subiaco through his AFL connections. He knew what was happening and went and bought Mustard at a rock bottom price. It made no sense whatsoever to go to Perth and buy a shit little caterer, but he knew it completely. It was a brilliant, cunning, cunning acquisition – inside information at the highest level.'

The insider said Spotless's contract renewal at the MCG in the mid-1980s was also secured with a wink and a nod. He said Evans had wined and dined two senior Melbourne Cricket Club (MCC) officials at the Adelaide Grand Prix where 'a deal was done under the table. There was no tender. I was there and privy to it all.'

By 1998, Evans was the AFL Commission chairman and would continue to cash in on the lucrative Spotless MCG arrangement until his death in March 2007.

'On further renewals of the contract there was psychological pressure brought to bear by Ron on the MCC,' the insider said. 'It was, "I'm the chairman of the AFL and we are having multiple conversations about the number of matches and funding and commitments." It stank and what it meant was that the MCC, and by extension the AFL, were compromised in their interests.'

Evans' conduct was again called into question in 1999 when his former club, Essendon, was investigated by the league for salary cap breaches in 1995–96. AFL commissioner David Shaw, who had succeeded Evans as Essendon president in 1993 before also joining the commission in 1997, ultimately bowed to pressure from the salary cap investigation and resigned from the commission, despite declaring that 'two of the alleged breaches relate to player contracts, the terms of which were agreed many years before I became president'. The Bombers were fined $276,000 and penalised draft picks but shattered club figures insist to this day that Shaw had been made a 'scapegoat' and that Evans was protected.

'There's a few things that Ron should look in the mirror about,' former Essendon premiership player and director Don McKenzie told 3AW radio in 2003. 'One day somebody might write the full story. It would make a good book.'[13]

In season 2000, Evans was again a beneficiary of a major management contract awarded to a subsidiary of Spotless at the new 54,000-seat Docklands Stadium in Melbourne.

'[Managing the whole venue] was something they had never done before,' a Spotless insider said of the Docklands deal. 'They had never, ever had a major management contract at a stadium. So how did they get their first one there?'

Supposedly, Evans would leave the room whenever the league commission discussed the arrangement with Nationwide Venue Management (NVM).

But his compromise was exposed after the stadium's opening was plagued by problems.

'He is not about to criticise, or even publicly demand answers, from NVM as it could damage his own hip pocket,' journalist Michael McGuire wrote at the time. 'Apart from being managing director, Evans also owns a 6.25 per cent stake in Spotless, which is valued at about $42 million. The AFL patently needs someone who is above such perceptions of self-interest, someone not tainted by such an obvious conflict of interest.'[14]

Evans' successor, Mike Fitzpatrick, would follow suit many years later when one of his private companies took a controlling stake in Sydney's Olympic Stadium, which was used for AFL matches. Fitzpatrick, like Evans, vowed to refrain from discussions relating to the stadium around the AFL Commission table and league officials openly scoffed at suggestions the chairman's conflict was even an issue at all.

The AFL's complete authority over Australian Rules was secured in 1995 when the NFL was dissolved. Total power now lay with the AFL Commission and within a generation it would morph into something its founding fathers did not foresee.

The clubs would soon live in fear of the very body they had created to represent them.

And it was in the name of 'integrity' that the modern AFL first learnt to flex its muscle. A fading force called Carlton was the first to find out.

# CHAPTER 4

# Brown paper bags

Victorian premier Jeff Kennett rose early on the morning of Saturday, 18 September 1999, ate breakfast and headed for the driveway of his Surrey Hills property.

A Brunswick-green picket fence stretches across the front of the Kennett residence in Melbourne's leafy inner-east, buffering an established garden bursting with camellias, clivia, box hedges, oaks and copper beeches. The red-brick Federation house has been the Kennett's suburban 'oasis' since the early days of Kennett's political life as the member for Burwood in Victoria's Liberal Hamer government.

And on this clear spring Melbourne morning, Kennett did what he always did on election morning: he washed his car.

'I cleaned it to within an inch of its life, inside and out, and then headed out, nice and relaxed, to the ballot booths,' Kennett told me.

It was the calmest of beginnings to an extraordinary day that would turn the state of Victoria on its head.

At voting stations from the Mallee to the Mornington Peninsula, and in the face of opinion polls, punters turned on Kennett's two-term state government, handing little-known Labor leader Steve Bracks the keys to the fifty-fourth Parliament of Victoria.

Bracks' upset election victory, confirmed almost a month later after three independents sided with Labor, condemned the Victorian Coalition to the opposition benches for the next eleven years.

But the shock was nothing compared to the epic boilover that played itself out that same afternoon at the home of football, the MCG.

In one of the biggest preliminary final heists in Australian Rules history, rank outsider Carlton defeated premiership fancy and traditional enemy Essendon by a solitary point to advance to the 1999 AFL Grand Final.

The powerhouse Kevin Sheedy–coached Bombers had shortened in the betting markets to $1.18 on the eve of the match, but failed to fire against a vastly less talented Blues team in front of 80,519 fans.

The climax to the Essendon horror show came in the game's dying seconds when Bombers defender Dean Wallis charged through the centre and was dragged down in a desperate tackle by Carlton midfielder Fraser Brown.

As the post-siren euphoria spilled into the Carlton dressing rooms beneath the MCG's Great Southern Stand, Blues president John Elliott threw himself into the thick of the celebrations.

Elliott, once touted as a future Liberal prime minister, had fuelled the flames of an already bitter rivalry in the build-up to the match by suggesting Essendon had 'cheated to win the flag' six years earlier when they thrashed Carlton in the

1993 Grand Final. The barb was a reference to salary cap breaches committed by the Bombers between 1992 and 1996, prompting Sheedy to declare that people like Elliott were the reason 'why you have a Labor Party'.[1]

It was a shirtfront typical of the passions and rivalry that had powered the game in Victoria for more than a century.

The Blues would be emphatically beaten by North Melbourne the following week, and the famous victory over Essendon – later dubbed the 'prelimiership' by *Herald Sun* journalist Trevor Grant – would prove one of the last great days of the Carlton empire.

A new salary cap storm was set to swallow Carlton whole and shake the foundations of the AFL competition.

Loud, brash and rarely without a cigarette hanging from his mouth, Elliott was the embodiment of Carlton arrogance. A product of Carey Baptist Grammar and the University of Melbourne, Elliott worked for global management consultants McKinsey & Company, which included a brief stint in Chicago with them, before masterminding the purchase of Tasmanian-based food products company, Henry Jones IXL. In 1972, at the age of just thirty-one, he raised $36 million for the takeover and became its managing director based at the Jam Factory in South Yarra. Through a series of subsequent acquisitions, mergers and manoeuvrings, Elliott emerged as executive chairman of a new company, Elders IXL, and launched a $1 billion takeover of Carlton and United Breweries.

Elders became Australia's second biggest company, a multi-billion-dollar conglomerate with 20,000 staff worldwide across the brewing, agribusiness, resources and finance sectors.

But Big Jack wanted more.

'Elliott is like a general without a war,' journalist Andrew Rule once wrote. 'He used to listen to tapes of Winston

Churchill in his car to inspire him to fight them on the bourses in his stock market raids of the 1970s and 1980s.'[2]

He joined the board of mining giant BHP (after Elders acquired a 19 per cent stake) and was enlisted as federal president of the Liberal Party. In 1988 he flirted with a run for the leadership and was touted as a potential prime minister as part of a plan to replace Roger Shipton as the member for Higgins.

Blue blood ran deep at Carlton.

Prime minister Sir Robert Menzies, the club's long-time number one ticket holder, was a die-hard Carlton man. After Menzies suffered a stroke and became wheelchair-bound in the early 1970s, the club built a ramp in the Robert Heatley Stand at Princes Park so he could watch his beloved Blues play games from the passenger seat of his chauffeur-driven Bentley.

Liberal prime minister Malcolm Fraser was another loyal Carlton fan and top ticket holder, seen regularly rubbing shoulders with players and administrators in the dressing rooms.

In 1981 and 1982 when Carlton claimed back-to-back VFL flags, Fraser hosted player celebrations at The Lodge, the prime minister's residence in Canberra, where pieces of cutlery and fine china were alleged to have gone missing amid the revelry.

Big Jack had swept to power at Princes Park at the start of the 1983 season, replacing Ian Rice as president. The halcyon days of the Elliott era netted premiership success in 1987 and 1995, but by the time the Blues had knocked off Essendon in that manic preliminary final of 1999 the walls were closing in.

Through elaborate company trust structures – or just brazen under-the-table cash payments – Carlton had been systematically cheating the AFL-policed salary cap for years under the orders of senior board members, including Elliott.

Two directors were given responsibility for the scheme, which also involved senior club executives. Carlton was intent on circumventing footy's socialist framework.

A moratorium in 1994 had given clubs cheating the salary cap the chance to confess their sins, but Carlton – and other clubs – continued on.

Inaugural VFL commissioner Dick Seddon said the Blues had declared from the start that they could beat the salary cap. 'John Elliott disagreed with the philosophy of the salary cap as he was averse to any shift of power away from his club to the VFL administration,' he said.[3]

Essendon and Melbourne were investigated and punished for salary cap breaches in the late 1990s but it was Carlton that would cop the full wrath of an AFL Commission determined to stamp out illegal payments once and for all.

But first, Elliott's business empire came under attack.

The seeds of destruction had been planted back in 1989 when Elliott's private company, Harlin Holdings, launched a bold takeover bid of Elders, which backfired spectacularly.

The National Crime Authority (NCA) launched an investigation into a series of other Elders transactions and by 1990 Elliott had quit the company, stepped down as Liberal Party president and dropped out of the BRW Rich List.

He was charged by the NCA in December 1993 and acquitted three years later over allegations involving fraud and conspiracy, but the court case and a counter-claim against the NCA cost Elliott his public standing and millions of dollars. As his empire burnt, the ambitious young merchant banker and Carlton director Mike Fitzpatrick saw his opportunity.[4]

A three-time Blues premiership ruckman, and captain of back-to-back premiership teams in 1981 and 1982, Fitzpatrick joined the Carlton board in 1989 after a stint in New York working for investment banks Merrill Lynch and Credit Suisse First Boston.

A Rhodes Scholar, Fitzpatrick had worked as a senior adviser in the state treasury department for Victorian Labor premier John Cain in 1984 and briefly commentated on VFL matches for ABC radio. His soaring self-confidence was on show in 1992 during negotiations for the sale of the Loy Yang B Power Station by the State Electrical Commission of Victoria to a US energy giant. Worth $1.4 billion, it was the first partial privatisation of Australia's power-generation assets and Fitzpatrick was in the thick of the action representing Credit Suisse First Boston, the Electrical Commission's primary adviser.

'The stakes were high. It involved a plethora of government officials, corporate entities, bankers, lawyers and expert advisers,' a Melbourne finance figure recalled. 'During a meeting in Melbourne attended by multiple parties, Mike Fitzpatrick, after having made an effective point, proceeded to throw his arms behind his head, puff out his chest and elevate his feet off the ground and onto the table. Everyone in the room was gobsmacked but the meeting continued on to the next point notwithstanding the fact the soles of his shoes were firmly in everyone's line of sight. The contempt and disrespect afforded to his fellow professionals was extraordinary.'

In early 1995, at a Carlton board meeting held in a stand named in Elliott's honour on the northern side of Princes Park, Fitzpatrick stunned his fellow directors by calling on the embattled president to stand aside.

Businessman and Blues board member George Varlamos recalled Fitzpatrick pulling him into a side office on the way in. 'He sounded me out a few minutes beforehand,' Varlamos said. 'I gave Mike a little bit of advice that I didn't think it was appropriate what he was doing and he shouldn't be doing it. I didn't support him and I didn't think it was the right thing to do. Elliott was still an innocent man. He hadn't been found guilty on any charges and eventually was found not guilty.'[5]

Another board member, who asked not to be named, said the confrontation that unfolded was seared into his memory. 'Elliott was under the pump with all sorts of court actions and Fitzpatrick tried to shoot him in the head,' the director said. 'He moved a resolution, but he was totally unprepared. It was just total and absolute bravado. He lectured Elliott for about five minutes – "You've been charged with doing this and charged with doing that, you're before the courts, you're letting the club down and neglecting your job and you're no longer fit to be president and you should stand down until it's all resolved." It was a blockbuster.'

Elliott sat back in his chair, uncharacteristically quiet. He'd been tipped off about Fitzpatrick's intentions.

'I couldn't believe that he was so restrained, I thought he might have stood up and told him to fuck off, but he listened to it for a bit,' the board member said.

Although the challenge to Elliott failed this time, the fact that Fitzpatrick had the gumption to do it was a window into his boundless self-belief: a master of the AFL universe in waiting.

Carlton committee member, Peter Kerr, who also attended the meeting, said: 'Fitzpatrick didn't make any approach to me before unsuccessfully challenging Elliott. No one at the meeting supported him except for Ken Hunter. A few days later Ken squared off with Elliott and was reinstated to the committee.

'It was most unfortunate all of this happened when, under Elliott's leadership, the club was enjoying continued success, we were never out of the finals and went on to win the flag in 1995.

'And because of this, Fitzy had no option but to resign from the committee, but by then I think he had really set his sights on an even bigger prize at the AFL.'[6]

His ambush dead in the water, a sheepish Fitzpatrick headed for the door. His days at the Blues were done but it didn't bother him much. He was already chairman of the Australian Sports Commission, was building a business empire as founder and managing director of Hastings Funds Management, and would join the AFL Commission in 2003 after playing a major role in the financing of footy's new $460 million Docklands Stadium.

Asked about Fitzpatrick's input during his time as a Carlton director, an unnamed Blues board man offered bluntly: 'His contributions didn't match his reputation'.

\*\*\*

Football's tectonic plates shifted profoundly on April Fool's Day 2000.

AFL football operations boss Ian Collins, a tough back-pocket in Carlton's 1968 premiership team, announced he was quitting to become chief executive officer of Docklands Stadium, the inner-city venue that had replaced Waverley Park in Melbourne's outer east as Victoria's second-biggest football ground.

His successor was a man named Andrew Demetriou and footy would never be the same again.

Then-commissioner Bill Kelty said Demetriou had proved his credentials by doing the 'right thing not taking advantage of the goodwill we had generated in making a really big, first offer' in the 1999 pay negotiations with the AFL Players' Association.

'He had not abused us, but he could have,' Kelty told me. 'He honoured his word and he was a great official and understood footy, so we said, "We are looking for somebody tougher than [CEO] Wayne [Jackson]" – that's it.

'And we also wanted to divulge some of the authority away from the hands-on commission approach. Graeme Samuel was doing all of the negotiations behind the scenes. We wanted somebody who was much tougher to deal with Channel 7 and the media, and someone much tougher to deal with the stadiums and someone much tougher to deal with the governments.

'We wanted a bit more animal.'[7]

Collins' move to the Docklands Stadium also signalled the end for Elliott.

Despite having worked loyally under the Carlton president at the Blues before becoming AFL football operations boss in 1993, Collins had joined the coup that would do what Fitzpatrick had failed to achieve in 1995: kill off Big Jack.

The Blues had split into two factions, with poker machine king and prominent Blues supporter Bruce Mathieson leading the charge to boot Elliott out. Mathieson's hatred of Elliott went back a decade and erupted in a heated exchange of words after a chance encounter in a Melbourne restaurant. The pokies king believed Elliott had put himself above his club to help foster his own interests.

The feuding boiled over at the same time as AFL investigators began taking a closer look at Carlton's books. The Blues had been fined $125,150 for salary cap breaches relating to the 1998 and 1999 seasons, but it was nothing compared to the scam AFL investigators were about to uncover.

A long-service-leave claim lodged against the league by Carlton midfielder Fraser Brown after his retirement at the end of the 2000 season fuelled the league's suspicions. The amount Brown's agent David Allison suggested his client was paid in his final season was different from the amount submitted by the club to the AFL.

Allison later detailed the brazen delivery of brown paper bags stuffed with cash to his Royal Parade office in Parkville across multiple seasons. 'Across a five-year period – there would be no doubt in my mind it would be three-quarters of a million bucks,' Allison said. 'It was always cash and it wasn't only me that was paid that type of money.' Pressed on the identity of the bagman, Allison said: 'A very wealthy businessman. I can't say who, mate.'[8]

Elaborate company structures designed to hide the flow of money to Carlton stars managed by rival agents were also discovered, triggering the interest of the Australian Taxation Office.[9]

Demetriou got to work and used the fear of prosecution over tax evasion as a weapon to convince some players to confess. By August 2002 the Carlton salary cap scandal had exploded into public view.

To help manage the fallout and messaging, the AFL reached out to a young communications consultant called Elizabeth Lukin.

Blues hard man Brown, who had retired at the end of the 2000 season, refused point-blank to cooperate with league investigators and was threatened with bans from attending AFL venues. But three players did play ball and the game was up.

Stephen O'Reilly, Blues defender and a chartered accountant who did not want an investigation over undisclosed payments to linger, was the first to fold. Then Stephen Silvagni, the champion fullback who was the son of club great Serge Silvagni, and star teammate Craig Bradley also confessed that they had agreed to – but supposedly not received – undisclosed payments.

Under AFL rules, a breach is committed when a club makes the offer of an under-the-table payment, whether it's paid or not.

An offer of a tax indemnity, conditional on the surrender of documents and signed statutory declarations admitting to the scam, sealed the deal and the league moved in for the kill.

Salary cap cheating charges against Carlton were laid by the AFL on 11 November 2002, and the following day Elliott and his three remaining boardroom allies – Wes Lofts, Barry Armstrong and Peter Kerr – resigned.

The anti-Elliott 'Carlton One' ticket assumed control of the club, with Collins installed as president. Elliott's twenty-year reign at Princes Park was over. His inglorious demise was front-page news, but the worst for Carlton was yet to come.

On the night of Friday, 22 November, Demetriou formally presented the league's findings on the salary cap investigation to a marathon hearing of the full AFL Commission. Collins pleaded Carlton's case but there would be no leniency.

At a 2 o'clock media conference the next morning, commission chairman Ron Evans, flanked by AFL chief executive Wayne Jackson and Demetriou announced that Carlton had been fined almost $1 million and stripped of the next two years of prized draft selections, including picks number 1 and 2 in the next day's national draft.

It was a sledgehammer punishment.

Jackson declared that Carlton 'deserved everything they got, and arguably some more'. Evans was even more direct: 'Carlton members and supporters ought to feel betrayed by the actions of their club.'

The sense of loss for Carlton fans was immediate as they watched Brendon Goddard head to St Kilda with the first pick in the draft and Daniel Wells land at North Melbourne with the second.

But at least two commissioners, Bill Kelty and Chris Langford, opposed the severity of the penalties, warning their fellow members that Carlton would be damaged for years.

'Chris Langford and I opposed it,' Kelty told me. 'We said this is simply too hard. There is a new regime at the club, they are trying to clean the deck and this penalty will really, really hurt them. It was just brutal. But they went the other way. I think they thought a compromise wasn't good enough. They thought there had to be a demonstration of the AFL being tougher.

'It was just terrible. And I said this will cost them ten years. Carlton will be buggered for a decade and I left in the end saying if you want to make this decision, I'm not. That's why it went for so bloody long. Andrew [Demetriou] was keen on the penalty, but he didn't participate a lot.'

Even with the benefit of hindsight, then-commissioner Graeme Samuel insisted the Blues copped the right whack. 'It was completely outrageous, there was an extraordinary amount of rorting going on,' Samuel said. 'We were given the report of the investigation, Carlton came in to give their view, and one of the recommendations was that there be a penalty of nine hundred plus thousand dollars and I remember saying, "That is nothing to them. The financial penalty is not the relevant one." And that's when we imposed the draft penalties – and that really hurt them.

'For some reason, someone must have said to them that "Graeme took a really hard line" at the commission and I do recall thinking enough was enough. They were furious and always blamed me for the decision.'

As Kelty had predicted, the fallout was devastating, triggering a two-decade run of misery for one of footy's proudest clubs. Many connected to Carlton have still not forgiven those who spilled the beans, chiefly Silvagni.

But Demetriou emerged from the crisis with an enhanced reputation. He had shown the football world, and more importantly Evans and the key members of the commission, just how formidable a force he could be.

Carlton was rightfully punished for years of brazen cheating, but the Blues were adamant they had been unfairly targeted by the AFL because of their status – and because of Elliott.

'We'd been pretty vocal and successful – and I'm not saying it was tall poppy syndrome – but it was all probably to take us down a notch or two,' Blues director Kerr said. 'I think we got singled out for special treatment – and a special penalty.' As for Elliott, Kerr said: 'Personally, I thought someone had to stand up to the AFL and not be a bloody patsy all the time.'

The Carlton salary cap scandal would be an instructive episode. The battlelines were becoming clearer to everyone. The AFL had prevailed, a club had been put firmly in its place and Demetriou's strength was on show for all to see.

No longer were Melbourne's power clubs calling the shots over head office. The worm had turned.

## CHAPTER 5

# Sliding doors

WAYNE JACKSON WAS THE 'JIMMY CARTER' OF AFL CHIEF executive officers, stepping into leadership following a period of great upheaval. But unlike the US president who is credited with brokering a historic Middle East peace agreement, Jackson's strength wasn't in deal-making and he made no secret of his shortcomings as a negotiator.

At a meeting with a prospective sponsor at the MCG in the late 1990s – and to the horror of two league officials who accompanied him to the discussion – Jackson let slip the amount of money the incumbent sponsor was coughing up.

There would be no bumper payday this time.

'Wayne openly said to [AFL lawyer] Jeff Browne and myself: "On the difficult commercial deals I want you to do the negotiations. I am not a good negotiator,"' said foundation commissioner Graeme Samuel.[1]

After a decade of turbulence under hard-nosed league chief executive Ross Oakley, Jackson's ascension to the AFL's top job in 1996 had been no coincidence. He was already a member of the AFL Commission when he got the job.

'What Wayne was good at was offering a softer community view, relative to Ross,' Samuel explained. 'Ross had an extraordinarily difficult task to turn the competition around, make the AFL a national competition, query the number of clubs in Melbourne – it was really tough.

'We decided then that what we needed was someone who could reflect a warm community football approach – it was a bit like bringing Jimmy Carter in as president following Richard Nixon. We needed someone to calm the horses a bit.'

On 15 April 2003, Jackson announced his decision to retire at the end of the season. His seven-year reign was the least contentious of any league boss, before or since.

'Wayne was much underrated,' retired Sydney Swans chairman Richard Colless said. 'He had a thirst for knowledge and didn't believe that he knew it all. He had an absolute passion for the game. He hadn't captained an AFL side to a premiership but he'd played senior football for West Torrens in the SANFL and coached the seniors and reserves teams. He was twice an All-Australian amateur. So he knew more about the less glamorous side of the game and it gave him a genuine common touch.

'He didn't have a political bone in his body and was never jostling for position with the chairman as to who was going to get their head in the shot or be quoted. But because of his humble demeanour I didn't think he was accorded the recognition that he deserved.'[2]

A commission subcommittee was formed to help identify Jackson's replacement, but Andrew Demetriou was chairman Ron Evans' preferred candidate and the red-hot favourite.

Demetriou had relished the AFL football operations role that he had worked in from May 2000. He did not back away from conflict, and his self-certainty in the role led to some memorable stoushes. Retired Sydney Swans player Dale Lewis rudely discovered what it meant to go up against Demetriou after an interview with the *Herald Sun*'s Mark Robinson in March 2002. The retired Sydney Swans star made the startling claim that up to 75 per cent of AFL players had dabbled in the use of illicit drugs. Speed, marijuana, cocaine or ecstasy – you name it, they've used it, Lewis declared.[3]

The firestorm was ferocious and it was Demetriou leading the attack. 'The suggestions of drugs being rife in the AFL are inaccurate and exaggerated,' Demetriou declared dismissively in words that would come back to haunt him. Lewis, he said, was 'incredibly naive and incredibly stupid'.[4]

Not everyone agreed.

At the end of his first presidents' meeting at AFL House in 1999, Collingwood boss Eddie McGuire warned the game's leaders that illicit drugs had become an increasing problem in the community and among the next generation of young footballers.

A few weeks before the Lewis story, Demetriou paid a visit to the St Kilda Football Club, who had stunned the football world midway through 2001 by sacking coach Malcolm Blight after just fifteen games at the helm.

The Saints had wooed Blight out of retirement with a $1 million advance on his contract payment, but quickly questioned his commitment and made the bold call to terminate his employment.

Grant Thomas, the club's director of football and Demetriou's old North Melbourne teammate, was installed as coach. Growing up in Frankston and later Mount Eliza,

Thomas had attended St Bede's College in Mentone, played for Frankston YCW and debuted for St Kilda in 1978. He played centre halfback, had one and a half years at North Melbourne and one at Fitzroy before coaching Warrnambool to four flags in five years.

Out of courtesy, Thomas asked the club to arrange for Demetriou to visit St Kilda's Moorabbin headquarters to outline their post-Blight strategy.

The meeting was a disaster.

'Demetriou adored Blighty and we invited him down to let him know what we were doing and why we were doing it,' Thomas said. 'We told him, "We're going for draft choices, we're picking young kids and we're going to build from the bottom. We need to endure some short-term pain to achieve long-term gain. It's never been done right at St Kilda. We need to be disciplined and methodical and engage the AFL and show transparency." We sold him the vision that we had put in place for the club.

'Demetriou was just sitting there and then he leant back and scoffed, and I said, "What are you laughing about?"' Thomas continued. 'And he said, "I've heard all this before." And I just said to him, "Who the flying fuck do you think you are? We invite you to come down here, out of decency, to let you know what our plans are. You are nothing but a fucking administrator for our game – get that straight. You've come into our home and we're telling you how we are going to run things here. How dare you fucking undermine what we are saying."

'He said, "I don't have to be spoken to like this," and I said, "You're dead right – you don't. Stand up and fuck off."

'He stood up and left and I looked at [president] Rod Butterss who was as white as a ghost, [chief executive] Brian Waldron had his eyes hanging out, and they said, "Thommo, what have you done?" And I said, "What I've done is draw a line in the sand for the St Kilda Football Club – we do not get talked about like that ever again."[5]

Waldron confirmed witnessing the clash between Demetriou and Thomas, but said both men had been out of line.

'There was always an issue between those two,' Waldron said. 'Grant disrespected Andrew that day, but Andrew was also a very autocratic-type bloke. He was very much confrontational with us ... it was a pretty awful situation.'[6]

A few days later, Evans called Butterss and requested a meeting with him and Waldron.

'We went to see him at his place in East Melbourne,' Waldron said, 'and he said, "Boys, we want you to be successful, but you can't fight city hall." The penny dropped with Rod, and I went to see Andrew and we made peace, which was fantastic because he was absolutely brilliant in helping me in my role there.

'When you work with them they are great, but Thommo thought we were weak in doing that.'

Veteran North Melbourne board member Peter de Rauch was another to cop the wrath of the AFL's fierce football operations boss when Demetriou was new in the role.

De Rauch was four when his family migrated to Australia from war-torn Hungary in July 1949. They started out in a displaced persons camp in Parkes, New South Wales, before his father, Charles, landed a job on the Snowy Mountains hydro scheme at Cooma. In 1952, the de Rauch clan moved to Melbourne and rented a small house in North Melbourne Football Club heartland, at 277 Flemington Road, a drop punt away from the club's Arden Street headquarters.

It wasn't long before Peter's new-found mates at St Michael's primary school indoctrinated him as a die-hard Kangaroos fan. 'Everything was tribal back then, if you didn't support North Melbourne around there, they'd throw you off the balcony,' he quipped.

De Rauch made his fortune in the lighting game and was approached to join the North Melbourne board at age forty-four in October 1989. He would devote almost twenty years to the cause and pour over $2 million of his own hard-earned money into the club, which defied its underdog status by claiming AFL premierships in 1996 and 1999.

His first clash with Demetriou was in mid-2001 when an AFL delegation made a visit to the club. 'The commission would come out once a year to visit the clubs and on this occasion Demetriou came with them,' de Rauch explained. As the discussion turned to the size of North Melbourne's annual AFL distribution, de Rauch piped up. 'I said, "We need more. Why can't you make it more? Is that the best you guys can do?" And he, Demetriou, turned to me and said something like, "We'll decide what you get." I just felt like he was showing off to the commissioners that he was in control. It was always up to the AFL how much money we would get or what direction we were going in.'[7]

Soon after, de Rauch was sitting on the interchange bench at a game in Manuka, Canberra, as he had done for most Kangaroos matches, including the two flags in the 1990s, when he got a tap on the shoulder from club chief executive Greg Miller.

Demetriou and Miller were watching the match not far from the bench in the Manuka outer. 'Greg said, "Andrew doesn't think it's a good idea you sitting on the bench,"' de Rauch said. 'I politely declined [to move] but they soon made a rule banning board members from sitting down there.'

The pair would soon lock horns again.

You won't find it anywhere in the history books, but the AFL Commission narrowly escaped a fatal self-inflicted wound during the 2002 football season.

Riding high on a sense of superiority, the league quietly committed to stage eleven games a year for fifteen years at Sydney's Homebush Stadium, home of the 2000 Olympic Games. The extraordinary arrangement was struck notwithstanding the Sydney Swans' commitment to play nine games a year at the rival Sydney Cricket Ground (SCG).

The deal was a stinker but the story never got out and it was the Swans who helped the AFL unwind it. 'It was a binding contract and we invested six months getting out of it and burnt a lot of bridges doing so,' then Swans chairman Richard Colless revealed.[8]

'The point here is the AFL would've had to find, on at least nine occasions, a home team to play at Homebush. The Swans could have been the home team for two of the eleven games but where were the others going to come from? The financial and reputational damage would have been enormous, and if the contract had stayed on foot the AFL wouldn't be the powerhouse that it is today.

'Kelvin Templeton, who was the Swans' CEO, was basically working on this full-time and I was heavily committed to it and to this day, I don't think either of us have ever received anything remotely resembling an acknowledgement of what we pulled off,' Colless said. 'I think the AFL Commission's mentality was, "We don't make mistakes like that" and it was expunged from their collective memories.'

Demetriou's biggest backers in the race to replace Jackson were Evans and Kelty.

'In truth, he has been doing many of the CEO's jobs for more than eighteen months,' journalist Caroline Wilson said of Demetriou in *The Age*.[9]

Evans had become somewhat of a mentor to Demetriou. 'He would meet with him, talk through business with him and guide him through life. They were very close,' an associate of Evans told me.

But as the weeks dragged on, word spread that the commission was divided.

Some in clubland weren't in favour either.

John Elliott, who had run into further corporate strife with the collapse of his rice growing business, Water Wheel Holdings, made no secret of his thoughts, declaring on *The Footy Show* that he didn't think Demetriou 'was anywhere near good enough' to be given the job.[10]

Long-time league lawyer Jeff Browne said it was Jackson who led the push for Demetriou. 'Wayne really groomed Andrew for that job,' Browne said. 'He selected him as football ops boss because he was running the players' association. He really liked Andrew from the start and liked his energy and foresaw that the connection with the players was a direction the league had to go in.'[11]

WAFL Commission chairman Neale Fong and Geelong chief executive Brian Cook made the final three – although at one stage businessman Sir Rod Eddington's name was mentioned – but on 30 July 2003, it was Demetriou who prevailed.

'I know what football means to so many people and to be able to make a contribution means a great deal to me,' Demetriou declared at his official unveiling.

Samuel said that he was the obvious choice. 'The only thing that was ever raised against him was the fact that he'd been with the AFL players' union, but that was also the greatest asset because he knew what the players were about.[12]

'He was an extraordinary negotiator. He negotiated the enterprise agreement with the players against the AFL – and the AFL had as its negotiators Wayne Jackson and Bill Kelty. It was an extraordinary deal that was very much in favour of the players, and so we figured, well, if Andrew can do that – bring him in and let him negotiate for the AFL.'

In reality, Demetriou had negotiated a favourable pay deal with a self-confessed weak negotiator and the head of the Australian union movement, who was sympathetic to the players' position.

Kelty confirmed the AFL had opened its negotiations with Demetriou by offering the playing group a generous pay rise. 'When Andrew took over, we went to them with a big deal,' Kelty told me. 'We said, "We want to raise the odds, so we'll offer the players a lot of money." He [Demetriou] had a great starting point but he was very good at negotiations. It [the final deal] was entirely consistent with what our approach was.'[13]

After the soft-touch of Jackson, Samuel said, 'it was absolutely fundamental that we needed someone stronger. I was spending sometimes forty hours a week on the AFL, and at the same time I was trying to properly fulfil the role of the president of the National Competition Council. Every day I was down at the AFL, into the carpark, into the office helping out.

'That's when we brought Andrew in. Andrew was the standout guy.'

Some have a different view.

Colless said overlooking Cook was the AFL's 'sliding doors moment'.

'My recollection is that there was a deadlock on the commission between Cook and Demetriou,' Colless said.

'Ron [Evans] was very, very strongly supportive of Andrew and he deferred the vote – and I think he then lobbied his colleagues.

'If Brian Cook had become CEO there's no doubt that the AFL would have been run differently. I think it would have been a far less confrontational approach. I can't say Brian would have been a better manager – it's all hypothetical – but his style based on his experience of being CEO of two successful clubs would have been significantly different.

'I think one of Andrew's disadvantages is that he'd never been involved in the administration of a club let alone having occupied a senior position in one,' Colless explained. 'That said, Andrew was a very effective CEO and I think he would agree we had a very good working relationship.

'Publicly he was a strong person but privately he was very good company and you knew where you stood with him.'[14]

The anointing of Demetriou was followed by a second profound arrival at AFL House.

Graeme Samuel was forced to retire his post as an AFL commissioner after almost twenty years to become chairman of the Australian Competition and Consumer Commission. His last stand was a key role in negotiations over the $450 million redevelopment of the MCG.

Mike Fitzpatrick, the man who had tried and failed to see off Big Jack Elliott, was selected to replace him.

'One can only do one's best, but I doubt I'd take the sort of profile and have the day-to-day involvement that Graeme had, and my view would be very strongly that the executive take the lead on those sort of issues,' Fitzpatrick declared at the time.[15]

How right he would be.

Jackson stayed on until grand final day, declaring at the 2003 North Melbourne breakfast, 'I believe Andrew

Demetriou, who at any time now will become the father of twins, will make a wonderful CEO.'

The Jackson era had seen the introduction of the league's sixteenth team (Port Adelaide), the sale of Waverley Park, the building of Docklands Stadium and a $500 million TV rights bonanza in 2001, but much was overseen by hands-on commissioners like Evans and Samuel.

'Wayne is a very nice and decent man,' foundation commissioner Dick Seddon said. 'He delegated a lot and did not have the greatest control over all management matters. He was absolutely run over by Andrew Demetriou when Andrew was president of the players' association. He was not able to push back against Andrew and this is the era when the players' association began to grow and increase its power and influence. And the power of Demetriou over Jackson increased even further when Andrew joined the AFL as the football operations manager.'[16]

Terry O'Connor recalled attending a farewell dinner held in Jackson's honour in Melbourne eighteen months after his own exit from the commission. 'The main speaker was Andrew Demetriou and when I came away I thought to myself, "They all think that the competition exists for them and the clubs are their servants."

'It appalled me that I may have been part of that without realising it. I think the commission forgets at times that it is a creature of the clubs and the clubs seem to forget it as well.'[17]

As Jackson walked off into the sunset, a star strategic planner he had hand-picked from Andersen Consulting in mid-2000, a towering South Australian–raised amateur footballer called Gillon McLachlan, was making his own name at league headquarters.

His rise would be as rapid as Demetriou's.

The Carlton salary cap debacle, the realignment of power relations between the AFL and its clubs, the ratcheting up of the financial stakes, the diminished power of the clubs and the rise and rise of Demetriou established the organisational culture that would prevail for the next decade.

And the fight against drugs would become the next big battleground.

# CHAPTER 6

# Three strikes

It was a hot April afternoon in Melbourne and Carlton's Laurence Angwin was off his face.

He was wearing a jumper and tracksuit pants despite the heat, and his teammates incredulously double-checked the speedometer on his exercise bike as they observed him riding 'at 100 miles an hour'.[1]

Downstairs in the showers at Carlton's Princes Park headquarters in leafy Parkville, teammate Karl Norman was seen staggering about, eyes rolling in his head.

The Blues duo had hit the town the previous night and then attended the club's compulsory recovery session under the influence of the party drug ecstasy.

Seething Carlton chiefs took matters into their own hands and drug tested the pair on the spot.

Angwin was sacked and Norman retained (because of a cleaner rap sheet), but after this incident early in the 2004 season, drugs and footy were back in the headlines.

For the AFL's top brass, who had become increasingly concerned about the use of illicit drugs in the player ranks, it was the final straw.

In February the next year, league chief executive Andrew Demetriou unveiled his illicit drugs policy; a radical testing regimen designed in conjunction with the players' union he once ran.

Former North Melbourne club doctor Harry Unglik, Demetriou's close friend (who would later enter a portrait of the league boss for the Archibald Prize), and AFL chief medical officer Peter Harcourt helped devise the scheme.

It was a three-strikes system, whereby players who tested positive for a third time during a set period would be named, shamed and suspended for twelve weeks. The first strike would be made known only to Harcourt and required the player to attend confidential education and counselling sessions.

The same applied for a second strike, but this time the player's club doctor would be informed to assist in his rehabilitation.

Testing began on 14 February 2005, and was carried out for forty-four weeks of the year but the policy was primarily aimed at education and rehabilitation and was starkly at odds with the World Anti-Doping Agency (WADA) system. Under the WADA code, players who tested positive to illicit substances on game day faced instant suspensions.

The issue erupted in June 2005 when the AFL refused to sign a revamped global WADA code on drug use in sport.

The league's policy, Demetriou declared, was better.

'The AFL's drug-testing regime is probably the most vigilant of any sport in the world,' he said.[2]

But failure to be WADA compliant would come at a heavy price – the withdrawal of up to $3 million in annual federal funding, future infrastructure cash grants and potentially access to stadiums like the MCG.

The stand-off reached flashpoint at a meeting in Melbourne on 28 June where Demetriou and Evans faced off with federal sport minister Rod Kemp and officials from the Australian Sports Commission.

More than 160 nations, including Australia, had already signed the WADA accord in the fight against drug cheats, but the AFL wanted amendments made around the use of cannabinoids and anti-inflammatory agents, supposedly because of a belief some of its players were using marijuana.

'I told them my door was always open but that they wouldn't receive any funding for AFL grounds or access to the AIS [Australian Institute of Sport] until it was signed,' Kemp recalled.[3]

Battle lines between Demetriou and the Howard government had been drawn five months earlier when the league boss was invited to deliver the John Batman Oration to mark Australia Day at the Melbourne Convention Centre.

Demetriou used the speech to take aim at the government's tough immigration policies and spoke of the 'days without prejudice' when his Cypriot parents arrived in Australia as migrants in 1951.

'The next decade is a watershed for us as a country,' Demetriou said.[4] 'It will see the transition from the Howard era to another era: what will come after John Howard? All I can do is hope that next generation of our leaders – whether Liberal or Labor – will think broadly, and challenge their values and our values, rather than building barriers between us and a world in need.

'If a *Tampa* suddenly appeared on our borders today, I'd like to think we might ask how we embrace the people on board, rather than how to rid ourselves of the problem. I'd like to think we'd respond as we did when the tsunami struck, rather than how we did when the *Tampa* arrived uninvited on our shores.'

In his weekly column for Melbourne's *Herald Sun*, 3AW broadcaster Neil Mitchell declared that Demetriou 'sounded more like he was applying to be Mark Latham's replacement than he did the leader of the most successful sports organisation in the country'.

'Andrew Demetriou is a powerful and charming man. But he is deluded if he thinks the AFL is a political weapon rather than a bunch of blokes who can organise a decent game of footy,' Mitchell wrote.[5]

The arrival of Demetriou's parents, Mitchell pointed out, had come during the days of the White Australia policy.

The piece de resistance of Demetriou's speech came when he took aim at the Australian flag. 'I want our flag to be our flag, and our country to be our country,' he said.

Treasurer Peter Costello, Essendon's number one ticket holder and a close friend of commission chairman Ron Evans, was the first to fire back.

'He's entitled to his views but, you know, Andrew's strengths are probably more in the AFL area than in political history,' Costello said.[6]

Federal Liberal MP Sophie Panopoulos urged the AFL boss to stick to football 'unless Mr Demetriou sees an ALP pre-selection coming his way'.[7]

Hostilities were just warming up.

Apart from the fight about WADA, the Howard government had diagnosed Demetriou's AFL as blatantly Labor-aligned. Senior Victorian Liberals began referring to AFL House as 'the Docklands branch of the ALP' or 'Kremlin House'.

Even the AFL's own could see it. 'I've had the view for a while that the AFL Commission was the Labor Party at play,' former commissioner Terry O'Connor said. 'I have been concerned from afar that they really seem to regard themselves as primarily a group responsible for social change. One can't necessarily object to all of that, but it seems to me that the focus is more on that sort of thing than the good of football. The clubs appointed the commission to run football not be an agent of "Woke" ideology.'[8]

As the years rolled on, the AFL under Demetriou drifted further into championing social issues.

A league official appeared to be deadly serious when he opined to a group of Melbourne businesspeople that because of the demise of the Catholic Church 'Australians now look up to the AFL for guidance'.

'Because of the strength of the code it does have responsibility in terms of how we perform and our attitudes, but conversely, the AFL have allowed themselves to become the social bellwether on every issue, and it's wrong,' former Victorian premier Jeff Kennett said. 'It's there to administer the code.'[9]

The irony, of course, was that inside its own four walls, the conduct and behaviour of many of the league's top dogs was starkly at odds with the public preaching.

Outrage over the AFL's refusal to sign the WADA code was growing. Demetriou insisted his policy was better, and he rarely, if ever, retreated. But why wouldn't he sign? What was the motivation behind his alternative drugs code? Maybe his policy was better because it guaranteed the protection of AFL players who failed illicit drugs tests? Or maybe he knew that Dale Lewis, the man he had excoriated for daring to talk publicly about the extent of drug use within the AFL player ranks, was on the money? After all, as far as many were concerned, Demetriou could never tolerate being proven wrong.

Olympic swimming great Kieren Perkins warned that Australia's global reputation in sport was 'unravelling' over the league's drugs stance. 'To back away from this code is small-minded and irresponsible,' Perkins declared. 'For a sport that has built up a great reputation, this is so counter-productive and it's a shame for Australian sport.'[10]

WADA boss Dick Pound hit out, saying, 'the AFL has had their head in the sand over this and part of the deal in sport is you don't take drugs'. As for the league's three-strikes illicit drugs policy, Pound said: 'By the time you get the third or fourth offence, it is more like an intelligence test, not a drug test.'[11]

At a second meeting between the AFL, Rod Kemp and the Australian Sports Commission on 19 July, it was made clear to Demetriou that there would be no compromise in his stand-off with WADA.

League lawyer Jeff Browne, who had accompanied Demetriou to the meeting, recognised first that it was the end of the road.

'I turned to Andrew and whispered into his ear, "Mate, I think we're fucked."'[12]

Even Demetriou conceded he had lost.

'The result of it was we became WADA compliant,' Browne said. 'We needed to redevelop the SCG, we needed to redevelop the Gabba and we had a heavy reliance on government funding to do all that.'

It would be a long time before Demetriou would again suffer such a significant loss.

'They did have an attitude that because it's Australian Rules and they don't have to report to a world body, they are their own masters in a sense,' Kemp said. 'They didn't enjoy being forced to integrate into a world code. They made the judgement that they could stand apart from it – and it was a serious misjudgement.'

The AFL's contentious illicit drugs policy – kept in place along with the new WADA policy – came under fresh fire years later when it was revealed that players who had self-reported the use of illicit drugs before they were about to be tested had not received a strike. Multiple players had self-reported more than once in a deliberate abuse of the policy.

Years after his retirement in 2014, Melbourne and Carlton midfielder Brock McLean revealed he had registered just one positive illicit drugs test during his eleven-year AFL career despite dozens of weekend benders mixing booze, cocaine, ecstasy and speed.

Demetriou and his successor, Gillon McLachlan, often claimed that random illicit drug testing had been extended to members of the AFL Commission and the executive, but this fact was significantly overplayed.

'If it's good enough for them, it's good enough for us,' Demetriou said in 2011. 'The last time was probably over twelve months ago when someone came into my office and said, "Over here, into this toilet" – and away I went.'[13]

\*\*\*

After taking over from Jackson, Demetriou reshaped the AFL executive team, surprising almost everyone by appointing little-known Melbourne defamation lawyer Adrian Anderson as his football operations manager. Anderson was just thirty-one and had no previous experience in football administration.

'He might grow into it but he's one of a number of queue jumpers Andrew has surrounded himself with,' a club official was quoted as saying at the time.[14]

Another club boss lamented Demetriou's decision to hire Anderson over Port Adelaide chief executive Brian Cunningham.

Demetriou's former North Melbourne teammate – Ben Buckley – was elevated into the AFL's number two position as general manager of broadcasting, strategy and major projects, with McLachlan becoming general manager of commercial operations, Ian Anderson running finance and Dave Matthews in game development.

It was a high-octane workplace where Demetriou would have the Sky Racing Channel running on his office wall TV. Punting was a staple diet for many of Demetriou's top men. One league staffer recalled being shown the hand by the league CEO while walking into his office and interrupting the climax of a race.

In the mid-2000s, during an industry conference in Adelaide, McLachlan arranged for the executive and a group of AFL stakeholders to tour the Lindsay Park Racing Stable and Stud in the Barossa Valley, resulting in the purchasing of a horse they named Dealbreaker. It ran a few times, got injured, and was sold off.

'I really enjoyed working for Andrew because you always knew where you stood,' a long-time league staffer said. 'You've got to be pretty ruthless and be prepared to make tough decisions, but he'd put you in a role and back you in. He didn't interfere too much, he was there to help if there was a big issue, but he would definitely challenge you if he didn't like something that was going on. We were just a young and aggressive group getting an enormous amount of stuff done.'

They were the cream of the team Demetriou crowed about when he convinced commission chairman Ron Evans to entrust greater control to Wayne Jackson's executive at the meeting in Cape Schanck held not long after his arrival in mid-2000.

And once in the big chair himself, Demetriou wasted no time flexing his muscle in clubland.

At a meeting with the new-look Carlton board in mid-2004, the AFL boss outraged some in the room by pushing the club to agree to the league's desire for the Blues to shift a number of their home games to Docklands Stadium.

An official present on the night said the club was threatened with unfavourable TV slots if it did not relent. One director boldly challenged the league contingent to repeat the ultimatum in front of the TV reporters parked outside the club, an offer that was declined. 'They wanted us to go to the Docklands and we didn't want to go there,' the Carlton official said. 'It didn't matter what anyone else said or wanted.'

It was a combative style of leadership in total contrast to Jackson's.

A new sheriff was in town and it was precisely what the commission wanted.

'We knew that Andrew wanted to run his own race,' a commissioner of the day explained. 'He wasn't going to be listening to what we had to say every day, he would say, "I've got my own views and I will be the chief executive."'

During the second week of the 2004 AFL finals series when Geelong beat Essendon by ten points in a cut-throat semi-final at the MCG, it was revealed that Demetriou and Ron Evans had left the league's official function early in the first quarter in favour of a night at the opera.

The pair were spotted scampering across the nearby Rod Laver Arena footbridge at about 8 p.m. to catch a performance by the blind Italian tenor Andrea Bocelli backed by the Melbourne Symphony Orchestra and a 38-piece choir.

'Not a capital offence, but a bad call,' *Herald Sun* chief football writer Mike Sheahan wrote at the time. 'Demetriou is the face of the AFL. The sight of him and Evans walking away from the MCG to Rod Laver Arena would have been a conversation point for many who passed them.'[15]

North Melbourne director Peter de Rauch was the inaugural chairman of Melbourne sports radio station SEN, which hit the airwaves for the first time in January that year. According to de Rauch, the station made inquiries about bidding to broadcast AFL matches but was told there was 'no way known it would happen while I was involved'.

'I did the honourable thing for the sake of the company and resigned,' de Rauch said. 'The AFL operated a big boys' club business, and I wasn't in it.'[16]

Money was almost always prioritised over integrity, a bent that seriously hindered the Brisbane Lions' pursuit of a fourth successive premiership in 2004.

Thanks to a commercial arrangement struck between the AFL and the Melbourne Cricket Club guaranteeing that at least one preliminary final be played at the MCG each season, Brisbane was forced to play a 'home' prelim against Geelong in Melbourne. The Lions got through but were mowed down by Port Adelaide in the grand final. Legendary Lions coach Leigh Matthews refused to shake the hands of Demetriou and then AFL football operations manager Adrian Anderson after the siren.

'In my mind the AFL denied us our best shot at winning a historic fourth consecutive premiership and here were the league's two main office-bearers and decision-makers having the temerity to act friendly when clearly they'd been the enemy,'

Matthews later said. 'I was in no mood for diplomacy, frankly I felt more like punching them on the nose, and muttered to them, "You blokes have got to be kidding," before turning my back and walking away.'[17]

The MCG deal was rescinded soon after.

Midway through the 2005 season Demetriou took aim at the Sydney Swans and their coach Paul Roos over the team's defensive style of play. 'We don't tell football clubs how to play, but obviously we take notice of how things are going,' Demetriou said. 'And I guess I, like others, would like to see the Sydney Swans winning more games because it's a very important market for us.

'I think it would be fair to say in the early part of the season we saw some games that weren't attractive, and I think they've been described as ugly ... Unless the Swans change that style of play, they won't win many football matches.'[18]

This was the new way: a mob boss mentality where recalcitrants got 'whacked'. Under the leadership of Demetriou, the AFL made no secret that it was the boss and the clubs their subordinates.

But, embarrassingly for Demetriou, four months after slagging their style of play, Sydney, under the coaching of Roos, would beat the West Coast Eagles to claim the AFL premiership.

Angst over Demetriou's comments had lingered all season.

'I was probably surprised at the time that someone from the AFL didn't apologise or didn't say it was taken out of context or, "Look we've spoken to Andrew and it's not great for our brand for the CEO to say that,"' Roos said. 'But it wasn't that out of character. I liken it to the CEO of Coca-Cola saying, "Oh, look – I wouldn't be drinking Coca-Cola in New South Wales – try Pepsi." It was just a strange thing for the CEO to say when we were doing so much work to promote the game in Sydney – to come out and basically tell people, "Don't go and watch the Swans play, they are terrible."'[19]

Roos suspected it was a part of a wider AFL agenda against the game's senior coaches amid the rise of defensive game styles. 'It soon became apparent that we were seen as the enemy, rather than allies,' Roos said. 'Andrew and his administration had a really clear vision and that's when all the rules started to change and Adrian Anderson became quite combative in the meetings, because they were really set on their views on clubs and coaches.

'One of the questions I would always ask was, "Well, what do you want the game to look like?" And they could never answer it. It seemed to lead into that combative era of the AFL versus the coaches. It was a strange approach. Why was it a combative era? I don't think any of us really know.'

In a profile story in *The Australian* on the day of the Swans–Eagles grand final, Demetriou was unrepentant about his attack on Roos. 'Nobody ever told me that as CEO of the AFL you shouldn't have an opinion and I expressed my view,' he said. 'That's just me. I can't artificially create a persona.'[20]

On nominating a pet hate, Demetriou said, 'Dishonesty. I won't tolerate it. Non-negotiable. That would easily be at the top of the list ... and greed.'

The 2005 article, written by journalist Michael Davis, described Demetriou as 'the super-confident, larger-than-life salesman'. It read: 'His detractors in the AFL's inner sanctum and among the sixteen clubs in the competition say woe betide anyone who criticises him. His supporters prefer to call him a benevolent dictator, a street fighter who is very good at thinking on his feet and who goes on the front foot when under attack.'

And while Demetriou had broken the mould of private school connections, Davis said, he 'does seem smitten with employing and rubbing shoulders with the private school set'.

Essendon coaching legend Kevin Sheedy soon began referring to Demetriou (half-jokingly) as 'Vladimir' and the AFL as the 'Kremlin'.

'Why so many references to [being a] dictator?' football journalist Mark Robinson asked him years later.

'You'd have to ask them, but I suspect it's the nature of the role of having to make tough decisions,' Demetriou said. 'And some people can construe that as having far too much influence or power. And I don't. Hopefully, decisions in this place are done with careful thought.'[21]

But Mark 'Bomber' Thompson, who became coach of Geelong ahead of the 2000 season – the same year Demetriou joined the league, said it was at this precise time when the AFL administration began to lose touch with its clubs.

Instead of focusing on how to best 'service' the teams, the AFL became obsessed with controlling its brand, he said. 'When Demetriou started that was when the AFL stopped listening and talking to clubs and coaches,' Thompson reflected. 'Instead it was just going in and being talked to. This is the way it's going to be and you're going to do it.

'And I thought from that moment on there was no input from any clubs. You had people there who had been in footy for a long period of time, [Kevin] Sheedy, [Denis] Pagan, [Mick] Malthouse – all these people with a wealth of knowledge just brushed over.

'The AFL actually didn't really care about individual clubs that much and that's exactly what their purpose was – to service the clubs, to put games on and administer the game. You'd never see them at club level. You'd maybe see them once a year.'

\*\*\*

Jeff Kennett never really left the public arena after his shock state election loss on preliminary final day in 1999, serving on various boards and as the inaugural chairman of national depression initiative, Beyond Blue. On 14 December 2005 he was elected president of the Hawthorn Football Club, replacing the retired Ian Dicker.

Kennett had some dealings with the AFL throughout his reign as Victorian premier from 1992 to 1999 but was floored by what he saw attending his first presidents' meeting at AFL House in early 2006.

'You're only one of a team but you became the one who represented the club at AFL meetings,' Kennett said of the role of a club president. 'So I was on a learning curve in terms of the other personalities from other clubs and the operation of the AFL. I was very conscious of, I guess, the strength of the code and became very much aware, very quickly, that the club presidents and commission meetings were orchestrated, that views were sometimes taken but almost always out of politeness, rather than listening, and that between the chairman and the CEO, they had their own agendas.

'It was almost as though they only met us because they had to meet us.'[22]

The lack of subtlety surprised Kennett.

'I was surprised at the clinical-ness of it. There was really no pretence,' he said. 'I also became very quickly aware of how some presidents were really neutered because of their dependence on the AFL for survival. There were only a few who could speak openly and honestly.'

Unsurprisingly, Kennett was one of those. He immediately took aim at the AFL over its three-strikes illicit drugs policy.

Kennett's concerns about the policy's secrecy were vindicated four years later when Hawthorn player Travis Tuck, the son of club great Michael Tuck, was found unconscious at the wheel of his car and treated for an alleged drug overdose. 'I knew it was wrong because we had an incident involving Travis Tuck, who almost lost his life, and I didn't know about it until then,' Kennett said.

'I knew through Beyond Blue that if one of my soldiers was in trouble and we knew about it, we could do something about it – and I'm not saying that the whole club should know but the president and the CEO should know.

'And it wasn't only for the interests of the individual, but he might have around him three or four others who were also in that sort of mix,' Kennett said. 'I argued and argued against it and at one commission meeting one of the other presidents said: "I don't want to be told, I don't want to know, it's not my responsibility."

'I couldn't believe it. It shattered me.'

Later in 2006, North Melbourne was in the market for a new chief executive officer after Geoff Walsh quit to take up a job as Collingwood football manager.

'We advertised the job and got about five or six applicants,' then Kangaroos director Peter de Rauch recalled, 'and at the next board meeting at 7 o'clock in the morning, Demetriou turned up and demanded that we appoint Mark Brayshaw.'[23]

Brayshaw, who had played thirty-two games for North Melbourne and worked in administrative roles at Fremantle, Port Adelaide and Richmond, had been interviewed for the position, but the majority of the board weren't keen.

Parachuting their own candidates into senior club positions has become an AFL art form, as was the case when lawyer Glen Bartlett was endorsed to take on the Melbourne presidency in 2013 and Gary Pert became his CEO five years later.

But on this occasion, North said no.

'Demetriou was acting like Nikita Khrushchev banging his shoes at the United Nations,' de Rauch said. 'He was getting louder and louder, saying we had to appoint Mark Brayshaw and I started saying, "Look, we decide, not you. It's our right. It's got nothing to do with you."'

The North Melbourne board duly appointed Rick Aylett, the son of legendary club president Allen Aylett, as CEO. 'He was the best of the lot at the time but I think Andrew would have been spewing,' de Rauch said.

Demetriou had a long memory, too, as retired Carlton hard-man Fraser Brown discovered in September 2006. Brown had been at the centre of the AFL's investigations into salary cap cheating at the Blues in 2002 and famously refused to cooperate with Demetriou's inquiries.

Four years on, and now in the big chair at AFL House, Demetriou boldly and publicly declared that the commission might use its powers to block a move by Brown to form a ticket and challenge Carlton president Graham Smorgon and his board.

'We do not know what Fraser Brown's intentions are but if he wants to join the Carlton board the AFL would have very serious concerns,' Demetriou said. 'And we have sought legal advice that we could act on those concerns.'[24]

Brown was never obligated to rat on his own club during an era where salary cap cheating was rife across the competition, but these were the new rules of engagement under Demetriou, even if he denied it himself.

'I'm not vindictive,' he later told the *Sunday Age*. 'I honestly don't go home and think about who I am going to have a grudge against, I'm thinking about which nappy to change.'[25]

St Kilda had thrived under the coaching of Grant Thomas, playing in consecutive preliminary finals in 2004 and 2005. But Thomas believes there is ample evidence to suggest the Saints were compromised during his coaching tenure because of his poor relationship with Demetriou. 'They kept sticking it to us through the draw, making it incredibly difficult for us every step of the way,' Thomas said.[26]

The bad blood spilled over in August 2005 when Thomas was fined $15,000 and the club another $5000 after he urged the game's umpires 'to put their ego in the locker when they start their career and pick it up when they finish their career'.

The Saints played Fremantle at Subiaco three days later and were bemused when the three officiating umpires entered the change rooms in single file before the match, shook one player's hand, and swiftly exited. Usual procedure involved the umpires mingling for a few minutes with players and officials.

'They were in the rooms for no more than forty-five seconds and [assistant coach] Matt Rendell dug me in the ribs and said, "I think we're in for a hard one,"' Thomas said.

TV footage captured Thomas and Rendell laughing together in the coaches' box after a dubious first-quarter umpiring decision.

In the dying seconds of the match, Dockers forward Justin Longmuir took a pack mark and slotted a goal after the siren to hand the Saints a costly defeat.

As the umpires boarded a flight home to Melbourne, Channel 9 journalist Tony Jones alleged he heard one of the umpires say, 'Now I know what it feels like to have a victory.' A businessman seated near Jones who heard the exchange scrawled the comments onto his boarding pass, while several other witnesses came forward verifying Jones's claims, later dubbed 'Whispers in the Sky'.

It triggered an AFL investigation, which exonerated umpires Matthew Head and Brett Allen of any wrongdoing.

St Kilda match-up coordinator Mark 'Gus' Parker, sitting two seats in front of Jones, was among those interviewed by ex–Victoria Police officers working for the league's integrity unit.

'I had these two retired coppers come out to my office in Port Melbourne and they had no intention of doing anything about what I said,' Parker said. 'I could tell from the minute that they walked in that they were just treating me with disdain – and I am telling you now that one of those pricks fell asleep during the interview.

'He deadset shut his eyes and I looked at the other bloke and said, "What's going on here?" and he said, "Oh, we've had a lot to do, we had a few people to talk to and we're a bit weary."

'They just weren't interested. It just shows the power of City Hall.'[27]

Jones and the other witnesses stood by their claims, but the case was closed.

Nothing to see here.

The new rules of the game meant integrity, a fundamental of governance, was more about rhetoric than reality.

But across the country, in the wild west, a new scandal was rumbling that could not be contained.

## CHAPTER 7

# Born to rule

WHEN PRINCE CHARLES ROLLED IN TO SOUTH AUSTRALIA during a 1988 Royal Tour he was lent a broodmare called Julie to play in an exhibition polo match on the Waterloo Corner grounds of the Adelaide Polo Club.

Julie belonged to fourteen-year-old St Peter's College schoolboy Gillon McLachlan, the eldest of four brothers and progeny of one of the state's wealthiest families.

'Charles is a better than average player in deep defence,' McLachlan told a local newspaper reporter ahead of the Prince of Wales' visit. 'Boy, will I have something to tell the kids in form 10 ... I would have liked to have met Lady Di, but I don't think she's coming ... maybe she'll change her mind at the last minute.'[1]

Gillon was raised on the family's 2000-hectare sheep station of 'Rosebank' in the Adelaide Hills near Mount Pleasant – about an hour's drive north-east of Adelaide (the property was once used as a farm set for the hit TV soapie *McLeod's Daughters*) – and was destined for high achievement.

According to the AFL website, McLachlan's 'Gaelic-speaking great-great-great-grandparents migrated from the highlands of Scotland to South Australia in the 1850s'.[2] His great-grandfather Hugh Patterson McLachlan was a successful grazier on a property near Yunta, about 300 kilometres north-east of Adelaide.

'HP was a pretty hard man,' the league boss once said. 'He made a go of dry, tough country in the middle of nowhere in South Australia where it mightn't rain for three years, and where others hadn't been able to make a go of it. To do that, you have to be hard and make tough decisions.'

But HP's biggest claim to fame came in the spring of 1931 when White Nose, the racehorse he owned and bred, upstaged the legendary Phar Lap to win the Melbourne Cup. 'It's a great story, and one that is a source of immense pride to the family,' McLachlan would say. The Cup was handed down through the family and takes pride of place on the dining room table on Christmas Day.

Years later, McLachlan would re-register his great-grandfather's racing silks, boasting a white sash and the family tartan. 'It's a real thrill when you win with a horse you've bred, and you do it in the colours your great-grandfather used,' he said. 'It has a bit of meaning.'

Gillon's father, Angus, made his first-class cricket debut for Cambridge University in the United Kingdom in 1964, taking four wickets bowling leg spin, before returning home and taking charge at Rosebank at age twenty-six in 1971.

Angus's elder brother, Ian, also went to Cambridge, played first-class cricket, was a director at Elders IXL and president of the National Farmers' Federation before becoming the federal member for Barker and minister for defence in the Howard government.

It was Ian McLachlan who witnessed an alleged agreement between John Howard and future treasurer Peter Costello in December 1994, where Howard was said to have given an undertaking to hand over the leadership after one and a half terms if the Liberal Party took power.

The handover never took place and when the story broke in 2006, Ian revealed he had carried a record of the discussion around in his wallet for years. 'I made a note because Costello said to me one day: "I think we'd better make a note of that arrangement" and I said, "Good idea",' McLachlan said.[3]

Ian was a long-time president of the South Australian Cricket Association and a key driver behind the $535 million Adelaide Oval redevelopment completed in 2013.

Andrew Demetriou had led the charge in shifting football away from the decaying Football Park at West Lakes to Adelaide's city centre; a coup that required the buy-in of South Australian cricket.

'Andrew was seminal,' Ian McLachlan said later of the secret negotiations. 'He and [state treasurer] Kevin [Foley] decided that this was something that needed to happen for the good of the place, so we'd sneak off and have these meetings. It was fun.'[4]

Ian was the first man Demetriou thanked after the Adelaide Oval's reopening in 2014.

But it was Ian's nephew Gillon, a standout school student, who won the prestigious C.A.S. Hawker Scholarship in 1992, who would soon tower over all of the McLachlan clan.

In a citation on the scholarship's website written in 2016, McLachlan says: 'The Hawker Scholarship provided me with the opportunity to attend St Mark's at the University of Adelaide and Trinity College at the University of Melbourne. These experiences facilitated extraordinary changes in my life – a new environment, new market, new friends and new challenges. I finished my law degree in Melbourne, travelled for a year, then worked as a management consultant with Accenture in their strategy division working across different functions, industries and markets.'[5]

McLachlan spent time jackarooing in the Riverina region of New South Wales, and, like his father and uncle, was accepted into Cambridge University. But the big smoke of Melbourne called and he knocked Cambridge back.

Residing at Trinity College on the grounds of Melbourne University, opposite Naughtons Hotel on Royal Parade in Parkville, McLachlan starred as a gangly ruckman for the Uni Blues footy club in the top grades of the Victorian Amateur Football Association. He was club captain, a best and fairest winner, life member, committee member and state representative.

His Uni Blues coach, Grant Williams, and teammate Stephen Meade would later follow him to AFL House in senior positions as would state teammates Simon Lethlean and Andrew Dillon, from the rival amateur club Old Xaverians.

A St Kilda supporter (although photographed wearing a Crows scarf at a final at the MCG in 1998), McLachlan spent two years on Carlton's supplementary list in 1996 and 1997 but never played a game.

He had better luck in love.

At Trinity College he met Laura Blythe, the daughter of wealthy Spotless chairman Brian Blythe, whose long-time chief executive, Ron Evans, was an AFL commissioner and soon to be its chairman.

AFL chief executive Wayne Jackson met McLachlan at a small party at Jackson's East Melbourne home, and the AFL boss was impressed. Jackson, who also hailed from

South Australia, shared the same farming interests and was acquainted with his family, offered McLachlan a job in strategy at AFL House in 2000. But they were humble beginnings, sitting outside Jackson's office, learning the ropes, for the man who would rise to the top of Australia's biggest sport.

Lawyer Chris Pollard recalled attending a meeting at AFL House where a young McLachlan delivered the coffees. 'Wayne snapped his fingers and in he came,' Pollard said. 'They were cold and they were shithouse.'6

But by late 2006, Ben Buckley – Demetriou's 'heir apparent' – had been poached to run soccer by Football Federation Australia chairman Frank Lowy and McLachlan emerged as his unofficial second-in-charge.

AFL would never know such a formidable team.

# CHAPTER 8

# Flatlining in Las Vegas

FAIRFAX INVESTIGATIVE JOURNALIST ANDREW RULE WAS lying low at his Camberwell home in Melbourne's inner-east when a trusty old contact called out of the blue.

It was early March 2007 and Rule, enjoying a well-earned week off, had just completed a stint at *Good Weekend* magazine before a return to the *Sunday Age*.

With a contact book reaching deep into the police, business, criminal and sporting worlds, Rule knew where to hunt for a yarn.

But this one found him.

His contact told him about a West Coast Eagles player who had collapsed and 'flatlined' outside a Las Vegas hotel on a wild end-of-season trip in October 2006.

Rule called a second source with connections in Perth and the story ran as a strip on page one on 11 March 2007.

'Elite footballers are young, rich and often act as if they are above the law, but they are not invincible,' Rule's first paragraph read. 'A high-flying premiership player learned that the hard way last spring when he nearly died in an American hospital.

'The strange circumstances surrounding a super-fit professional athlete being revived after "flatlining" is a story most football insiders know – but none talk about publicly.'[1]

The source for Rule's story was a veteran football administrator who said he first told two senior AFL writers in Melbourne about the Las Vegas incident. Both, he said, declined to run it.

Rule's second source firmed up the yarn but wouldn't be quoted. 'Mate, it's right, but they'd hang me off the grandstand if I went on the record,' the figure told Rule. 'It's such a small world, football.'

The player who had 'flatlined' in Las Vegas, West Coast Eagles premiership midfielder Chad Fletcher, was not named in Rule's story, but it opened the floodgates.

The previous December, Eagles superstar and Brownlow medallist Ben Cousins had been arrested after being found intoxicated and dazed outside the Melbourne Convention Centre. A photograph of Cousins asleep on the street was plastered across the front page of the *Herald Sun*, but footy's ticking time bomb – the West Coast Eagles illicit drugs crisis – was yet to explode.

Cousins had quit the Eagles captaincy in February 2006 after abandoning his car and running from police near a breath-testing station in Perth but was still considered the club's 'spiritual leader'. Six months later he held the premiership cup aloft on the MCG alongside replacement captain Chris Judd after the Eagles defeated Sydney by one point in an epic grand final.

Within days, the Eagles boys were in Las Vegas snorting lines and smoking ice pipes on the football trip that would nearly cost Fletcher his life.

Rule's 'flatlining' scoop led to a bigger one.

He was contacted by an amateur soccer player who read the story and told Rule how he had come to the rescue of Cousins on the night he had collapsed near the Melbourne Convention Centre in December 2006.

The soccer player told Rule he had encountered a man 'shivering' on the street just after 2 o'clock. on a Saturday morning – 'and I realised it was Ben Cousins'.

Rule's second front-page story in a week was the lead story of the 18 March 2007 edition of the *Sunday Age*.

The West Coast Eagles drugs scandal was out of the blocks.

The soccer player offered candid details of Cousins' distressed state when he found him collapsed on the street. 'He was sweating and paranoid. He had his hands over his face and was looking around as if he was frightened someone was chasing him,' the witness said. 'I think I can tell the difference between drunk and drugs and I'd say he was tripping out bad – his brain was fried on some hard-core stuff.'

Rule's two big yarns, a week apart, coincided with another Cousins meltdown out west. On Tuesday, 20 March, the superstar midfielder was stood down by his club for missing a training session. His parents, Bryan and Stephanie, revealed their son was battling problems related to substance abuse and the following day he was suspended indefinitely after the Eagles found out he'd been out on a three-day bender.

On 22 March, the AFL held its annual season launch at the Carousel on Albert Park Lake in Melbourne. Andrew Demetriou and Gillon McLachlan were seen locked in heated conversation outside the venue before proceedings kicked off. A big Eagles problem was about to become a full-blown AFL crisis.

'I was a bit outside the magic circle and I worked out a way to write it,' Rule recalled of his Las Vegas yarn. 'There is no doubt that established football writers had known about it and were dismayed that it had broken elsewhere.

'And the Ben Cousins story really put the match to the fire and away it went. The AFL were really rattled by it, because Ben was the pin-up boy.'[2]

The gala Albert Park function, where the sixteen team captains were unveiled on a floating pontoon, was also Mike Fitzpatrick's first as AFL Commission chairman. Ron Evans, who had been battling abdominal cancer, had passed away on 12 March just a month after retiring from his position.

It was a seminal moment in the history of the game, unleashing a ruthless Fitzpatrick–Demetriou double act upon the competition.

The tributes for Evans flowed. 'He never lost his temper, he was never aggressive, but he led the commission through the most difficult issues and through an extraordinary period of change in a most determined, yet at the same time a most collaborative and consultative fashion,' retired commissioner Graeme Samuel told ABC radio.[3]

That would all change under chairman Fitzpatrick.

\*\*\*

Ben Cousins' spiralling drug addiction got the better of him before a ball had been kicked in season 2007.

On 31 March, he flew out to a Californian rehabilitation facility specialising in methamphetamine addiction. Returning home a month later, he appeared on national TV, admitted to substance abuse and apologised for his fall from grace.

In late June, Cousins convinced Demetriou and AFL chief medical officer Dr Peter Harcourt that he had overcome his issues before making a stunning 38-possession return in a game against Sydney at Subiaco Oval on 21 July. A hamstring strain ended his season in the qualifying final against Port Adelaide.

It would be an off-season from hell for West Coast and an AFL administration that would be determined to smother the extent of the scandal.

On the night of 1 October 2007, retired Eagles champion and Perth TV identity Chris Mainwaring was found dead from a drug overdose at his Cottesloe home. An investigation by the Western Australia state coroner found Mainwaring had died from a cocaine-caused seizure.

The coroner's report revealed Cousins had visited Mainwaring's home on two occasions on the day of his death and entered a bedroom where he 'saw a quantity of a substance which he believed to be cocaine on a plate'.[4]

Mainwaring's death devastated the Perth football-loving community, but was just the start of a shocking sequence of drug-fuelled events.

Fifteen days later, images of a shirtless Cousins being arrested for drugs possession and escorted to the back of a WA Police divisional van flashed around the country. The freshly inked 'Such is Life' tattoo splashed across his torso offered a window into the soul of a one-time football golden boy who had seriously lost his way.

It was the final straw for West Coast (and the AFL), who sacked him at an emergency board meeting the next night. Cousins, Eagles chiefs declared, was 'terribly sick' and needed to focus 'solely and only on his health'.

The drugs charges against Cousins were dropped but on 19 November the AFL Commission suspended him for twelve months anyway for bringing the game into disrepute.

Astonishingly, the drug-addicted champion had never failed an AFL illicit drug test throughout his career.

But when it came to drug abuse, the Cousins story was just the tip of the iceberg in footy's wild west – yet more proof that Dale Lewis, who had raised the alarm about the extent of drug use in the game, only to be savagely shot down, had been on the money.

And quite clearly, Demetriou's three-strikes drugs policy, the one he fought so fiercely against the government and WADA to implement, was a flop. Drugs were rife and full-blown addicts were escaping detection.

Determined to protect their brands – and themselves – senior AFL and club officials worked overtime to cover up a decade of rampant illicit drug use by West Coast Eagles stars. At its heart was the belief of many in football circles that the club's 2006 premiership was tainted by the widespread abuse of cocaine, speed, ice, ecstasy and marijuana.

In a move aimed at investigating the depth of the problem, but at the same time keeping it all in-house, the AFL Commission turned to retired Supreme Court judge E. William Gillard, QC. Gillard was appointed as a special investigator and spent three months uncovering incidents involving Eagles players and administrators dating back to the late 1990s before presenting his explosive findings to the league in February 2008. His secret 87-page report was one of the most closely guarded documents in football history, with just three hard copies ever produced.

Gillard's discoveries were shocking.

An internal Eagles investigation had found the earliest drug-related incident involved three senior players on a football trip to Spain in 1998 'observed behaving in a highly stimulated fashion despite not drinking alcohol'. Coaches at the club were warned by police as early as 2001 about players dabbling in drugs. Eagles bosses also knew of a prescription form stolen from a club doctor used by a star midfielder to buy fifty Valium pills – to help teammates 'prolong a high'.

And Gillard got to the bottom of Rule's big scoop about Chad Fletcher flatlining in Las Vegas.

Fletcher was in Vegas with eighteen teammates and five club officials who had extended their premiership celebrations with a trip to Sin City. On the final night of festivities, Fletcher collapsed outside the MGM Grand Casino and showed no sign of a pulse. He was revived by a club staffer before being rushed to hospital.

When the news broke at home, club bosses insisted Fletcher's illness was 'alcohol induced' or an allergic reaction from a yellow fever vaccination. 'We vehemently deny any drugs were involved,' Eagles president Dalton Gooding flatly declared.

But Gillard concluded that illicit drugs were indeed the cause of Fletcher's brush with death in the Nevada desert. 'On the morning after his admission to the hospital, Fletcher was observed to be in an unconscious state by two of the officials and was gravely ill. He was strapped into a hospital bed,' Gillard wrote. 'I interviewed Fletcher on two occasions. In the second interview, I informed him that I had a provisional view that drugs were involved in his collapse and I invited him to produce his medical records,' Gillard reported. 'He refused to do so.'[5]

Gillard's report fully detailed Fletcher's denial. 'Fletcher ... told me that he did not know what caused his problem. He was very ill and he recognised that he had had "a very moving and very life-changing event".'

Gillard's report outlined statements from other sources involved that helped inform his findings. 'Evidence was placed before me that a few days before the incident Fletcher was openly displaying in a bar a photograph on a digital camera screen which appeared to show a supply of a substance that looked like the drug ice ... he was observed to be highly stimulated ...

'I gave Fletcher the opportunity to comment on this evidence and he denied that it had occurred. I do not believe him. I have no reason to disbelieve the source of the information.'

Gillard's summary was unequivocal: 'In my opinion, the totality of the evidence leads to the conclusion that Chad Fletcher was taking drugs in Las Vegas and that the taking of the drugs was a cause of his serious illness. Fletcher was not penalised.'

Gillard was scathing in his assessment of both the club's handling of the issue at the time and the evidence of its players and officials. 'This whole episode reflects upon the club,' Gillard said. 'It exemplifies the attitude which had persisted for some five years previously, and that was to ignore any suggestion of drug-taking. The official line was there was no evidence of drug-taking. But the circumstantial evidence cannot be ignored.'

In his summary, Gillard wrote: 'Too much time was spent in my investigation on this incident. It was difficult to ascertain the truth ... The club adopted what it had done in the past and moved into damage-control mode. It hid behind the fact that it was alleged it could not prove that Fletcher had taken drugs in Las Vegas despite all the circumstantial evidence pointing to it ... and let the incident pass without any form of penalty. Again, the wrong message was sent to all the players.'

A spree of other undisclosed incidents, including a car crash and lies to police about who was behind the wheel, were also uncovered. But on-field success and commercial riches led the club's senior management to ignore it all.

'The culture developed over a number of years and could be traced back to about the year 2000,' Gillard said in his report obtained by the *Herald Sun* in 2017. 'It was based on success, arrogance, a belief that what the players did in their own time was their own business, and a failure by the club to properly punish players in a way that acted as a deterrent.

'It was a culture which emerged and developed during a period when some players were taking illicit drugs, a fact that would have been known to the playing group and which was ignored by the club. The club did not take a stand on illicit drug-taking, and once the [AFL] Drugs Policy came into operation in early 2005, there was no excuse for the inactivity. The inaction caught up with the club in 2006.'

Gillard found that the club's leniency towards Cousins and the protection of its star player was a major factor in his personal demise and the Eagles' own unravelling.

'Cousins took such quantities that he became addicted,' Gillard said. 'However, it was not until March 20, 2007, that the club took a strong public stand on the issue. The failure to deal with Cousins also fed the culture. The Cousins saga amply demonstrates and exemplifies the dangers in failing to respond to a problem early and nipping it in the bud. The sore festers and every effort is made to cover it up without confronting the real cause and seeking to eradicate it.

'All the background evidence suggests that he [Cousins] was in the grip of illicit drugs and that he took them regularly. Yet nothing was done at the club to take a stand against illicit drug use. Importantly, Cousins remained a member of the players' leadership group. This sent the wrong message,' the report stated.

Gillard later continued: 'The fact was that to deal with him in an adequate and appropriate way would have derailed the club's campaign on the field.'

Eagles chief executive Trevor Nisbett, who kept his job and continued in his role for years, and coach John Worsfold were condemned for allowing a toxic off-field culture to 'fester'.

'During the period from 2001 to 2007, there were no set procedures laid down within the club to deal with players' off-field misconduct,' Gillard wrote. 'Each incident was dealt with by an official although as Mr Nisbett stated, he dealt with the more serious actions of misconduct and some were dealt with by the board ...

'Mr Nisbett emphasised the difficulty involved in seeking to establish the facts. I have some difficulty in accepting that players and especially officials are not forthcoming when dealing with the CEO or the coaching staff in relation to misconduct.'

Of Worsfold, who coached the club's 2006 premiership side, Gillard said: 'Coach Worsfold was told by at least three fairly reliable sources in 2002 that some players were taking illicit drugs and were mixing with undesirable persons and could get themselves into trouble. Two names were mentioned, Cousins and [Michael] Gardiner. They were spoken to by the coach, and the players responded that there was nothing to worry about.'[6]

Only after the Eagles were knocked out of the 2007 finals did the coach read the riot act to his players about illicit drugs. 'After West Coast Eagles were defeated by Collingwood in the finals series in September 2007, coach Worsfold addressed the players and after congratulating them and thanking them for their efforts in what was a very close-fought semi-final, proceeded to severely criticise a number of players, who he named, as derailing the team's efforts for season 2007,' Gillard said. 'It was clear that the coach was extremely disappointed and angry that the season had not ended on a winning note, and in particular talked about the taking of drugs and stated in a belligerent manner that "he would rather die than take a drug".'

'There is little doubt that by the end of the year 2003, there was a culture at the club which gave rise to the scheduled conduct,' Gillard wrote. 'The culture could be described as the view held by players and the club, that if they were successful on the field, what they did outside the club was of little consequence and was in their own private time, and if trouble resulted, the club would take steps to minimise the gravity of the misconduct and impose a fairly lenient sanction, especially if the player concerned was one of the better players.'

Gillard's scathing report had laid bare a toxic drug-fuelled crisis and yet no charges were ever laid by the AFL against the West Coast Eagles or the club's management.

Why?

Frantic correspondence between the AFL and Eagles bosses exposed the league's extreme paranoia that the Gillard report would be leaked.

With good reason it turned out.

Quizzed by 3AW's Neil Mitchell over the emergence of Gillard's findings in March 2017, McLachlan claimed Gillard had cleared West Coast of 'conduct unbecoming'. 'The recommendation of the Gillard report to the commission was there was not enough evidence to charge the club with conduct unbecoming,' McLachlan said. 'That was the conclusion and the recommendation by the independent judge.

'His brief was to write an independent report. He did that and his recommendation to the commission – under the rules at the time the one thing they could have been charged with was conduct unbecoming – and his recommendation was there was not enough evidence.'

What McLachlan failed to tell Mitchell and his listeners was that Gillard's explicit directive under the terms of reference for his probe was to only consider incidents that took place post April 2007 when determining if the club should be punished.[7]

In effect, Gillard had been restricted by the AFL Commission and could only recommend charges for indiscretions that took place at West Coast long after the worst of the drugs storm had passed.

Everything that took place before that was off limits – and Gillard's report was unequivocal in concluding that the club's management had 'covered up' years of blatant illicit drug abuse and allowed a rotten off-field culture to fester before 2007.

That West Coast was never punished for governance failings or for bringing the game into disrepute defied logic.

'They made a mistake but how far do you want to go with clubs?' retired AFL commissioner Bill Kelty reflected. 'Carlton is a prime example. Do you want to go in so hard against a club and put it out of business for twenty years or do you want to fix up the problem? The decision on Carlton was too hard and the decision on West Coast might have been marginally too soft.'[8]

An unspoken conflict of interest throughout the West Coast Eagles illicit drugs crisis was Demetriou's business relationship with the club's chairman Dalton Gooding.

There are no public references to their association, but Demetriou and Gooding are long-time directors of global acrylic teeth import company, Ruthinium Group Pty Ltd. Demetriou was the company's managing director before moving into football administration – but has maintained his shares and directorship, while Gooding has been chairman since 1998.

The pair went into business after Demetriou sat next to another West Coast Eagles director, Perth stockbroker Tim Lyons, at a lunch in Melbourne before the 1994 AFL Grand Final. Demetriou told Lyons he was looking to raise money for his dentures company and Lyons later mentioned it to Gooding as a potential investment opportunity.

Australian Securities and Investments Commission documents reveal Demetriou has been a Ruthinium director since June 1991 and Gooding since April 1995.[9] Demetriou and Gooding are listed among a small number of Ruthinium directors, with the company's registered address transferred from Demetriou's 46th floor Rialto Tower office to Gooding's William Street headquarters in Perth on 24 January 2002. Since 2012, Demetriou and Gooding have been the firm's only two Australian directors. The third is based in Rovigo, Italy.

In 2007, the year the Eagles crisis peaked, Ruthinium reported revenues of $13 million and a profit of $2.1 million.

Did Demetriou ever disclose that conflict of interest to the commission or the other members of the West Coast Eagles board? And if so, what discussion took place about it?

One Demetriou associate confirmed the commission had a conflict declaration policy at the time, but believed the Ruthinium link was insignificant.

'It was a pre-existing arrangement. It didn't compromise the way the Eagles were dealt with,' the associate said. 'Andrew was very good at separating his personal arrangements with his work.'

Nevertheless, Demetriou led the AFL response to the crisis and was involved in the decision to keep the Gillard report secret. The least he should have done was disclose his business arrangement with Gooding to the football public.

When asked about his business association with Demetriou, Gooding told me: 'I can say categorically and absolutely that we were given no special treatment by the AFL.

'We were very much left on our own by the AFL executive to deal with the drug issue in 2006 and 2007. And we knew that there were problems at other clubs, but we, as a board, decided not to point the finger and just get on and try and fix the problem.'[10]

Gooding said he strongly disagreed with the suggestion West Coast had got off lightly. 'The process that we had to go through to get Ben Cousins reinstated to play was particularly onerous as well,' he said. 'That took a lot of negotiation and a lot of letters backwards and forwards.'

While serving at the AFL and collecting his bumper seven-figure salary, Demetriou stayed on as a Ruthinium director and was also non-executive chairman of the Baxter Group, a waste management company listed on the Australian Stock Exchange in 2003 with a market capitalisation of $40 million. It sold to waste giant Transpacific for a massive $260 million in 2006.

'I'm very grateful to the AFL for allowing me to continue to have my own business outlets while performing my tasks in football,' Demetriou said in 2004. 'I believe my outside business experience complements my expertise in running the AFL.'[11]

In November 2007, as Gillard was delving deep into the West Coast Eagles cover-up, Demetriou splashed out more than $7 million on a Toorak mansion complete with a lap pool, wine cellar and five-car garage.

Demetriou's business links returned to the news pages in 2014 when it was revealed he and commission chairman Fitzpatrick had misused AFL resources to lobby the Victorian government on behalf of a mining company they part-owned.

AFL government relations staffer Phil Martin had emailed the office of energy and resources minister Nick Kotsiras regarding issues affecting Creswick Quartz Pty Ltd. Fitzpatrick was the company's chairman and Demetriou a shareholder.

Both Demetriou and Fitzpatrick acknowledged that the letter from an AFL email account was an inappropriate use of the league's resources.

Fitzpatrick told *The Age*: 'An email about a personal investment of mine shouldn't have gone out from an AFL email address. I wasn't aware that had happened until it was pointed out to me by you. It should have been sent from a private email address just to be completely clear that the issue we were dealing with had nothing at all to do with AFL matters.'[12]

Again, it didn't pass the sniff test, but few batted an eyelid.

The football world was immune to such matters.

\*\*\*

Mike Fitzpatrick had his own deep roots in Western Australia. He grew up in Perth and played ninety-seven games for Subiaco in the WAFL competition before crossing to Carlton and the VFL in 1975.

Fitzpatrick graduated from the University of Western Australia with a Bachelor of Engineering, and studied at Oxford in the United Kingdom on a Rhodes Scholarship, missing almost two seasons at the Blues in 1976 and 1977 to do so.

He knew his way around Perth and fully understood the power of the West Coast Eagles in a two-team AFL town.

But Justice Gillard wasn't worried about any of that when he presented his scathing 87-page report to the AFL Commission in early 2008. His damning dossier came complete with a list of extensive recommendations to the AFL's top body; and they failed to act on a single one of them.

'I think there is much merit in having a separate body, independent of the AFL Commission and the clubs, to deal with serious misconduct,' Gillard concluded in his report. 'It should be chaired by a person who has substantial experience in trial litigation, assisted by a former player and a former administrator.'

Gillard might have been a respected Supreme Court judge but he was naive to think the AFL would ever agree to hand control of serious integrity issues to an independent body.

To this day, the AFL Commission remains the game's ultimate disciplinary authority: judge, jury and executioner.

Fitzpatrick confirmed receipt of the Gillard document in March 2008 but would only say publicly: 'We thought the report was thorough and tough.'

Into the bottom drawer it went; with just a single copy given to the club along with a demand that the names of all Eagles directors and legal advisers given access to it were handed over.

Nothing to see here. Move along.

Tellingly, the Gillard report, which would only surface publicly nine years after he handed it over to the AFL Commission, also took aim at the three-strikes illicit drugs policy that Demetriou had trumpeted to the world in 2005. 'There are strong and powerful arguments that testing should be 365 days per year and the secrecy of positive readings reduced to the second reading,' Gillard said.

It would take another eight years for the AFL to adopt Gillard's recommendation for a two-strikes policy, but by then Demetriou was long gone.

# CHAPTER 9

# Blind Freddy

THE MELBOURNE TANKING SCANDAL BROKE LIVE ON national TV just after 8 p.m. on Monday, 30 July 2012.

Brock McLean, the former Demons hard-nut midfielder, who had shifted to Carlton at the end of the 2009 AFL season, wasn't even supposed to be on the tube that night but, as fate would have it, he was a late fill-in for star teammate Chris Judd in the third segment of Fox Footy's Monday night AFL analysis program, *On the Couch*.

The interview unfolded like any other until McLean was quizzed on suggestions he was part of a team that had 'tanked' to deliberately lose matches in his final season at the Demons in 2009.

'Circumstances that happened in the second half of the year never really sat well with me,' McLean flatly admitted. 'They don't call it tanking, we would call it "experimenting" or whatever it was. It just went against everything I was taught as a kid, taught as a footballer and as a person.'[1]

Pressed on whether winning hadn't been a priority at Melbourne in 2009, McLean said: 'Definitely, and I think you would have to be Blind Freddy to not figure that one out.'

It was a big admission, which triggered a media frenzy that forced the AFL to launch an investigation and finally get serious about what had really gone on at the Demons in 2009.

AFL chiefs watching at home understood immediately the fire McLean had lit.

At the heart of the tanking issue was a contentious priority pick system introduced by the AFL Commission in 2006, guaranteeing clubs a national draft selection before their first overall pick if they won fewer than five games in a season.

Whispers of teams manipulating games – or more bluntly, deliberately losing – in the back end of seasons to secure a priority pick had dogged the competition ever since; but AFL chief executive Andrew Demetriou staunchly disputed that tanking was a problem in the game.

The issue, and the AFL's refusal to even acknowledge it, had been an open secret for some time.

'Demetriou's head is so deep in the sand he should be able to see China,' *Herald Sun* chief football reporter Mike Sheahan wrote of the tanking issue in July 2009.[2]

Dean Bailey, who had coached the Demons that infamous year, had raised eyebrows after his sacking in 2011 when he declared: 'I had no hesitation at all in the first two years in ensuring the club was well placed for draft picks. I was asked to do the best thing by the Melbourne Football Club and I did it. I put players in different positions.'[3]

At the time, AFL football operations boss Adrian Anderson moved quickly to hose down Bailey's comments, telling radio stations he had spoken to the sacked coach and been assured he was only referring to playing players out of position as part of their long-term development.

But McLean's confession in 2012 could not be ignored, particularly given the AFL's responsibilities to the Victorian Commission for Gambling and Liquor Regulation.

Betting on footy was big business. Australians blow almost $30 billion a year on sports betting – a fair percentage on AFL games. Suggestions of compromised matches would put at risk the AFL's right to pocket a slice of the action.

McLean was swiftly interviewed by AFL integrity manager Brett Clothier and a formal investigation was launched.

Two weeks later, on 17 August 2012, fresh claims about tanking at Melbourne emerged. The allegations focused on a suspect game at Manuka Oval in Canberra in Round 17, 2009. The Demons lost to Sydney after making seven changes from the previous week. Six players were listed as injured or ill, and another was dropped.

Figures connected to the club confessed that they were privy to a conversation with a senior Melbourne official the night before the match that indicated steps had been taken to reduce the prospect of a win. The conversation at a Canberra hotel centred around concerns a Demons win would cost them a priority pick. 'We'll be right, we've made eight changes,' a Dees official said.[4]

True to form, Demetriou ridiculed the claims on his weekly slot on 3AW radio.

But over the course of the next six months, following the August 2012 allegations, the league's integrity unit investigators, Clothier and Abraham Haddad, would interview fifty-eight Melbourne players, coaches and administrators. They seized computers, files and emails and called witnesses back for second and sometimes third interviews if stories weren't adding up.

What they found was starkly at odds with Demetriou's public derision.

Secret interview transcripts uncovered six years later revealed multiple senior Melbourne staff had blown the whistle on a conspiracy to lose games during the 2009 season.

The files included a stunning confession from Bailey, who later died after a battle with cancer in March 2014. Bailey, who had initially denied that the team had tanked, admitted he was repeatedly threatened and pressured to ensure the team kept losing.

'What was said to me was, if I win games I would get sacked,' Bailey told Clothier and Haddad during his third interrogation in the Adelaide offices of law firm Minter Ellison on 14 November 2012. 'I was threatened. Yeah, I didn't like it. I think it was a terrible thing to be bullying and harassing not only me but the rest of the staff. Absolutely, I knew if we won those games, I felt that I would get sacked.'[5]

The damning tanking documents, hidden away in an over-flowing bottom drawer at AFL House for years, revealed eight senior Demons officials had admitted the club's football department was directed not to win more than four games in order to secure a priority pick.

Bailey confessed that players who were not seriously injured were kept off the ground during matches to stymie interchange rotations, while another club staffer surrendered internal reports detailing how 'fake injuries' were used to rule players out of team selection. Several staff also confirmed that players were sent early for season-ending operations as part of a ruse some accepted was designed to weaken the team.

A major focus of the secret AFL probe became the club's Round 15 win over Port Adelaide at the MCG – Melbourne's third win of the season, and the second in succession. As the players sang a raucous rendition of 'It's a Grand Old Flag', Bailey recalled seeing Demons chief executive Cameron Schwab enter the change rooms with his head bowed low.

'There was no question I wanted to win [but] I remember Schwaby walking in and puts his head down,' Bailey said. 'I can't remember exactly what he said, but it was something like, "Fucking Jesus, Gee", you know, shaking his head. I thought, "We are okay, we won." He mumbled something about "difficult, hard, what we're doing to get to the end of the year, gotta think of the club's future", something to those words, to that effect.'

According to Bailey, CEO Schwab was not alone in his consternation.

He also fingered Melbourne's football general manager Chris Connolly. 'I can't remember the words. Chris said something to me about "Fucking Jimmy had just fallen out of his bloody hospital bed" or something. Oh right, I just ignored Chris to be honest.'

'Jimmy' was a reference to Melbourne chairman Jim Stynes, who was undergoing treatment for cancer, which killed him three years later. Stynes and his fellow board members were never implicated in the tanking scandal, but Connolly's reference to the club president in his 'hospital bed' suggested the conspiracy to lose had been rubber-stamped from the top.

Bailey's version of events was backed up by the club's personal development coach Ian Flack, who described Schwab's post-match body language in the win over the Power as 'very negative'.

A meeting of senior football staff the next morning in a shed at the Demons' Junction Oval training ground dubbed 'The Vault' became critical to the investigation.

Several present at the meeting told Clothier and Haddad that Connolly had launched into a rant, threatening Bailey and his coaching team with the sack. Melbourne's brazen strategy, they said, was to lose enough games in 2009 to secure star juniors Tom Scully and Jack Trengove with the first two picks in the national draft.

'Chris is good with colour texta, he loves writing things on boards. He wrote up Scully and I think he wrote Scully's and Trengove's names up on the board,' Bailey said. 'Sometimes Chris has a joke and a laugh, but he was not in a joking mood that day. We just sat back and thought, "Fucking hell, is he serious?"'

Asked whether Connolly was 'giving a direction that the club wasn't to win more than four games for the year', Flack told his interrogators: 'Yes, absolutely.'

Regarding the involvement of CEO Schwab in the plan to lose games, Bailey said: 'Cameron mentioned to me a couple of times that "The future of the Melbourne footy club is in your hands".'

Schwab and Connolly flatly denied giving orders to lose, but the evidence of a conspiracy was overwhelming.

While the AFL would later announce that there was no 'match-day' foul play, the secret transcripts revealed Bailey had told investigators that interchange rotations were deliberately compromised.

'Chris [Connolly] was very controlling during that period, of blokes on the bench. I've got no doubt about that,' Bailey claimed. 'And when he rang a couple of times upstairs to say they were fucked, they can't come back on, I found that a bit odd, because the doctor would say give me five minutes, I am going to give an injection or walk downstairs underneath, to either manipulate, physio, or they do hips or ankles or calves.

Calves are ones where they normally test, normally calves can take five to ten minutes, but it was very much, no, they're not going back on, they're done, they're done for the day, and I reckon that was the explanation for the low rotations.

'[Stefan] Steffy Martin, I remember one game Chris saying he can't come back on, I can't remember what was wrong with him. But it wasn't. It was something he said was wrong with him. I just took it. After the game, or during the week, he didn't show any signs.'

The AFL's investigators had cracked an open and shut case of tanking.

'Let's call it what it really is. Tanking is a nice word [but] it's match-fixing – I don't get why we dance around it,' retired Geelong champion Jimmy Bartel declared when the transcripts came out in 2019. 'You can't go out and deliberately stack a game so your side doesn't win for a future draft pick, that is match-fixing at its finest.'[6]

AFL legend Leigh Matthews said: 'If you can prove a club deliberately wasn't trying their hardest ... you would have thought that's about as big an offence as you can have in footy.'[7]

But that's not how it played out when AFL deputy supremo Gillon McLachlan fronted the press to announce the findings of the league's investigation in March 2013.

'I actually don't know what the definition of tanking is,' McLachlan declared in a line that will live on in football infamy. 'In the AFL rules it talks to performing on merits and the best of their ability. In my view, there was no tanking on match day,' McLachlan explained. 'There is no allegation that is able to be sustained that Dean Bailey didn't coach on his merits or any players didn't play to their utmost abilities. To be clear, Dean Bailey, on match day, coached to the very best of his ability.'[8]

The truth contained in the tanking transcripts told a completely different story, but it would be years before they surfaced.

Neither the club nor its coach had set out not to win, McLachlan said.

The end result was charges against both Bailey and Connolly for 'acting in a manner prejudicial to the interests of the AFL'. Schwab and all other club officials were cleared of wrongdoing. Bailey was banned from coaching for the first sixteen rounds of 2013, Connolly suspended from the game for a year and Melbourne fined $500,000 for employing them.

McLachlan and the AFL had spun the unspinnable.

But the obvious question was why?

What was it that spooked the AFL so much about admitting that tanking had taken place, not just at Melbourne, but at several other clubs while the priority-pick carrot was being dangled?

The answer, as always, was money.

The AFL banks millions of dollars a year from its association with the lucrative Australian sports betting industry. It pockets a slice of every single bet placed on an AFL match.

Corporate bookmaker CrownBet paid $8 million a season to become the AFL's official wagering partner in 2016 – a deal the league quietly extended for another five years in early 2020.

Monash University gambling researcher Dr Charles Livingstone found that $280 million was lost by Australian punters on AFL matches in the 2018–19 financial year alone. 'The sports administrators are absolutely in bed with the bookies,' Dr Livingstone said. 'But the losers are their supporters, who are bombarded with messages they don't want to hear. The way forward – to protect sport from potential corruption, and to protect kids – is to reduce dependence on gambling losses by sporting bodies. It may be necessary and desirable to ban advertising and sponsorship, as was done, effectively, with tobacco.'[9]

Until that happens, the riches will flow from football gambling into the AFL's coffers, but a proviso for the league is to present a product free of corruption and manipulation.

A finding that tanking had taken place at Melbourne in 2009 would have had dire consequences for the AFL and its responsibilities to the Victorian Commission for Gambling and Liquor Regulation, which polices the integrity of wagering on AFL matches.

So, the AFL did what it always does: it conjured an alternative outcome.

It wasn't until after Bailey's death, at age forty-seven, that the extent of the threats made to him to accept sanction and take the blame for the tanking saga fully came to light.

Bailey's lawyer, Chris Pollard, was in Melbourne in mid-January 2013 when his client called from Adelaide. Bemused, Bailey, now working as an assistant coach with the Adelaide Crows, told Pollard about a voice message he had received from McLachlan.

'McLachlan flew in to Adelaide unannounced and rang Dean direct on his mobile and told him he wanted to meet him at his uncle's office in the city,' Pollard recalled.[10] The 'uncle' was Ian McLachlan, the former Federal MP, prominent landowner and South Australian powerbroker, whose office sat in a CBD tower high above the City of Churches.

'Dean called me and told me about McLachlan's message and I rang the AFL's lawyer, David Poulton, and said, "What the fuck is going on here?"'

'He said, "Gill is a big enough boy to look after himself, I haven't got a problem with that," and I said, "Well, I've got a fucking problem with it."

'It was just extraordinary. Totally inappropriate ... Gillon should have and would have known that. It was just intimidating, bullying behaviour. I told Dean not to attend and we arranged a meeting in Melbourne the following week where I would be present.'

On Friday, 25 January, at the offices of Melbourne law firm Russell Kennedy in La Trobe Street, McLachlan, Bailey and Pollard came together in a conference room.

Pollard said McLachlan 'waltzed in like John Wayne' and put Bailey on notice that the AFL was poised to charge him with four counts of serious misconduct; but could 'do a deal if he agreed to plead guilty to one charge'.

'He laid it all out and stood up when he was leaving and said, "Mate, I don't think you're getting good legal advice here. I strongly suggest you accept the deal, because if you don't you'll never work in footy again."

'I couldn't believe it,' Pollard recalled.

'I said, "What is going on here, Gill? My client has still got legal rights and we reserve those rights." And he just walked out. He was a law unto himself. The arrogance was breathtaking.

'We put them on notice that we were going to issue Supreme Court proceedings, but in terms of dollars we just couldn't afford to take them on.

'Incredibly, the AFL Coaches Association had been told to withdraw their funding of the matter, which I was told followed a threat by the AFL, who were funding the organisation and its employees.'

Pollard's account of the McLachlan meeting was corroborated in a book, *Breakfast with Bails*, written by former AFL player and ex–Adelaide Crows high-performance manager Paddy Steinfort.

'Dean, we want to protect you,' Bailey recounted of McLachlan's blunt directive. 'We've got the others – Schwab, Connolly. They've confessed. Got them. The club's in trouble. But, mate, we want to protect you, so we want to put an offer to you. And that offer is sixteen weeks suspension.'[11]

As McLachlan headed for the door, Bailey fired back: 'Hey, Gill, I'm not a cheat. I know that for sure and I won't pretend that just for you to save face. So, nah, we're not going to accept. Sharpen your pencil and come back to us, pal.'

'I've made my recommendation to the commission,' McLachlan countered, 'and we can't alter that – it's too late because they meet on Monday. You either accept it, or this goes all the way.'

'And with that, Bails was left with a long weekend to ponder his future in the game he loved,' Steinfort recounted. 'He would feel the pressure of McLachlan's hand on his shoulder, and the words that came with it, every second.'

Pollard described the AFL's justice system as 'a disgrace'. 'There was no justice. It doesn't exist,' Pollard said. 'They are a powerful organisation and it's pretty rare for anyone to take them on. And if you do take them on, they'll run you out of town.

'The tragedy of it all is that Dean was a very, very decent man; a family man, and a good guy – people that football needs.'

The AFL's eagerness to restrict blame for the tanking fiasco on Bailey and Chris Connolly, and no one higher up the Melbourne food chain, Pollard said, was also driven by a desire to protect the club's licence to operate a poker machine venue in the suburb of Bentleigh.

Schwab was a director of the holding company that was licensed to run the pokies pub, which was crucial to the club's financial viability. By clearing Schwab and the board, both the AFL and the Demons' gambling licence would be protected.

There is no doubt the AFL was considering charging Schwab at one point. A submission to the AFL as the league investigators closed in reveals the Melbourne Football Club board attempted to wash its hands of the alleged conduct of Schwab, Connolly and Bailey. The club's directors told the league they could not be held responsible for the trio's actions during the 2009 season if a guilty verdict was reached.

'It goes without saying that none of Mr Schwab, Mr Connolly and Mr Bailey had any authority, express or implied, to engage in conduct in contravention of Rule 1.6 or 1.7,' the submission said. 'In these circumstances ... none of the alleged conduct of Mr Schwab, Mr Connolly and Mr Bailey could be attributed to MFC, at least under common law.'[12]

As it turned out, the board had no need to worry. Bailey and Connolly went down, Schwab and the board were protected, and the show went on.

It was a patsy strategy that would repeat when the big daddy of all AFL scandals broke at Essendon in February 2013.

Lawyer David Galbally, QC, said the scapegoating of Bailey was symptomatic of the AFL's boys' club system.

'Bailey was not within the family – and therefore he was expendable,' Galbally said. 'That's the way they work. And if you are a part of the group of accepted individuals, they will always find a way to look after you; to get you through to safety with minimal consequences.'[13]

A confounding aspect of the AFL's tanking investigation was the lack of interest shown by the state's gambling watchdog, the Victorian Commission for Gambling and Liquor Regulation (VCGLR).

After the AFL handed down its verdict in the case – and McLachlan's astonishing straight-faced admission that he didn't even 'know what the definition of tanking' was – the VCGLR announced it had conducted an inquiry of its own, which rubber-stamped the league's findings.

Six years later, after the emergence of documents exposing how multiple club figures had actually confessed to a conspiracy to lose matches in 2009, the VCGLR launched a fresh 'investigation', which again determined that the AFL had not breached its obligations.

State opposition leader Michael O'Brien declared that the regulator's 'nothing to see here' verdict 'beggared belief' before two VCGLR whistleblowers came forward to claim the Melbourne tanking scandal had not been properly investigated.

The pair referred their concerns to Victoria's Independent Broad-based Anti-corruption Commission, alleging the tanking probe and two other AFL-related gambling issues had been whitewashed.

'It doesn't happen by accident,' one of the whistleblowers confessed. 'The regulator is deliberately set up to fail. The AFL is treated like it's above the law. How can the AFL be allowed by the regulator to do its own investigation into match-fixing? The independent regulator should be doing the investigation. And how can the AFL be allowed to clear itself of wrongdoing when a coach admits to match-fixing? It's a cover-up and the VCGLR are involved.'[14]

Central to the fiasco, too, was the fact it was the AFL Commission's own fundamentally flawed priority-pick system that had motivated some clubs to tank. While some sports in the USA use a draft lottery giving bottom-placed teams a random chance at securing the No. 1 pick, the AFL simply refused to acknowledge that it had dangled a carrot some clubs found too juicy to ignore. By protecting Melbourne, the AFL were protecting themselves.

Veteran Sydney Swans boss Richard Colless said of tanking: 'Andrew and Gill treated it in such a cavalier fashion. It all seemed to be a bit of a joke and we'll laugh it off – but it was rorting the system in plain sight and everyone knew it was going on.

'Tanking – it's the word we can't use: "Ha, ha, ha". And I suspect it was because the implications of it were pretty enormous, so you find a softer landing. In racing they have a term about not allowing a horse to run on its merits. The penalties for which are pretty harsh. That's essentially what tanking is.

'But it's so misguided; what it does to general morale and individual reputations dramatically outweighs any benefit you might get from an earlier draft pick. It's not only corrupt behaviour, it's dumb and irresponsible.'[15]

The tanking saga was another stain on the Demetriou–McLachlan era, but nothing compared to what was to come next.

## CHAPTER 10

# Cashed-up bogans

THE SECRET BRIEFING THAT SET OFF THE BIGGEST SCANDAL IN Australian sports history went down in a secure room at the Australian Crime Commission (ACC) in Canberra in the final week of January 2013.

Novak Djokovic had just defeated Andy Murray in four sets at Melbourne Park to claim a fourth Australian Open title, while prime minister Julia Gillard, copping a hammering in the polls, was preparing to call a federal election.

In a notification from the ACC, AFL boss Andrew Demetriou, his deputy Gillon McLachlan and the league's integrity services manager Brett Clothier were summoned to a meeting in the nation's capital on the morning of Thursday, 31 January.

What happens in the days and hours that follow the confidential briefing is a window into the AFL's infinite strategic capabilities and inimitable arrogance.

\*\*\*

The first the public learnt of the brewing storm was the next Tuesday when the Essendon Football Club announced a snap press conference at the AFL's Docklands headquarters for 2 p.m.

It was 5 February and Demetriou, McLachlan and Clothier had been busy boys.

Six days earlier, the trio were asked to surrender their mobile phones and sign a confidentiality agreement before entering the secure crime commission briefing room. There they were informed of a secret investigation tracking the importation of banned performance-enhancing substances into Australia.

Reading from carefully selected excerpts of a classified report, the ACC told them that the probe had led them to an unnamed AFL club that had taken WADA-prohibited substances in a team-based program.

They revealed a major announcement was to be made at Parliament House in Canberra on Thursday, 7 February, blowing the whistle on alleged links between organised crime and the use of banned drugs across multiple sporting codes.

The AFL had long suspected it had a problem, but now it knew for certain.

'Is it Essendon?' McLachlan asked the ACC point blank.

'Say no more,' investigator Paul Jevtovic replied.

A Federal Court judge would later describe it as the 'wink and a nod' to everyone present that McLachlan had got it right.[1]

Under national secrecy laws it is a criminal offence punishable with time in prison to disclose any information relating to an ACC briefing; but within weeks league chiefs would be accused of doing precisely that.

The AFL's master plan to get ahead of the pending crisis was hatched within moments of the trio leaving the crime commission briefing room.

There was simply no time left to waste. Potentially, forty-seven Essendon players were involved and the AFL understood precisely the Armageddon scenario that presented.

Should a large number of Bombers players be wiped out for doping for one or two years – thus preventing the club from fielding a team – the league would be in breach of almost all of its multi-billion-dollar contractual obligations.

It was a catastrophe too chilling to contemplate, so the AFL got to work doing what it does best: devising a strategy to protect the empire. Forget due process or the possibility that the players might be innocent; they would take matters into their own hands.

And in the case of Essendon, league chiefs knew exactly where to start.

\*\*\*

David Evans is the softly spoken son of a giant of Australian Rules. His father, Ron, was a star full-forward for Essendon, kicking 210 goals in sixty-eight games between 1958 and 1962, topping the league goal-kicking on two occasions. But it was in business and football administration where Evans Sr truly excelled.

He made his fortune as the managing director of Spotless Services and served as Bombers chairman before joining the AFL Commission, which he chaired from 1998 until his death from cancer, aged sixty-seven, in March 2007.

His son David was an Essendon tragic and handy cricketer, not good enough to play at the top level, but smart enough to follow in his father's footsteps to the 'Paris End' of Collins Street. A career in finance, a friendship with James Hird and some good old-fashioned nepotism saw him rise to the presidency of the Bombers in 2009.

By the morning of Friday, 1 February 2013, Evans Jr knew all about the secret drugs investigation that was about to consume his club and throw the Australian sporting landscape into chaos.

The high-stakes strategy sold to – and agreed to – by Evans triggered a series of unstoppable events that would tear apart his world, stain the game and ruin the lives of many of his closest friends.

The AFL's cunning plan involved the Essendon Football Club voluntarily coming forward and 'self-reporting' to the league and the Australian Sports Anti-Doping Authority (ASADA) about the potential use of inappropriate substances at the club during the 2012 season.

Evans made a series of his own inquiries, including several conversations with veteran club doctor Bruce Reid, and on the night of Monday, 4 February, held a crisis meeting at his Hawthorn home with a group of senior club officials: coach James Hird, chief executive Ian Robson, football boss Danny Corcoran and Reid.

Evans informed them of a major report about to be released accusing Essendon of using performance-enhancing drugs before taking a phone call. After hanging up, Evans declared to the group: 'They're definitely saying we've taken them.'[2]

The 'tip-off' allegations and Essendon's decision to 'self-report' is critical to the crisis that would ignite.

It meant the club had little ability to defend itself from the tsunami of leaks and revelations that flooded the nightly news, footy talkback lines and the front and back pages of the national newspapers for years.

'We're guilty of something,' the club was effectively saying, 'we're just not quite sure what.'

More crucially, Essendon's decision to 'self-report' would permit the AFL to conduct a joint investigation with ASADA, giving the league control of and access to all confidential information. Demetriou and his men would know almost everything ASADA knew.

But what was in it for Essendon? As it turned out, absolutely nothing but years of pain.

Evans has never spoken publicly about what transpired during those early days of February 2013 or of allegations he betrayed his club, but surely, with the benefit of hindsight, he realised his obligation was to protect Essendon and its staff; not the AFL and its self-interests?

Why didn't Essendon stand firm and defend itself, as NRL club Cronulla would later do, and call on ASADA to deliver the proof about the use of performance-enhancing drugs?

The truth is that Evans, the son of football royalty but insecure about his own place among Melbourne's ruling elite, chose to side with the AFL strategy and in doing so threw his own club and its staff under a bus.

Evans and his board escaped sanction for what went on at Essendon in 2012.

'My last six months at Essendon I saw what I thought was a breakdown in ... I suppose governance is the word,' ex-Bombers director Beverly Knight later reflected of her departure from Evans' board in 2010. 'I think the chairman [Evans] was in a hurry to get to a premiership and then maybe take his rightful position on the [AFL] Commission.'[3]

Just after 10 a.m. on Tuesday, 5 February 2013, Evans, Robson, Hird and Essendon media manager Justin Rodski walked into AFL House and signed their club's death warrant.

Hird didn't know it, but the events of the next five hours would deliver a fatal blow to his chances of defending himself from allegations of overseeing a 'pharmacologically experimental' injections regimen.[4]

The AFL's strategy was rolling out beautifully.

Waiting for the four Essendon figures as they entered the league's second-level boardroom was Elizabeth Lukin, by now a vastly experienced spin doctor in scandals involving the AFL.

Evans had agreed to engage Lukin to help manage the inferno about to spark. With a background in managing public relations for trade unions, Lukin had first advised the AFL during the Carlton salary cap scandal before assisting in the fallout from the West Coast Eagles illicit drugs scandal after the 2006 Grand Final.

Demetriou was absent, attending a second meeting with sports heads, the ACC, ASADA and senior federal bureaucrat Richard Eccles in the Qantas Lounge at Melbourne Airport; so it was McLachlan and Lukin who did the talking.

The conversation was recounted in a Supreme Court writ filed by Hird's lawyers six months later.

'You can't say Essendon did not use drugs, because my information is you have used them,' McLachlan told Hird.[5] 'Brett Clothier knows the names of the drugs and he will be here soon. The club should come forward to the AFL and ask for an investigation. Essendon should go public about the uncertainty surrounding its supplement program in 2012. The Australian Crime Commission is going to hand down a report. There is going to be a meeting of all the codes. If you come forward earlier and invite ASADA to investigate, then the investigation will look better for you.'

Robson, who has also never spoken publicly about his role in the saga, fully embraced the 'self-report' strategy. He picked up the phone and called ASADA chief executive Aurora Andruska, triggering the joint investigation.

Robson then called Corcoran back at the club's Windy Hill headquarters and ordered him to stand down high-performance boss Dean Robinson, a central figure in the supplements program.

At 2 p.m., to an explosion of camera flashes, Evans, Hird and Robson walked into the Mike Sheahan Media Centre on the ground floor of AFL House and did what they were asked.

'I'm very disappointed, shocked is probably the best word,' Hird said.

'As a coach I take full responsibility for what happens in our footy department. If there have been goings-on within our football department that are not right, we want to know.'

There would be no going back.

\*\*\*

Essendon was rightfully disgraced as shocking details of its disastrous 2012 supplements regimen leaked out in February and March of 2013.

More than forty Bombers players had been repeatedly injected with a range of substances over a period of months under an ad-hoc program overseen by sports scientist Stephen Dank and Robinson.

Some injections took place off-site, with players asked to sign consent forms listing the names of the drugs and the precise amounts to be administered. Details about curiously named substances such as AOD-9604, thymosin, cerebrolysin and CJC-1295 began to emerge.

But while governance of the program – aimed at aiding performance, boosting recovery and helping players sleep –

had been calamitous at best, players and club staff insisted nothing prohibited under WADA rules had been used. 'I can honestly tell you that everything I took I knew 100 per cent that it was within the WADA and AFL doping regulations,' senior Bombers player Mark McVeigh said.[6]

ASADA and AFL investigators got to work within days of Essendon's decision to 'self-report' conducting dozens of exhaustive joint interviews.

'I have confidence in our processes at our footy club that we'd get it right,' Hird declared on 6 February. 'Our players are moving on, we're training hard and we're looking forward to the start of the season.'

Behind the scenes the AFL machine moved into overdrive.

On 9 February 2013, McLachlan, Clothier, Robson and Evans travelled to Canberra to meet with ASADA and Eccles.

For the first time, the AFL's end game became crystal clear.

Andruska's handwritten notes, later produced in the Federal Court, revealed Eccles asked McLachlan and Clothier, 'What is it you are after?'[7]

McLachlan replied: 'Come to arrangement ... players found to be innocent ... this is the outcome ... Sanctions against Essendon ... hold individuals accountable.'

But for it all to work, they had to have a patsy: a big scalp to prove that the AFL took the injections debacle seriously.

His name was James Hird.

\*\*\*

A front-page story in *The Age* newspaper in Melbourne on Thursday, 11 April 2013 screamed that Hird had been accused of injecting 'the WADA-black listed drug' hexarelin as part of the club's experimental supplements regimen.[8]

The explosive story, citing 'information gathered by ASADA' and an interview with Dank, was a game changer. On top of the claims against Hird, it was alleged that Essendon players were injected with a pig's brain extract and anti-obesity drug AOD-9604.

A WADA expert panel, the story claimed, had told ASADA that AOD 'should be considered as a prohibited substance under one of its controversial catch-all rules'.

Hird was under attack.

The next morning Demetriou told 3AW that the Bombers coach should consider standing down while the investigation unfolded.

'As he goes through his thought process ... that is an option he has to consider,' Demetriou declared.[9] 'He's entitled to be able to put his position forward, which he will get the opportunity [to do] next week with ASADA.

'In the interim, those are the things that will have to cross his mind when he's contemplating what he's going to say to ASADA.'

The same day *The Age*'s 'hexarelin' story dropped, Essendon's newly installed crisis manager Elizabeth Lukin also suggested to Hird that he should think about standing down. The next day, *The Australian*'s Patrick Smith wrote that the Bombers coach 'had no choice but to walk away'.[10] Hird's initial lawyer, Tony Nolan, SC, was also contacted by Tony Hargreaves, a lawyer acting for Essendon, passing on a message that Hird should consider standing down.[11]

It was a clearly orchestrated campaign, and for the first time Hird began to comprehend that he was being positioned for execution.

Not only was there the ASADA investigation for Hird to deal with, but Evans also commissioned former Telstra chief Ziggy Switkowski to conduct an independent review of Essendon's governance processes.

As Hird and his team travelled to Perth to play Fremantle in Round 3, his wife Tania called top employment lawyer Steven Amendola.

Hailing from the inner-city Melbourne suburb of Carlton that is famed for its Lygon Street restaurant strip, Amendola attended St Joseph's Christian Brothers in North Melbourne, achieved honours in law at the University of Melbourne and a Master of Law at Monash. Sharp and street smart, Amendola worked as an associate to Federal Court judge Sir Reginald Smithers in the 1980s and rose to prominence acting for the Commonwealth in the brutal waterfront dispute against the Maritime Union of Australia.

Amendola, then a senior partner at top law firm Ashurst, had endured years of heavy-duty industrial disputes, but it was nothing compared to what he would experience dealing with the might of the AFL.

He accepted the brief just two days before Hird fronted AFL and ASADA investigators at Docklands Stadium at 9 a.m. on 16 April.

Hird told him everything, including the revelation that Evans received a phone call from Demetriou at the club's crisis meeting in Hawthorn the night before the club 'self-reported'.

Hird's suspicions were raised further on the eve of his ASADA grilling in a conversation he had with Evans. 'You can speak to them [ASADA] about anything but don't tell them what Andrew told me,' Evans told him.[12]

However, Hird did exactly that, testifying to ASADA investigators that Demetriou had told Evans that Essendon was the club being investigated over the alleged use of performance-enhancing drugs before it became public.

Corcoran made the same admissions during his own interview.

It would turn the Essendon drugs scandal on its head.

\*\*\*

In a front-page story on Thursday, 25 July, under the headline 'Night of Crisis', the *Herald Sun* revealed ASADA investigators had been told about a 'tip-off' phone call made by Demetriou to Evans in the days before Essendon 'self-reported'.

Demetriou vehemently denied any wrongdoing and declared to Neil Mitchell on 3AW radio that morning that he could not have tipped off the Essendon chairman. 'And I did not for one simple reason,' Demetriou said.[13] 'I didn't know who the club in question was. The AFL wasn't aware of who the club was in question because the ACC, who briefed us a few days earlier on the Thursday, wouldn't disclose to us who the clubs were.

'There absolutely was a discussion that I had with David Evans because I'd spoken to him throughout the day and I did ring him that night because I was returning his phone call. But it wasn't tipping off David Evans that Essendon was the club because we didn't know who the club was.'

Demetriou's glib dismissal was later contradicted by evidence provided in a Federal Court proceeding.

All-out war between Hird and the AFL had erupted.

Hird calmly fronted the cameras that morning and said he had told the truth to ASADA about everything he knew. 'I know I've told the truth to ASADA and I know other people have as well, so the truth will come out over time,' Hird said.

The storm was too much for Evans to handle. He collapsed in the change rooms after suffering a physical breakdown following Essendon's Round 18 loss to Hawthorn at Docklands

Stadium and resigned as chairman the next morning. 'What is happening at our club right now is a tragedy, but I know that it will survive,' Evans said.

Lukin resigned from Essendon the same day.

Over a year later, in December 2014, Lukin was employed full-time by McLachlan to become the AFL's most senior spin doctor. Interestingly, Ray Gunston, a former chief financial officer of the Tatts Group, who was appointed as interim Essendon chief executive after Robson's resignation, also bobbed up in a senior position at AFL House in July 2015 as McLachlan's general manager of finance and major projects.

The drugs story had become far more than just a tale about a club that had allegedly used performance-enhancing drugs. It was two runaway trains on a collision course.

On one side was what Essendon had done to its players. On the other, a new scandal about what the AFL had done to protect its own commercial interests and to manipulate outcomes in its favour.

A flurry of bitter legal letters were sent between the AFL and Hird's legal team.

Amendola wanted assurances of confidentiality. He alleged Hird was the victim of months of strategic leaks and innuendo, including a front-page report in *The Age* on 17 July 2013 alleging Clothier had 'warned' the Essendon coach about the use of peptides in August 2011.[14]

'The article contains various allegations which are false or misleading and highly defamatory,' an email from Amendola to the AFL declared.[15] 'What is more concerning to our client is that the article purports to disclose matters which are clearly within the knowledge of the investigation team. It is clear that information provided by our client and the views of one or more people involved in the investigation have been leaked. As such, the confidentiality of the investigation process has been compromised.'

An entry in the secret ASADA interim report appears to verify Amendola's claim that the 17 July 2013 story was the direct result of an AFL leak.

The story was first published online at 3 a.m. and appeared in that morning's newspaper. The deadline for the article was the evening before, on 16 July, but an email from Clothier to ASADA recounting his version of events from the August 2011 meeting with Hird, which matched *The Age* report, was not sent until 12.33 p.m. on 17 July 2013 – nine and a half hours after the story went up.

*The Age* knew about it before ASADA did.

Significantly, the story about Hird's peptide 'warning' was published the morning after talk show *AFL360* co-host Gerard Whateley revealed on Fox Footy that ASADA had previously provided advice that the drug AOD-9604, the substance then at the centre of the scandal, was not a prohibited substance when used by the Essendon players.

The AFL was aware of what Whateley was going to put to air, giving them ample time to plant a counter story.

It was a pattern of deflection and retaliation that would repeat over and over as the saga wore on.

David Evans was still Essendon president when Whateley's AOD information surfaced. He and his wife, Sonya, had taken a quick break in the United Kingdom to attend the second cricket Test between England and Australia at Lord's. To their surprise, McLachlan turned up in London unannounced to take in some cricket with them.

An associate of Evans believes the surprise visit was an example of the careful 'management process' of the businessman that would continue for years to come. To this day, Evans has never talked publicly about what he knows of the AFL's behind-the-scenes meddling in the drugs saga or the alleged 'tip-off'.

Further breaches were alleged by Amendola against the AFL on 22 July after the publication of another damaging article about Hird.

In an email to Clothier, Amendola wrote: 'It is difficult to see how [the media] could make such an unequivocal statement without being privy to evidence obtained by the AFL throughout the course of the investigation.

'We say this because we are confident that ASADA investigators are complying with their statutory confidentiality obligations.'

Amendola then asked the AFL to explain 'what arrangements are in place' with journalists at *The Age* and *The Australian* and to detail the information the newspapers had been provided.

Clothier wrote back: 'The AFL rejects any suggestion that it has provided confidential information to the media about the investigation. We point out that the investigation has been going for almost six months and now involves over 130 witness interviews. In accordance with standard practice, a great deal of information has been disclosed by the investigators to witnesses in order to test or corroborate evidence. Your deduction that ... [they] must be privy to information obtained by the AFL is simply incorrect.'[16]

Four days later, Amendola replied: 'To be frank, the response contained in your letter is hard to believe.'

The gloves were off and the pressure mounting.

\*\*\*

Elizabeth Lukin thrives in managing footy scandals.

In the five-day window the AFL was presented to get ahead of the supplements storm, the veteran public relations expert was one of the first put on the payroll.

But who exactly was she representing?

Supposedly it was Essendon.

She was in the thick of the action on day one in the AFL boardroom at the mid-morning meeting on 5 February before the Bombers took the plunge and 'self-reported' to ASADA.

Lukin had trumpeted her wares and close links to the league's top brass in an online bio prior to the story breaking. 'My five years experience providing issues management advice for AFL leaders Wayne Jackson and Andrew Demetriou has underlined to me how important it is to protect their reputations while managing their campaigns,' she wrote.[17]

At a meeting with Evans, Robson and Bombers football department staff a month into the investigation, it was claimed Lukin outlined a plan to sell a 'rogue operators' strategy that would finger the bulk of the blame for the saga on Dank and Robinson. The conversation was captured in court documents filed by Robinson's lawyers.[18]

Bombers strength coach Suki Hobson asked: 'So aren't we concerned with what actually happened?' To which Lukin allegedly replied: 'No, it won't help us moving forward.'

Dank would receive a lifetime ban from the AFL, but incredibly Robinson was never charged by the league or ASADA, despite being a central player in the injections program. Instead he walked away from it all with a $1 million payout.

But how?

Robinson's lawyer, David Galbally, QC, had read the play superbly. In a wrongful dismissal action against Essendon,

Galbally had issued Supreme Court subpoenas against Demetriou, McLachlan, Evans, Robson and Lukin.

In the blink of an eye the case was settled, Robinson was rich and landed a job with AFL auditor KPMG for his troubles.

AFL officials don't do courtroom appearances under oath.

Incredibly, in 2017, the NRL gave approval for Robinson to return to sport as a fitness consultant because there was no black mark against his name.

Two key documents were relied upon by the AFL to punish Essendon for the supplements scandal.

The league was quietly confident all Bombers players would be spared from suspensions, but came good on their promise to hammer club officials responsible for the program. Except for Dean Robinson.

The first report that condemned the football department (but strangely not Evans nor any members of his board) was Ziggy Switkowski's probe into the failures of the club's governance structures.

A condensed executive summary of the Switkowski report released in May 2013 found that the club's poor handling of the 2012 sports science program allowed it to mushroom into a 'pharmacologically experimental environment never adequately controlled or challenged or documented'.

It was a sexy sentence but nothing compared to the contents of a contentious 400-page ASADA interim report that was lobbed at AFL House on 2 August 2013.

Eleven days after receiving it, Hird, Corcoran, Reid and senior assistant coach Mark 'Bomber' Thompson were all charged with conduct likely to bring the game into disrepute. A hearing date was set for Monday, 26 August, at AFL House, but a frenzy of secret negotiations were already underway, aimed at getting Essendon and its officials to roll over and accept sanctions.

Essendon chairman Paul Little, the billionaire businessman who had replaced Evans after his collapse, spent hours and days on the phone and in person with McLachlan.

It's hardly due process, but this is justice, AFL-style.

As stories began to emerge about the behind-the-scenes negotiating, Demetriou assured the public: 'I want to state very clearly: there has been no predetermination of this matter by the AFL Commission.'[19]

The facts would tell a different story.

At a crisis meeting on 8 August at Windy Hill, Little detailed a heated discussion held with McLachlan the night before. A secret tape recording of the 11.30 a.m. meeting captured how the Bombers felt the AFL was threatening them to either accept sanctions or be 'stood down' as a club.[20]

'That's the gun at our head,' Little declared. 'I rang him [McLachlan] last night and I said, "You know, you've really upset me here, because you've gone back on your word, Gill." He said, "No, no, I haven't, I haven't." I said, "You have. You told me one thing, and now you're doing something else."'

Hird's fury poured out. 'They're a pack of fucking lying pricks – and they have done from the start,' Hird mutters of the AFL's top brass.

Little said: 'So, I think what they're saying is … if we don't cooperate they have the power to stand [us] down. And we don't know if that refers to individuals or the club. But they have used that as a veiled threat.

'Every single issue that I agreed on with Gill McLachlan, and I met with him the other night, has pretty much been reversed now in this note here.'

The leaked tape also gave insight into McLachlan's belief that the thirty-four players would escape suspension.

'Then we spoke about getting the players cleared, "unconditionally" was the word I used,' Little said. 'And he said, "What do you want from me?" And I said – no, he then said to me, "There is a 99 per cent chance that the players won't be charged."

'And I said, "Well, I'd like to believe you, but are you happy for me to use that language in front of the players?" And he said, "Oh no, you can't do that." And I said, "Well, fuck, you're telling me one thing and over here we can't say anything to the players."

'And he said, "Let me work on it. I will try and give you some language that will give you the comfort that the players so desperately need."'

Thompson was up for the fight. The two-time premiership coach saw the AFL's veiled threat of standing down club officials as brinkmanship. 'Let's crack 'em. Let's crack the fuckers,' Thompson urged. 'Don't panic. Don't jump to conclusions that they think they know everything. They actually know very little, because otherwise it would've been done a long time ago with players. You know what we have to do, mate? We have to find out what actually happened. Don't fucking believe what's in the [ASADA interim] report.'

Referring to the ASADA interim report, handed to the league just six days earlier, Hird said, 'Every bit of advice we've been given by everyone we know is that that is not a legal document. It cannot be used. It is in breach of the ASADA Act.'

Little responded: 'And it's questionable whether ASADA should have even handed it over to the AFL ... You know, to give someone an interim report where 20 per cent of it is blacked out and you can't even read it is a fucking joke, and then make a decision based on that ...

'And Gill McLachlan says, "Oh, by the way, the redacted parts, we'll give them to you in a day or two." Oh, fuck, I haven't seen them, they haven't come. You know, so, mate, that story can be told and the fact that [Andrew] Demetriou has put himself up as being not able to talk to us because he's conflicted. Well, fucking what's happened to his confliction for the last six months?'

Little declared that 'the gloves are off' and vowed to work with Hird's legal team and others to block the AFL's attack.

'We need a council of war now because if the AFL get the initiative here and start throwing these bloody charges around, it may be that we can't stop anything. So we've got to get out there first,' he said.

'It's us against the world.'

\*\*\*

Lawyers littered the landscape and on the eve of the finals all hell broke loose.

After another Whateley bombshell the night before revealing a sports medicine specialist had been advised by ASADA in February 2013 that the peptide at the centre of the crisis – AOD-9604 – was not a banned substance, retribution was swift.

Just after 11 a.m. on 21 August, the AFL published a damning 34-page 'statement of grounds' detailing the full allegations against Essendon and its officials. It was devastating stuff.

The drugs crisis had become a schoolyard game of tit for tat, prompting Little to declare war on Demetriou and McLachlan.

In an astonishing press conference on the top floor of South Yarra's Olsen Hotel, the Essendon chairman called on AFL chairman Mike Fitzpatrick to 'step in and take over this process, as I along with a significant percentage of the football public have lost total confidence in the AFL executive to handle this matter'.

It was an unprecedented broadside fired directly at the AFL's two most senior executives.

What happened the following morning on Eddie McGuire's Triple M breakfast radio program became one of the most contentious, and critical, episodes in the drugs saga.

A distraught woman called 'Sarah' rang through to the show, claiming to be the mother of a young Essendon player, and she took direct aim at Hird.

'It's all right for James and the board of Essendon to say they have not cheated,' said 'Sarah'. 'The whole question is not about cheating. The whole question is about morals, it's about ethics and it's about the trust that the parents put in the club.'

A senior AFL official listening in to the call declared it to be the 'game changer' and it probably was.

The emotional peak-hour interview helped swing public opinion back against the Bombers and Hird.

The only problem was, nobody at Triple M, including the vastly experienced McGuire, bothered to verify if the caller was a mum or an actress.

'Sarah' called on a private number and refused to provide information regarding her identity. 'I spoke to her before she came on air extensively,' McGuire later explained.[21] 'I was convinced enough to put her on air at a very volatile time. If she was an actress, she was the best actress in Australia.'

McGuire, president of a rival club Collingwood, had his

own conflict in footy's greatest scandal; he sat on the advisory board of David Evans' investment firm, Evans & Partners.

AFL commissioner Bill Kelty and Melbourne financier John Wylie, whose secret backroom role in the saga was yet to emerge, were also members of Evans' advisory panel.

To his credit, Kelty recused himself from the AFL Commission deliberations on the Essendon matter because of his close friendship with Evans. 'When Ron was dying, one of the things he said to me was, "Please look after David,"' Kelty said. 'Nobody else had that. He was like a son to me so I separated out. I had a very significant level of conflict and I got out.'[22]

In yet more ties that bind, two other AFL commissioners, Richard Goyder and Paul Bassat, sat on the investment committee of the global disruption fund for Evans & Partners.

Evans, Wylie and McGuire were also board members of the Melbourne Stars T20 cricket team in the Big Bash League.

Small town, Melbourne.

Hird's lawyer, Steven Amendola, pulled the trigger at 10.50 a.m. on 22 August.

He filed papers with the Victorian Supreme Court claiming his client had been denied natural justice and repeated, this time in sworn court documents, that Demetriou tipped off Evans.

The statement of claim sought injunctions, both interlocutory and final, restraining the AFL from allowing Demetriou to sit on any tribunal in judgement of Hird. It also asked for any AFL commissioner given access to the ASADA interim report to be banned from future hearings.

But the league had another card to play. Western Bulldogs boss Peter Gordon read a statement on behalf of the seventeen other clubs declaring their support for the AFL.

'In our view, it is of paramount importance that every effort be made to resolve these matters within the AFL industry', Gordon said.

Then it was McLachlan's turn to step in.

On the morning of Sunday, 25 August, Hird and Amendola attended a secret meeting at the AFL deputy CEO's Prahran home.

There was supposed to be a hearing before the full AFL Commission at 9 a.m. the next day to hear the evidence and determine penalties for Hird, Reid, Thompson and Corcoran, but due process counts for little in an AFL firestorm.

That wasn't how it was done in the Demetriou–McLachlan era.

Hird and Amendola were escorted through a garage at McLachlan's property, packed with polo sticks and equine equipment, and led to a large room at the rear of the family home.

They were met by McLachlan and his former VAFA state teammate, the AFL's general counsel Andrew Dillon, and it became clear very early in the discussion that a proposed twelve-month ban for Hird was non-negotiable.

It was all about the 'optics' the Bombers coach was told, because the scandal required a face.[23]

Hird and Amendola held their ground and the meeting adjourned while McLachlan went upstairs.

As Hird made his way to his car he checked his phone to discover Little had sent him a text message asking him what he was playing at. Hird's refusal to bend had already been passed on.

The next day's commission 'hearing' in the AFL boardroom was a farce.

Fitzpatrick opened the proceedings, declaring: 'I will open the hearing of what is a very unfortunate matter.'[24]

'I almost started laughing because they had no intention of hearing and determining the matter,' Amendola said.[25]

Fitzpatrick's high-powered fellow commissioners included Wesfarmers managing director Richard Goyder, Rio Tinto chief financial officer Chris Lynch, Seek co-founder Paul Bassat, future Victorian Governor Linda Dessau and the game's first female commissioner Sam Mostyn, but there would be no formal proceedings that day. Or any other day.

Instead, the AFL's lawyers called for an adjournment and Hird, Thompson, Corcoran and Reid were siloed into offices scattered across the second floor of league headquarters.

Essendon chairman Little had turned.

Despite waging war against the AFL just a week earlier, he was now encouraging Hird and co. to accept their penalties.

Their lawyers pushed back and with Melbourne's frenzied football media camped on the street below, the day was called off.

Everyone returned the next morning and one by one, Corcoran, Thompson and finally Hird yielded to the pressure.

After dark on 27 August 2013, the AFL announced that Essendon had been slapped with the biggest raft of penalties in football history. The club was fined $2 million, banished from the finals and stripped of a suite of prized draft picks for governance failings. Hird was suspended for twelve months, Corcoran for six months and Thompson fined $30,000.

With the prospect of doping charges being laid against the Essendon players now considered remote, many believed the drugs saga to be over.

Their belief would soon be shattered.

***

Human rights lawyer Julian Burnside, QC, represented Hird at the two-day commission 'hearing'.

He emerged distressed by what he had witnessed.

'I don't like what I saw ... not a great sense of natural justice. What I saw worried me a lot,' Burnside told a Melbourne radio station. '[It was] astonishing how much sensitive material was leaked to the press. I'm not sure who leaked it, but I'm pretty sure it wasn't the players or the club.'[26]

In an interview six years later, Burnside said: 'It was pretty clearly a stitch-up. They just wanted a scalp and James was the bloke that they wanted to get. Looking back it surprises me that things were so much controlled by Demetriou.'[27]

The footy finals rolled on and Hawthorn beat Fremantle at the MCG in late September to claim the 2013 premiership, but questions lingered about what had transpired over the course of that crazy month of August.

Why did Little go from a declaration of war at the Olsen one day to a full surrender the next? Why did Hird, adamant he would never admit to a crime he had not committed, relent and agree to sanctions and then apologise for his role in the scandal to the AFL Commission? Why did the AFL drop its charges against Reid when he refused to do a deal and instead took his case to the Supreme Court?

The answers were exposed three months later in a stunning set of revelations that laid bare the duplicity of the AFL's 'justice' system.

On 4 December 2013, under the headline 'AFL Secret Offer', the *Herald Sun* blew the lid on the extent of the secret negotiations that had led up to the two-day 'hearing' at AFL House and the involvement of Fitzpatrick and his old mate, Australian Sports Commission boss John Wylie.[28]

A similar story ran on the front page of *The Australian*.

Secret documents and a bombshell email showed the behind-the-scenes inducements offered to Essendon and Hird as the AFL worked frantically to pressure them into accepting penalties. In one document presented to Hird on 23 August, amid negotiations between Wylie and Little, the Bombers coach was offered 'an outstanding career development opportunity' in return for dropping his legal action against the AFL.

The University of Oxford, where both Wylie and Fitzpatrick had studied as Rhodes scholars, was suggested but Hird later settled on the prestigious INSEAD business school in Fontainebleau, France. Amid the horse trading he was also offered a two-year contract extension, guaranteeing him employment once his suspension was served.

An outrageous offer of 'no player sanctions' and 'no double jeopardy' despite the ongoing ASADA investigation was also discussed.

An embarrassed Wylie confirmed to *The Australian* that he was asked by Little and Fitzpatrick 'to assist in communications between the AFL and Essendon at a time when direct communication between them was difficult' – a shocking look for the head of a commission with oversight of ASADA.[29]

Wylie was a mate of Fitzpatrick but he also knew Little, having advised him on his company Toll Holdings' 2006 takeover of the Patrick Corporation stevedore business.

Fitzpatrick said nothing of the revelations – he was accountable to no one – but the optics for the head of the commission were appalling.

Based on an interview he gave after his retirement in 2017, Fitzpatrick had made up his mind about what went on at Essendon well before the August hearings were scheduled. He said he had been told by a rival player that the Bombers had presented in the 2012 season as though 'they had done five pre-seasons in one'.[30]

'And I think that kind of summed it up,' Fitzpatrick said. 'My point of view was that it was almost certainly performance enhancing ...'

The damning exposé about the AFL's dealings included the fact that Hird was still being paid his full salary, despite serving a twelve-month suspension.

Demetriou turned up again on Neil Mitchell's 3AW morning program to shoot down the entire story: 'There's no deal. The deal was what was announced on the day.'

But a dozen years at the top of Australian sports administration was taking its toll on Demetriou. He made a fatal mistake in declaring to Mitchell that Hird was not being paid.

'Neil, I want to make it very clear,' he said. 'The sanction to James Hird is twelve months suspension ... suspension without pay. So it is incorrect that he is being paid by the Essendon Football Club. He is not allowed to be paid money ... I can categorically tell you that part of the sanction from the AFL is that he is suspended without pay ... Neil, that is one thing I will go to my grave on: I know 100 per cent that the AFL is not paying [Hird] and I know that Essendon is not paying.'[31]

Demetriou was flat out wrong.

Essendon was continuing to pay Hird's salary and the agreements signed by the club and the coach on 27 August made no reference to his wage.

In the frantic discussions that had taken place at AFL House that day, with throngs of media camped outside waiting for an outcome, the league had attempted at the last minute to include a provision that Hird would not be paid during his suspension.

The attempt was flatly rejected by the Hird camp.

McLachlan kept it secret, hoping it would never get out.[32]

Demetriou had been made to look a fool and went on the attack.

Despite the fact the AFL had entered into a binding agreement with Hird that made no mention of pay, the AFL announced on 12 December that it was withdrawing all funding to Essendon until the issue was resolved.

Hird's wife, Tania, spoke outside the family's Toorak home and accused the AFL of a 'total disregard for the truth' and 'appalling' behaviour throughout the drugs saga.

'James took a twelve-month suspension because he was threatened,' she said. 'The club was threatened, he was threatened. In the end the club said, you know, it's in the best interests of the club, we need to move on, which is what we did. Of course he's being paid, that was the deal. Andrew Demetriou knew it, the AFL knew it.'[33]

A ludicrous compromise was reached when Hird was paid his full $1 million entitlement for 2014 on the eve of Christmas 2013, supposedly in keeping with Demetriou's wrong declaration that Hird would not be paid during the 2014 calendar year.

Rather than an apology for getting it wrong, they manufactured another farcical outcome to save face.

It stank but barely a journalist on the AFL beat batted an eyelid.

When Tania had the temerity to express an opinion about the AFL's bullying of her husband she was savaged by multiple industry figures starting with Eddie McGuire. The Pies president and morning radio host expressed the view that

James would lose his job and ought to be held responsible for his wife's comments. It was appallingly sexist and prompted Hird's media adviser Ian Hanke to suggest it was McGuire who should stand down.

McGuire hit back in the belittling fashion that constitutes standard AFL industry operating procedure. 'The Hirds have been getting advice from Ian Hanke, who is a political bomb thrower,' McGuire said. 'He is a guy who shaves his head going into elections.'

Football journalists including Caroline Wilson and Patrick Smith joined the pile-on. 'If Hird thought he was smart allowing his wife to speak for him then he has outsmarted himself,' Wilson wrote. Smith wrote: 'Grab a pen. Get a pad. We are going a jotting. Take this down for starters. You and your suspended coach of a husband need to leave the club immediately. Just walk away.'

As the ABC's Louise Milligan responded: 'It might as well have started "Sit down, girlie".'

Demetriou survived the summer but knew he was on borrowed time. On 3 March 2014, after a decade in the job, he announced that he was walking.

Defiant to the end, the Coburg kid turned AFL supremo scoffed at suggestions his own conduct had contributed to the Essendon malaise. 'I will tell you what I didn't do, I didn't inject anyone,' Demetriou barked. 'I do not accept any responsibility for people who seek to infiltrate the game to inject young men with God knows what substances to introduce practices that are abhorrent to the game and to families.

'Our job is to try and put as many preventative measures in place as we could and even as good as our integrity department was we didn't pick that up.

'And that is not a fault, you don't catch every speeding fine, you don't catch every person who breaks the law. The AFL's in much better shape today as an industry because of what we learned last year.'

Demetriou could rightly point to a string of achievements during his time in the hot seat of Australian Rules: the competitive balance fund (assisting poorer clubs), a fully funded salary cap, the football department soft cap and major stadium deals at the Adelaide Oval, Carrara and Perth.

But he was also an AFL chief executive who behaved as he pleased and was permitted to do so.

'Somewhere in the final years of the Demetriou decade the AFL started to believe its glowing publicity and mistake competence for omnipotence,' columnist Richard Hinds wrote of Demetriou's farewell press conference.[34]

'Even the anodyne questions of the media created the feeling Demetriou could be judged by only two standards – absolutely superb or simply fantastic.'

A recruitment firm was engaged to identify Demetriou's successor, but it was money down the drain. Everybody knew the man who would replace him was occupying the office across the hall.

Richmond chief executive Brendon Gale and Geelong boss Brian Cook (who came close a decade earlier) were interviewed, but never seriously considered.

On 30 April, less than two months after Demetriou's announcement, McLachlan was installed as the AFL's chief executive officer.

'He is indeed the best man for the job,' Fitzpatrick declared at his unveiling.

'This appointment is fitting reward for the hard work, commitment and leadership we've seen from him in his time at the AFL. It's particularly pleasing to be able to appoint a candidate developed from our own game.'

McLachlan promised to be an accountable leader for the fans.

'I understand the honour, I understand the responsibility, I understand the privilege of leading this code and this game,' he said.

He even gave a little ground when pushed on his part in the Essendon debacle. 'With respect to me specifically, I am sure there was some skin taken off me,' he said. 'There was skin taken off a lot of people. It was an incredibly tough period ... we ended up in a position that I don't think was edifying for a lot of people and it certainly wasn't great for the game.'

Few knew, in terms of skin loss, the game was about to get shredded.

A crack cop who oversaw Australia's investigation into the Bali bombings and ran the police component of the peace-keeping mission in the war-ravaged Solomon Islands emerged as the game breaker in the Essendon drugs saga. The AFL's plan hatched in those manic days leading up to the Bombers' 'self-reporting' press conference in February 2013 may have gone askew, but at least the players injected with Dank's mysterious drugs had escaped doping charges. That all changed when Ben McDevitt rode into town.

On 9 May 2014, sport minister Peter Dutton unveiled McDevitt, an Australian Federal Police detective with almost thirty years experience, as the new chief executive of ASADA. 'As Australians, we all love sports and we all hate cheats,' he declared ominously on his first day in the job.

While the AFL had pushed and prodded and been caught red-handed in the early days of the drugs investigation attempting to save the Essendon players from suspension, it had no clout with McDevitt.

In early June 2014, McDevitt sent shock waves through the AFL by indicating show cause notices were set to be issued against multiple Bombers players who had taken part in the injections program.

'In relation to Essendon we are talking weeks, not months,' McDevitt declared. 'I am as keen as everybody else to see these matters progress to finality.'[35]

He came good on his word a week later when thirty-four Essendon players, including the club's captain and 2012 Brownlow medallist Jobe Watson, were officially charged with doping.

Less than twenty-four hours later, Hird and Essendon launched a stunning Federal Court counter-attack.

The doping charges were put on ice in a case aimed at proving ASADA's controversial joint investigation with the AFL was unlawful and in breach of the *ASADA Act*.

'Enough is enough. We will not be bullied and we will not let our players be hung out to dry any longer,' Little said. 'They have suffered enough.'

The three-day trial before Justice John Middleton in Melbourne's Federal Court in early August was a show-stopper.

Piles of dirty laundry from the drugs investigation were laid bare for the Australian public.

ASADA chief executive Aurora Andruska's carefully handwritten notes obtained by Essendon's lawyers under discovery, captured the precise moment when McLachlan directly asked the ACC whether Essendon was the club under suspicion for using prohibited WADA drugs.

In a submission to the court, lawyers for Essendon and Hird asserted: 'This was the confirmation to all those in the room that the EFC was the club under suspicion.'[36]

During his cross-examination of Andruska, Essendon counsel Neil Young, QC, asked: 'When these words were said you immediately recognised there had been a clear identification by the ACC that one of the clubs was Essendon, didn't you?'

'I agree,' Andruska said.[37]

McLachlan would dismissively declare it all 'noise' and 'distraction', saying the case has 'sort of got nothing to do with us'.

Andruska was grilled for five hours and blew the lid on her covert dealings with the league between February and June 2013. Meetings were held in Canberra and twice in the AFL boardroom. On most occasions, Richard Eccles, the senior federal bureaucrat from Canberra, was in the room or in the background.

In an email discovered by Essendon's lawyers, Eccles said to a lawyer for ASADA on February 13: 'Spoke with Gillon – not sure he was fully in the loop. But I think he is now ...

'Where ASADA forms a view that the defence of no fault or negligence is available ... ASADA and the AFL agree that they will support the application ... before the relevant tribunals as far as was possible and a really good thing.

'And all he [McLachlan] then needed was an assurance that the AFL Tribunal would view things in a certain light, and it is as locked in as it can be.'[38]

Documents also revealed that then-sport minister Kate Lundy and her advisers had conveyed to ASADA that the stalled investigation was hampering the government's chances of re-election.[39]

In notes taken in one meeting, Andruska wrote: 'Lundy: needs something, deal with AFL, support staff sacked, points off, players off. Know can't do without ASADA agreeing.'

The fate of thirty-four players had become a political football.

After leaving politics, Lundy emerged as a director of the Bastion Group, where Demetriou was also a board member and shareholder.[40]

The trial reached fever pitch when Hird took the stand, repeating under oath that both McLachlan and Demetriou were behind his club's decision to 'self-report'.

Hird told the court he had been pressured into accepting his twelve-month ban. 'I signed the deed of settlement [with the AFL] under great duress, threats and inducement,' he said.[41]

Essendon also came clean, formally acknowledging that it did not 'self-report' to the AFL and ASADA on 5 February 2013, but rather was told that there would be a joint investigation into the club's 2012 supplements program.

'By 1 February 2013, ASADA and the AFL had devised and agreed to conduct a joint investigation,' the Bombers confessed in a submission. 'This occurred without any invitation or involvement of Essendon or Hird.'[42]

But while the truth had finally surfaced, the case was lost.

Justice Middleton ruled that the AFL and ASADA had not been in breach of the Act when they joined forces to investigate the Bombers, clearing the way for McDevitt to reissue his doping charges against the thirty-four Essendon players.

McLachlan would later claim repeatedly that the Federal Court verdict was a vindication of the AFL's conduct, but that was simply not true.

Justice Middleton merely found that the basis of the joint investigation was lawful; he made no determinations about the AFL's behaviour or its Machiavellian tactics.

The Middleton decision saw Essendon and Hird go separate ways. Defying orders from his club, Hird lodged an appeal with the Full Court of the Federal Court. It was a bold play leading to a report in *The Age* claiming Hird had been sacked. The report was wrong, but the Essendon coach was hanging on by his fingernails.

Hird's legal team were adamant Middleton had got it wrong and that an appeal would be successful.

Essendon was back in the bosom of the AFL and Little arranged a private meeting between Hird and Fitzpatrick at the commission chairman's South Yarra mansion opposite the botanic gardens in a bid to convince Hird to drop the appeal.

'Once seated in his house, he [Fitzpatrick] looks at the Essendon coach as though he is a stain on the carpet,' journalist Chip Le Grand wrote of the encounter.[43]

The Hird appeal process would run for months but ASADA would not wait.

On 17 October, they hit the thirty-four Bombers players at the centre of the storm with fresh show cause notices alleging use of the banned peptide thymosin beta-4, sourced from China, in 2012.

The AFL Anti-Doping Tribunal – an independent judiciary of the league – was convened in December to hear ASADA's case against the players. Across seventeen days of hearings, closed to the media and the public, the full chaos surrounding Essendon's 2012 injections regime was presented to a three-man tribunal panel chaired by retired County Court judge David Jones.

The evidence was damning but the tribunal ruled it could not be satisfied the thirty-four accused Essendon players had been administered the WADA-banned peptide thymosin beta-4. In March 2015, the tribunal cleared all thirty-four players of doping but the saga was far from done.

McDevitt made a trip to WADA headquarters in Montreal and on 11 May the world anti-doping agency announced it was appealing the AFL tribunal decision to the Court of Arbitration for Sport (CAS).

The appeal signalled the end for Hird, who resigned in August after his shell-shocked team, with the prospect of two-year bans hanging over them, dropped their bundle.

A 110-point smashing at the hands of lowly St Kilda in Round 14 at Docklands Stadium was the final straw.

'There are certainly some people within the AFL industry that I have no time for – who I think are ordinary individuals and don't speak the truth,' Hird said on his way out the door, 925 days after the scandal broke. 'They have agendas and drive really hard towards their own agendas.'

The CAS hearing – again held in secret – began on 16 November 2015 and in January 2016 the WADA appeal was sensationally upheld. The Essendon thirty-four were guilty of doping and handed two-year backdated bans wiping them out of the entire 2016 AFL season.

The AFL's Armageddon moment had arrived after all.

\*\*\*

The drugs scandal was the most destructive period in the Demetriou–McLachlan era.

It took its darkest turn on the night of Wednesday, 4 January 2017, when Hird attempted to take his own life. He was rushed to the Cabrini Hospital suffering from a drug overdose.

Friends accused the AFL of hounding him to suicide. 'I walked out of that ICU and just felt the total despair of how systemic bullying and harassment of a person had caused him to fall into such a dire state,' former Bombers football staffer Danny Corcoran said, breaking a four-year silence after a visit to Hird's bedside. 'I can't believe it. He's in ICU in a secure ward.

'A great man, a great champion, reduced to this … it's just horrendous to think that it's got to this point.'[44]

Corcoran claimed the AFL's four-year pursuit of Hird had triggered a post-traumatic stress disorder, leading to the near-fatal incident. 'The persecution of James Hird was a construction that started very early in the process,' he said. 'He told me that Gillon McLachlan and Andrew Dillon told him, "James, you haven't done much wrong, but we need to put a face to this as it is all about the optics."'

Long-time league critic Grant Thomas savaged the AFL for its silence after Hird's overdose. 'There is one reason the AFL has not commented, one reason alone; it's called hypocrisy. They are perplexed about supporting a guy they nailed to the cross,' Thomas tweeted. 'Polo, couta boat racing, wineries, horse racing, cricket, tennis – there is plenty on to keep the execs busy.'

Corcoran detailed an explosive conversation he said he held with Fitzpatrick in Hampton on 19 March 2016.

'I saw Mike Fitzpatrick by chance at an auction,' he said. 'I approached him and asked if there was any chance I could speak to him about having some involvement back in the game. He never answered my question, he simply turned and said to me, "Your mate Hird will never get back into football."'[45]

Fitzpatrick confirmed speaking to Corcoran, but denied making a comment about Hird. 'That part of the conversation did not happen,' a league spokeswoman said.

Told of Fitzpatrick's denial, Corcoran said: 'That just shows you what we are dealing with. I will sign a stat dec that those were his exact words.'

In the days after Hird's hospitalisation, it emerged he had been told that the AFL had blocked a move by the radio station SEN to recruit him for its 2017 football broadcasts. But while the league denied any interference, Hird had found many of the Melbourne doors he once waltzed through were now slammed shut.

A shattered Amendola declared at the time of the overdose: 'From what I have observed over the past number of years, it seems that you can glass your partner, you can sleep with your best friend's wife and the path to forgiveness will always be open in AFL land – but if your name is James Hird that path will be blocked.'[46] The veteran lawyer said he would forever maintain that the facts of the drugs saga presented to the AFL Anti-Doping Tribunal and the CAS did not justify the targeting and scapegoating of Hird.

'Before any hearings or any determinations of anything had ever occurred, James Hird was the architect of the supplements program, he drove the program, he was responsible for the program – whereas in the formal submissions of the AFL, ASADA and WADA he barely rated a mention in terms of the prosecution of these anti-doping offences,' Amendola said.

The only evidence relating to Hird lodged with the two tribunals was an email he had sent to club officials in January 2012 demanding that all supplements be approved by the AFL, WADA and club doctor Bruce Reid, Amendola said.

'What those submissions went on to say was that Stephen Dank ignored that,' he said. 'So contrast what was put before a quasi-judicial tribunal compared to the way in which he was effectively tried, convicted and executed by the AFL and their crony mates in certain sections of the press.

'To the AFL and those certain sections of the media I say shame on you. Shame on all of you in terms of the way in which they still consider him to be public property.'

Amendola had taken on the might of trade unions before but had never encountered a machine like the AFL. In an interview with the ABC's Louise Milligan in March 2014, he declared that 'they looked to behave like a bunch of cashed-up bogans who thought they could do what they wanted'.

After its damaging encounter with Amendola, the AFL would move to try to 'conflict out' a number of Melbourne's major law firms; in other words, retain a selection of top firms on their books so that any future opponents might be unable to employ those firms for themselves. This would theoretically limit the likelihood of being exposed by such a formidable foe again.

In addition to its preferred representatives, Minter Ellison, the league has also engaged firms such as Corrs Chambers Westgarth, K&L Gates, DLA Piper and Gordon Legal.

Mark Thompson's life would also spiral into the abyss in the wake of the peptide scandal. After walking away from the game at the end of the 2014 season, he spent years fighting in the background in the hope of exposing what he believed were the 'injustices' of the investigation. But the mission would consume and ultimately overwhelm him, leading to the destruction of his marriage and the abuse of methamphetamines living alone in his Port Melbourne warehouse apartment. After police raids in 2018, Thompson was convicted of drug possession and sentenced to a 12-month community corrections order. 'It [the ice] just took pain away. I was just happy to go anywhere,' Thompson would later lament.[47]

\*\*\*

The Essendon saga was the most damaging in AFL history.

The injections program was reckless and deserving of ASADA's full scrutiny, but the AFL's decision to manipulate and contaminate the investigation, within twenty-four hours of a secret crime commission briefing, in the hope of concocting an outcome favourable to the commercial interests of the game blew up in their face.

League supremos always believe they are the smartest people in the room, but on this one they outsmarted themselves. Or as foundation commissioner Peter Scanlon said: 'I think they got caught out. They thought they could solve it in a much simpler way and underestimated the vehemence of ASADA.'[48]

That the scandal continues to dog the AFL so many years later stands as the ultimate lesson that it should allow events to unfold in an independent and transparent manner rather than interfering in the justice process.

Demetriou's favourite line as the saga raged was 'I'll tell you what I didn't do – I never injected anyone'.

He was right.

But what he did do (with David Evans riding shotgun) was set in train a disastrous, self-serving strategy that helped rip the game to shreds.

## CHAPTER 11

# Inconvenient truths

ON MONDAY, 4 FEBRUARY 2013 – THE DAY BEFORE ESSENDON 'self-reported' to the AFL and ASADA – Melbourne Football Club doctor Dan Bates and sports scientist Stephen Dank continued a near twelve-month long exchange of text messages.

Between 6.49 a.m. and 4.33 p.m., the pair, seemingly oblivious to the drugs storm about to hit, discussed the use of supplements by Demons players, a train breakdown causing gridlock at Kensington, a training session at the club's AAMI Park headquarters in Swan Street, Richmond, and a proposal for Dank's peptides supplier, Nima Alavi, to advertise his South Yarra Como Compounding Pharmacy business on the sleeve of polo shirts worn by Melbourne coaching staff and officials.

'When can we start Tribulus?' Dank asked Bates at 12.18 p.m. in reference to the herbal supplement popular among bodybuilders who believe it can raise testosterone.[1]

'Are you doing xenografts in Melbourne?' Bates queried Dank, referring to the transfer of cells, tissues or organs from one species to another, a few hours later.

'Not at the moment. But that may change soon. What do you have?' Dank replied.

The SMS conversation continued into the next morning, Tuesday, 5 February, the same day Bombers chairman David Evans walked into AFL House, fronted the cameras and nervously revealed he had asked the AFL and ASADA to investigate 'slightly concerning' information about supplements given to his club's players in 2012.

'I have secured the worldwide rights to the human world for TB-1000,' Dank told Bates at 8.36 a.m. that day.

It would be the last text he sent the Demons doctor.

At 2.59 p.m., Bates messaged Dank and gave him a heads-up about the Essendon press conference going down at league headquarters.

Dank's escalating involvement at Melbourne was stopped in its tracks.

ASADA and AFL investigators would discover more than five hundred text messages sent between the duo starting in March 2012 when Dank was still employed at Essendon. The messages showed that by the time Dank had been let go by the Bombers in early September 2012 – months before the club 'self-reported' – he was deep in discussions with Bates about substances that would become household names during the Essendon saga, including Thymomodulin, AOD-9604 and cerebrolysin.

By year's end Dank had interviewed for a permanent role at Melbourne, had attended multiple pre-season training sessions and arranged for nine Demons players to be put on intravenous drips administering vitamins at an off-site facility at Gladstone Park.

Sound familiar?

'Okay. I have a way to put the high-performance unit as an R&D tax break,' Dank told Bates. 'That would mean a fair chunk of money coming back to the club. I was about to employ it at Essendon but held off. We will talk more about it on Tuesday night.'

On 12 November 2012, Dank told the Demons doctor that he had met with the 'AOD board' (a group with rights to the product). 'I have also told the board of your involvement with me. By the time I finished I had you sitting at the left hand of God.'

Two day later, Bates wrote: 'Peter Roberts the head trainer called Como to get a quote on normal meds. We may have caused some confusion, you might want to talk to Neama [sic].'

Melbourne's injury-plagued captain Jack Trengove was a focus of discussion. 'Sorry you still up?' Bates texted at 10.38 p.m. on 12 December. 'Trengove is not going to Darwin so I don't need the Thymomodulin tomorrow.'

In Essendon's AFL Anti-Doping Tribunal hearing, ASADA asserted that Dank's use of the term 'Thymomodulin' deceptively referred to a different substance, the WADA-prohibited thymosin beta-4. Yet any use of Thymomodulin at Melbourne, also obtained from the Como pharmacy, was completely overlooked in the joint AFL–ASADA investigation.

'Should we consider AOD cream for Jack Trengove's navicular?' Dank asked the following morning.

'Yes,' Bates said. 'Can you email all the WADA stuff and the Thymomodulin stuff etc in the next 30 min?'

On 6 September, Bates asked Dank: 'Have you got any Thymomodulin I can get access to?'

'Of course, mate. Ring me on your break,' Dank replied.

Bates admitted to an ASADA investigator in 2013 that he had gained possession of Thymomodulin from Alavi.

'I've got some samples I chucked out,' Bates admitted. 'I went down to meet Nima. He gave me some cerebrolysin and he gave me some Thymomodulin.'

'Now the Thymomodulin, was that injectable?'

'Yes,' Bates said.

The Melbourne doctor had approved Thymomodulin for use by Melbourne players after reviewing scientific material provided by Dank. But if ASADA argues that the Thymomodulin used at Essendon was thymosin beta-4, what exactly was the Thymomodulin used by Melbourne?

The question was never asked by the AFL or ASADA and Trengove was not requested to attend an interview. ASADA did not even ask Alavi what the Melbourne club's Thymomodulin actually was.

On 12 December, Bates and Dank arranged for Trengove to pick up AOD-9604 from Alavi's Como pharmacy.

'Tell him to ring me and he can meet me there,' Dank said.

Bates then asked: 'Are we using the topical or injectable?'

To which Dank replied: 'Topical. It will penetrate very well around the ankle area.'

A week later, Bates wrote: 'Thanks for this morning. You got a massive tick from Jack. Great work. Dan.'

Intravenous infusions containing vitamin C, vitamin B and the peptide glutathione were administered to multiple Melbourne players before Christmas.

The use of other substances like ubiquinol, Actovegin, oxytocin and naltrexone was also discussed.

On 29 January, Bates said to Dank: 'Lynden Dunn would like an injection on Thursday if possible (good about Dunny asking, as he is doing it because the other guys have said they feel good).'

'Great. I will book him in ...' Dank replied. 'It is the happiest I have felt about football for three years ... I just wanted to thank you for all the support and the belief over the last five months. That is so important when the knockers line up.'

Bates responded: 'Mate, you have some amazing knowledge that has always stacked up with evidence from external sources. I am frustrated we are not further along at Melbourne but you can see from the list from tomorrow that they are all getting on board.'

When the Essendon story erupted, Melbourne issued a statement alluding to Dank's minor involvement at the club. 'He [Dank] applied for a job at the club late last year but he was unsuccessful. He has never had any direct contact with the players,' a club spokesman said.

Wrong.

When the ABC turned the spotlight onto the Demons in April 2013, publishing some of the texts between Dank and Bates, the reality was inconsistent with the club's original statement.[2]

After an exposé by investigative journalist Caro Meldrum-Hanna was aired, Bates immediately stood down. Serious questions were going to be asked of the Demons.

In a meeting with the AFL in February 2013, after Dank and Essendon had hit the front pages, Demons director David Thurin, who had begun an internal review into Melbourne's own supplements program, stated that no illegal substances had been used at the club.

On 1 May 2013, Thurin was accompanied to an AFL–ASADA interview by two Arnold Bloch Leibler lawyers, including Leon Zwier, known in legal circles as 'Mr Fix-It'. Thurin made clear to investigators that the upper echelons of the club had no knowledge of Dank's involvement at Melbourne. By his own admission, it was a complete failure of corporate governance. The 'suits' had been unaware that Dank was organising off-site treatment and reshaping the Demons' supplements program in Essendon's image.

Thurin also revealed that Trengove had received an intra-muscular injection of an unidentified substance. 'Jack Trengove went to Gladstone Park medical centre once only, one week after Darwin ... got one shot IM and intravenous shot. The receptionist told him to go to the back room ... Steve [Dank] and [doctor] Amir [Nekoee] were there ... they went to another room where a registered nurse gave the treatment.'[3]

Essendon's inability to identify certain substances administered to players contributed to unprecedented media scrutiny and massive governance penalties. But those same governance failings at Melbourne never resulted in any rebuke by the AFL.

Why not?

The supplements program at Melbourne was embryonic and smaller in scale than Essendon's but was of the same genus. Jabs, creams, off-site intravenous drips, experimental substances and procedures. Imagine the hysteria if it had emerged that an Essendon official had discussed xenografts over text messages with Dank?

In a rambling interview, Thurin also revealed that McLachlan had called Melbourne CEO Cameron Schwab, warning him about the Dank link on the day Essendon 'self-reported'.

'Gill rang up Cameron to say that, you know, be careful,' Thurin told investigators. 'I think that's the day when Essendon made the announcement. Gill said [he] heard there was an association with Melbourne footy club and if there was, stop it immediately.'

The AFL's response to the Melbourne–Dank links was timid and it is not hard to draw the conclusion that the AFL was content to simply let it drift away. One club became the pin-up boy of governance failings while the other was left alone; and the AFL has never had to explain why.

\*\*\*

When the AFL hierarchy was summoned to Canberra by the Australian Crime Commission on 31 January 2013, they became aware of a most delicate problem. ACC intelligence alerted them that not just one of their clubs was named in its Organised Crime and Drugs in Sport report. There were two.

And one of the clubs just happened to be their own expansion baby, the Gold Coast Suns.

Dank had been employed by the league-controlled Suns from November 2010 until February 2011 and a Gold Coast player, highly paid defender Nathan Bock, had admitted to the ACC and later to ASADA that he had self-administered injections of a substance from a vial given to him by Suns fitness boss Dean Robinson.

Dank and Robinson had first worked together assisting NRL club Manly with its 'sports science' program in the mid-2000s. Robinson's scientific approach to fitness caught the eye of Geelong in the AFL, and they hired him to oversee their own high-performance team for their premiership-winning 2007 campaign.

The Cats claimed another flag in 2009 before Robinson was head-hunted by the AFL to run the Suns' fitness unit ahead of its debut season in 2011. It was Robinson who convinced the Suns to engage Dank as a paid consultant in late 2010 before the pair reunited at Essendon a year later.

While all eyes were on the Bombers debacle, the use of dubious substances at the Gold Coast Suns flew under the radar. No 'self-reporting' there.

When a team of Suns executives and football department staffers visited Melbourne in mid-2013 to sell the club's blueprint for success to media organisations, none of them could explain who had hired Dank or acknowledge what sort of work he had done there.

The substance Robinson had given to Bock was later revealed as the WADA-prohibited peptide CJC-1295 – the same drug at the centre of ASADA's investigations into NRL club Cronulla, which led to players accepting sanctions.

Transcripts from Essendon and Dank's AFL Anti-Doping Tribunal hearings revealed Robinson suggested to Bock that he should tell a hospital pharmacy that he needed to collect syringes for his girlfriend – rather than admit that they were for himself, to fast-track his recovery from an Achilles injury.

In April 2016, Dank confessed to buying CJC-1295 at a Sydney compounding pharmacy in December 2010 and taking it with him on his flight to the Gold Coast. A cooler bag packed with dry ice sat on the seat next to him, containing 10-millilitre vials of the drug, to be injected 0.2 millilitres at a time. Some of the CJC-1295 vials were for Dean Robinson's personal use.

Significantly, Dank and Robinson maintain that Gold Coast doctor Barry Rigby approved Bock being treated with CJC-1295.

'I spoke to Barry Rigby on two occasions in his office at the Gold Coast Suns Football Club, which was adjacent to Dean Robinson's room,' Dank said. 'I had two discussions and he was fully aware of what we were doing and approved it. Plain and simple.'[4]

Asked what Rigby approved, Dank said: 'The use of the CJC.'

Rigby alleged the conversations with Dank never took place, and produced time sheets from the nearby Robina Hospital, showing he was on duty at the time Dank and Robinson suggested they had occurred. But Robinson told ASADA that Rigby would routinely drive the fifteen minutes from the hospital to the Suns facility during his shifts and check in on training days. Rigby's ASADA interview transcript was never produced at the AFL tribunal hearing into Dank's use of CJC-1295.

By the time the Dank–Suns link was exposed, the club's chief executive officer Travis Auld had joined the AFL executive as one of McLachlan's trusted lieutenants.

Bock and Suns officials were interviewed, but ASADA never issued Bock with a show cause notice for possibly using a prohibited substance. Neither was Robinson, for possibly trafficking a prohibited substance, despite Bock's and Robinson's full admissions regarding the procurement and administration of the substance they believed to be CJC-1295. Nor were the Suns ever punished by the AFL for any governance failings.

But ASADA did proceed against Dank for his role in the arrangement, alleging trafficking and attempted trafficking.

A vial passed from Dank to Robinson and then to Bock and was self-injected by the player. Three individuals implicated – only one accused.

As Hird's lawyer Steven Amendola declared, it was 'bare-faced hypocrisy'.

As mentioned, long before his association with Essendon, Gold Coast and Melbourne, Dank was involved with the Geelong Football Club. As occurred at Gold Coast and Essendon, Dank had been introduced to Geelong by the club's high-performance chief Dean Robinson.

In 2009, when coach Mark 'Bomber' Thompson had his team firing on all cylinders, Dank was in the background sourcing supplies of a substance named Actovegin. Club doctors administered injections of Actovegin into injured Cats players. Actovegin, an extract of calf's blood, is permitted for use by athletes in Australia and has been widely used by other AFL clubs, including Essendon.

After the previously undeclared Geelong–Dank link was revealed in 2015, the AFL and Cats were staunch in denying any impropriety. Both were determined to play down the dealings with Dank and what had taken place at the club. 'It is simply not true that Geelong employed the services of Stephen Dank,' former Cats football boss Neil Balme declared.[5]

Cats premiership star Cam Mooney said Dank 'never came inside the four walls', adding: 'We did supplement programs, like everyone does – powders and stuff like that. But as far as injections, we never got injections.'[6]

However, transcripts from the AFL Anti-Doping Tribunal hearing into Essendon's supplements program revealed an email from Balme to a club staffer sent in March 2010 that referred to Dank. 'If you need to talk to the creditor tell them that their man, Steve Dank, knows all about what should be charged etc,' Balme wrote.

Then Geelong assistant football operations manager Steve Hocking also referenced Dank in an email sent to Robinson and another club staffer in June 2008 relating to the payment of an invoice. 'Could you please help with this invoice as I believe it belongs to Steve Dank,' Hocking wrote.[7]

ASADA possessed two invoices that were sent to Geelong from companies linked to Dank and a Sydney doctor associated with him.

Dank later said he sourced the Actovegin from a company in the Ukraine and then sent it 'overnight express' to Geelong. 'You pack it in polystyrene boxes and ice blocks and things like that,' he said.

ASADA told the anti-doping hearing that Robinson had 'used the services of Mr Dank' while at the club.

But the AFL went into full shutdown mode.

'The AFL is aware that Actovegin was purchased [by Geelong]. Actovegin is not a prohibited substance,' AFL spokesman Patrick Keane said.

'The AFL joint investigation with ASADA fully and forensically investigated the Geelong Football Club, which included seizing all email, phone and computer records. The investigation found no evidence of any irregular supplement or injection program, and no evidence of any prohibited substances at the Geelong Football Club.'

A Geelong spokesman said: 'In 2008 or early 2009 Stephen Dank's professional services were recommended to the club. Our then assistant general manager of football operations Steve Hocking met with Dank in regard to this, but after that meeting the club decided not to engage Dank's services. At no time did Dank have a position with our club.

'In 2007 Max Rooke was sent to Germany for treatment on his hamstring injury ... part of that treatment was the injecting of Actovegin ... the success of this treatment led to the club's medical staff to use Actovegin to treat other soft tissue injuries. Later that year the club sourced Actovegin from a company that was connected to Dank. Dank had no connection with our players.'

But Dean Robinson did.

An email sent by Robinson to club staff, including Steve Hocking in July 2007, revealed that Robinson had proposed a series of blood tests to be conducted on Geelong players. Robinson requested tests for markers including insulin-like growth factor 1 (IGF-1), male hormone profile and other insulin-related diagnostics.[8]

Another email chain reveals more blood tests were conducted the following year at St John of God Pathology in Geelong seeking markers including the hormone dehydroepiandrosterone (DHEA), IGF-1 and IGF-2.

Robinson wanted the analysis done at an external New South Wales facility.

Dank and Robinson utilised similar blood testing at Essendon in 2011 and 2012. Those samples, too, were shipped off to New South Wales.

Yet the analysis of the Bombers' blood samples, for some of the same markers, were interpreted by AFL and ASADA investigators far differently from those at Geelong.

At Essendon, Dank's and Robinson's motives for performing them was a constant topic of discussion in ASADA's interim report, at the AFL tribunal and by WADA in its submissions to the Court of Arbitration for Sport (CAS) hearing.

The AFL's publicly released notice of charge to the Essendon Football Club, for breaching AFL Rule 1.6 by bringing the game into disrepute, also stated: 'The players' blood was analysed for, inter alia, Insulin Growth Factor 1, which is prohibited by the AFL Anti-doping Code and the World Anti-Doping Code. Analysing players' blood for Insulin Growth Factor 1 is inconsistent with the rational and legitimate analysis of players' blood in accordance with the reasonable practice of the medical departments of AFL clubs.'[9]

And WADA's appeal brief filed in July 2015 to the CAS and participating parties declared: 'These blood samples were not sent for analysis to the club doctors or any local doctor in the Melbourne area, but instead were sent to a doctor in Chullora, NSW – a doctor who never consulted, or had any direct contact, with any Essendon player.

'The doctor selected by Dank to receive and analyze the players' blood samples in November 2011 was none other than Ijaz Khan, the same doctor who had provided thymosin beta-4 treatments to [NRL player] Sandor Earl, with Dank's participation, in July 2011. Dr Khan analyzed the Essendon players' blood samples for, among other substances, testosterone and specific growth hormones, including IGF-1.

'These blood tests are consistent with recommendations from peptide clinics that "patients" have their blood tested before receiving a doctor's script for peptides – in fact, one Australian peptide clinic that sold thymosin beta-4 specifically recommended testing blood samples for IGF-1.'[10]

Ijaz Khan's Injury Care Pty Ltd issued invoices to Geelong in 2010.[11]

Geelong's Actovegin injections and surrounding practices involving Dank and Robinson, including blood tests for IGF-1, were almost certainly beyond reproach. And yet the same methods used during Essendon's supplement program were characterised as suspicious, reckless and dangerous.

On governance failings, the Bombers deserved to be whacked by the AFL. And they were. But the three other clubs with links to Dank, who were involved in practices ASADA, WADA and the AFL asserted were questionable or worse at Essendon, escaped scot-free.

# CHAPTER 12

# Sun burn

THE GREATEST CODE-HOPPING HEIST IN AUSTRALIAN SPORTS history was sealed with a secret kick-to-kick session on a public oval next door to the Melbourne Youth and Justice Centre in sleepy Parkville.

It was Saturday, 23 May 2009, the morning after NRL star Karmichael Hunt helped the Brisbane Broncos to a 20–18 win over the Wests Tigers at Campbelltown Stadium in Sydney.

Hunt and his partner, Emma, slipped quietly into Melbourne on an early-bird flight and were met at about 10 a.m. on the Parkville playing field by two retired AFL players, Nathan Buckley and Jason McCartney, Gold Coast Suns list boss Scott Clayton, AFL national talent chief Kevin Sheehan and league development manager David Matthews.

Buckley had retired in 2007 after a glittering career with Collingwood and was working in the football media as well as being an assistant coach of the elite AIS–AFL Academy Squad.

'We were on the back ovals there, so no one could really see us, unless maybe they were walking their dog around the parklands near the zoo,' McCartney recalled of the Hunt rendezvous.[1]

McCartney played 182 games for Collingwood, Adelaide and North Melbourne and was a survivor of the 2002 Bali bombings, where he suffered severe second-degree burns to 50 per cent of his body in the attack on Paddy's Bar.

His comeback game against Richmond in June 2003, in which he wore full-body bandages and protective gloves, was one of football's most inspirational nights. He announced his retirement within seconds of the final siren during an on-field TV interview.

Like Buckley, McCartney was working in game development for the AFL and was asked to play a small part in the audacious bid to steal Hunt from the NRL and sign him as a foundation player for the AFL's newly created expansion club, the Gold Coast Suns.

Their assignment was to take Hunt through his paces with some kicking and hand-balling drills using an Australian Rules Sherrin football.

But there was an early hitch.

'He actually turned up with jeans and thongs on,' McCartney said, describing the thirty-minute session. 'So he kicked with bare feet – he really did. Bucks and I did look at each other and think, "Interesting attire." But we couldn't do too much to be honest because he'd played a Friday night NRL game and obviously they belt the crap out of each other. It was just some basic stationary stuff, looking at technique more than anything. And he was fine, because he'd played before when he was at school in Brisbane and he was keen, you could see that.'

Embedding a team on Queensland's 'Glitter Strip' was the embodiment of AFL ambition. Andrew Demetriou, Mike

Fitzpatrick and Gillon McLachlan each played integral roles in the project's planning and execution.

A front-page splash in the *Sydney Morning Herald* and Saturday *Age* written by chief football journalist Caroline Wilson in 2008 revealed the league was set to introduce two new teams to the AFL competition – a club on the Gold Coast and another in western Sydney.

Gold Coast would be first, entering the AFL in 2011. Western Sydney was slated to come in a year later. The teams would eventually be unveiled as the Gold Coast Suns and Greater Western Sydney Giants. It was a brave but important decision for the growth of the Australian game.

TV riches from the extra home-and-away match played each weekend were estimated by the league at about $40 million a season, but perhaps more significantly, the AFL had determined to strategically encroach on rugby league heartland in south-east Queensland and western Sydney.

The AFL's initial plan was to induce the battling North Melbourne Football Club to relocate to the Gold Coast rather than starting a club from scratch. A $100 million carrot was dangled in front of the Kangaroos board in a bid to get them over the line but a complication was the club's ownership. Long-time director Peter de Rauch owned 34 per cent of the shares in the club.

Demetriou called de Rauch in April 2007 and asked to have breakfast with him. The AFL boss brought along commissioner Colin Carter, a man Demetriou knew de Rauch respected.

'We met in a café in the city and the AFL offered to buy my shares,' de Rauch recalled.[2] The offer was for $1 million but de Rauch said he wasn't prepared to sell, insisting the club should stay in Melbourne. 'I found out later that Demetriou organised a secret meeting with all the other North Melbourne shareholders at Crown casino and I wasn't invited,' he said.

But the Roos eventually rejected a shift to the Gold Coast, forcing the league to establish the Suns, while all of North Melbourne's shareholders returned their shares to the club free of charge.

'Demetriou is a left-wing Labor voter who lives in Toorak,' de Rauch said. 'The attempt to relocate North Melbourne to the Gold Coast insulted the passion of our supporters. It was a commercial plan that suited their national ambitions.'

Demetriou fully understood the strength of the NRL code in the northern states and was all ears as Queensland-based AFL development officer Mark Browning pitched a wild proposal to lure Hunt across to the Suns. Hunt had played a few games of Australian Rules as a student at Brisbane's Anglican Church Grammar School before becoming an NRL star with the Brisbane Broncos.

Browning kept his eye on him and learnt in February 2009 that Hunt was contemplating a move to play rugby union in Japan. Browning contacted Clayton and a stunning $1-million-a-season poaching plot was hatched. Hunt's management were keen and arranged the secret trip to Melbourne and a kick – in jeans and thongs – with Buckley and McCartney.

A report was filed commending Hunt's ability with the oval ball, he attended a St Kilda–Brisbane match in a corporate box and had afternoon tea with Demetriou at his Toorak home where the league CEO personally pitched his bold code-jumping vision.

By the time Hunt and his partner, Emma, departed Melbourne, the defection was all but on.

'I can see that Emma's mind is made up,' Demetriou declared. 'And if your partner is anything like my wife, well, I reckon you will be with us next year.'[3]

And so he was, on a bumper three-year, $3 million deal that put the fledgling Gold Coast Suns on the Australian sporting map.

\*\*\*

The Suns played their first game for premiership points in front of 27,914 fans on 2 April 2011, against Carlton at the Gabba in Brisbane.

Charlie Dixon kicked the club's first-ever goal before the Blues annihilated them by 119 points.

The team was based in the Gold Coast suburb of Carrara – joining the Brisbane Lions as the league's second Queensland club – but was forced to play its debut game at the Lions' home ground because its own stadium was undergoing redevelopment works.

It was a sign of things to come.

The Carrara stadium deal was the AFL's first big victory in its bid to win over the hearts and minds of the Gold Coast sporting public. The ground was the original home of the Brisbane Bears, formed by the league in 1987, but required significant upgrading. The final bill would top $144 million.

Through its powers of persuasion, the AFL secured $60 million from the Queensland government, $36 million from the federal government and $20 million from the Gold Coast City Council.

Billions of dollars in taxpayer funds have been funnelled into AFL projects over the years and the temerity with which some clubs simply expected it to be paid was laid bare in May 2011 when Victorian Sport Minister Hugh Delahunty paid a visit to North Melbourne's Arden Street headquarters.

The Kangaroos were lobbying for a major upgrade of Ballarat's Eureka Stadium, where the club hoped to play AFL games, and had invited Delahunty and the then deputy secretary of the Department of Sport and Recreation, Peter Hertan, to a briefing in the club's boardroom.

The club's chairman James Brayshaw, a former state cricketer turned media star, arrived late, casually dressed in pants and a sweater, before excusing himself early citing other commitments.

Delahunty and Hertan were surprised a short time later during a tour of the club's facilities to discover Brayshaw hitting golf balls in an office.

'It was his birthday, so James remembers precisely why he had to excuse himself,' a club spokesman explained when the story about 'North Melbourne's putting president' hit the newspapers. 'The office he was in was Adam Aiello's, who is our sales and sponsorship manager ... who does have golf clubs in his office, and he was talking to "JB" about Mazda. JB had to quickly see Adam before he went to a lunch with his family for his birthday before going on air for Triple M.'[4]

Needless to say, North never got the money.

At Carrara, the AFL put in just $10 million of its own and the league's seventeenth club was off and running.

The ambitious Gold Coast Suns project, dubbed 'GC17', was the responsibility of Andrew Catterall, a rising star strategist at AFL House.

Working alongside McLachlan, Catterall, helped set in place the foundations of the club, making regular commutes from Melbourne to the Sunshine state.

Smart and ambitious, he had a temper like a volcano.

As the AFL's general manager of strategy and marketing, he had followed a well-worn path to the rarefied air of the league executive. He studied engineering at the University of Melbourne and joined the Boston Consulting Group at 101 Collins Street before serving two years at sports marketing company Gemba. Shifting to the AFL in 2004, Catterall made an immediate impression on Demetriou and the league's top brass.

'He was a bit of a rock star,' one industry figure said. 'He was one of the most talented and dedicated operators you've ever met but there was a self-destruct button, too. He was basically the CEO of the Suns until Travis Auld got the gig in 2009 but even then he was overseeing him. If you made it to the executive level of the AFL it was like you were a made man in Demetriou's gang – it was bestowed upon you.'

But by mid-2012, during the Suns' second season, trouble was brewing.

A series of staff complaints about Catterall's conduct triggered an internal AFL investigation. AFL Commission members became aware of a pattern of behaviour, tolerated for years by senior league chiefs, involving repeated allegations of bullying by Catterall. Lawyers for the chief complainant – a male office worker whose name was never disclosed – pushed hard for action.

In early 2014, the AFL agreed to pay Catterall's victim a $200,000 settlement, plus additional costs for medical expenses.[5] In return, the staff member was forced to sign a confidentiality agreement preventing him from ever publicly discussing his complaint. Those close to Catterall's victim say the bullying had continued for months and had an enduring impact on the man.

But it meant little to the blokes in charge at AFL House.

Demetriou took Catterall to lunch at Lamaro's in South Melbourne in October 2012 and removed him, the same place where Adrian Anderson was taken before his own resignation six weeks later.

'After that no one would accept an invitation to Lamaro's,' an industry figure quipped.

An email sent to club bosses claimed Catterall had taken extended leave to plan for his wedding and go on holidays, but in truth Demetriou was left with no option but to force him out.

When the bullying payout was exposed three years later, it emerged that Demetriou had endorsed Catterall for a top role at Racing Victoria just weeks after his departure. Then–Racing Victoria chief executive Rob Hines confirmed Demetriou had provided a 'positive' reference for Catterall, making no mention of the allegations made by AFL staff against him.[6]

'He had a super mind, and when he was in charge of strategy at the AFL he worked on every major project,' Demetriou said in 2015. 'He worked day and night. I am absolutely one of his greatest fans. Sure, he might be a bit outspoken, but you can never doubt his ability.'

Catterall's victim also left the AFL but others who claimed they had been bullied stayed on. They expressed bewilderment in late 2017 when Catterall was seen regularly in the coffee shop in the foyer of AFL headquarters. He had been installed as chief executive of Racing.com, which leased prominent office space on the ground floor of AFL House.

A person close to one of his alleged victims said: 'It's extraordinary to think that an individual who has had allegations of bullying made against him – who left the workplace amid those allegations – is then allowed to return and rent an office at that workplace. How must [the victims] feel?'

Another senior industry figure questioned how members of Gillon McLachlan's executive team thought the deal to let Racing.com set up shop at AFL House would pass the pub test or if members of Richard Goyder's AFL Commission had been briefed about the complaint, the payout and eventual termination.

Catterall has repeatedly maintained he knows nothing of the bullying allegations levelled against him. 'I left the AFL on good terms. I've never been notified of any complaints, before or after I left,' he said in 2015. 'I stand by my record of managing people and my team.'[7]

For all his sins, Catterall was invited to attend a farewell bash for Demetriou held in Melbourne in 2014 before Catterall became chief operating officer of boutique sports and marketing firm, Beyond Boundaries Group, set up by Demetriou and former AFL executive Ben Buckley.

Once a mate, always a mate in the boys' club.

\*\*\*

Karmichael Hunt was one of the poster boys of the Gold Coast Suns.

When a group of Melbourne journalists was flown north to inspect the club's temporary facilities at Carrara Stadium in mid-2010, Hunt was rolled out to model the team's distinct red and gold jumpers.

'The Gold Coast is a place where you feel alive and energised, so the Suns is a fitting symbol that sets us apart from other teams,' inaugural chairman John Witheriff declared at the time. 'The sun is bold, it's fresh, it's dependable and it's relentless. It can also be fierce and uncompromising – what other AFL teams will learn to respect about the Gold Coast Suns.'

In a bid to get the league's baby off to a successful start, the Suns were handed a suite of generous draft and salary cap concessions. They got priority access to the best seventeen-year-olds in the land and a conga line of first-round picks in the 2010 national draft: selections 1, 2, 3, 5, 7, 9, 11 and 13 – all at the expense of other clubs. Years of compromised drafts had a spill-on effect to the rest of the competition.

A bulging salary cap also allowed the Suns to poach a string of established stars, none bigger than Geelong superstar Gary Ablett Jr on a five-year deal worth up to $9 million. Ablett would go on to win a Brownlow Medal for the club in 2013 but his greatness alone was not enough.

The Gold Coast has long been a graveyard for all professional sporting codes. The Christopher Skase–owned Brisbane Bears – the 'Bad News Bears' as they became known – were a disaster at Carrara before shifting to the Gabba in 1993, while rival soccer, rugby league and basketball franchises have also tried and failed on the holiday strip.

The most outspoken critics of the Suns described the Gold Coast as a 'tourist destination' where residents were too distracted by the sun and surf to get behind an Australian Rules team. But the AFL forged ahead anyway.

The Suns showed some early pluck, saluting for the first time in just their fifth AFL game against Port Adelaide at AAMI Park on 23 April 2011.

But they won just three games in their debut year and kicked off the 2012 campaign with a disastrous 14-straight losses, before Karmichael Hunt's greatest AFL moment arrived.

With four seconds left on the clock, in stifling conditions against Richmond at Cazaly's Stadium in Cairns, Hunt marked the ball in the left forward pocket and kicked truly after the siren. The Tigers had led by ten points with less than a minute to go, prompting former Sydney Swans coach Paul Roos to label their last-gasp fade out as the 'worst forty-seven seconds in footy history'.

Despite the moment, the Hunt experiment, which cost the AFL millions of dollars, ultimately failed. His time at the Suns ended in August 2014 but not before an end-of-season bender with teammates shone a light on the party culture that had infected the AFL's under-achieving club.

An explosive Queensland Crime and Corruption Commission investigation report leaked to the *Daily Telegraph*'s Phil Rothfield in June the next year revealed Hunt and a large number of Suns teammates had boozed and snorted large quantities of cocaine over a three-day period across the Gold Coast.[8]

Hunt had confessed to police how he would party for days without sleep, hide cocaine in his golf bag, meet his dealer outside a Domino's pizza shop and attend team functions while off his head. He coughed up the information, including admitting to the purchase of 'two eight-balls of cocaine' for 'a couple of grand', in exchange for a lighter sentence on four cocaine possession charges.

It was an exposé that rocked the foundations of the AFL franchise and deeply embarrassed league chiefs who had spent millions making him a face of the Suns. They clearly hadn't done their homework.

'When I was twenty-two or twenty-three I started experimenting using ecstasy when I was partying and drinking,' Hunt told investigators. 'A few years later I experimented with cocaine, again when I was out drinking at bye weeks, end of season or other extended time-off periods. Initially I would only be using it when other guys had got some and gave it to me but there were occasions a few years after that where I would buy some for myself.'

Just a week after the report was leaked, the Suns were rocked by a second drugs scandal involving star youngster Harley

Bennell, a former housemate of Hunt's. Graphic photographs of Bennell racking up lines of speed in a Tasmanian hotel room in the days leading up to the 2013 season were splashed across the national newspapers.

\*\*\*

The mistakes and miscalculations that cruelled the Suns were made long before they took to the field for the first time. Almost all of them can be sheeted back to their AFL masters in Melbourne.

The club was horribly under-resourced from day one. Generous government funding paid for the impressive upgrade of Carrara Stadium, but the league's own notoriously tight purse strings were never loosened.

'The AFL wanted everyone to think that they were funding it, but always did it on the cheap,' a club insider explained. 'Looking back, the view was that we just needed to get fifty games into the kids and everything would just take off from there. It was supposed to be a slow, linear growth that would keep people interested – but that didn't happen.'

The Suns had the smallest administration and football department in the game. The club never challenged the league-enforced soft cap limiting the amount teams could spend on off-field resources. A $1 million additional services allowance, permitting clubs to pay star players extra cash outside the salary cap for marketing and promotional purposes, was not used by the Suns until 2019.

In its first season, Gold Coast boasted just six coaches – senior coach Guy McKenna, three assistant coaches and only two development coaches.

Rival interstate clubs had up to a dozen coaches.

The critical area of player welfare was also shamefully neglected.

'When we started we had one welfare person, Simon Fletcher, for a group of fifty players, including 35-plus eighteen-year-olds,' the club figure said.

Greater Western Sydney (GWS), which entered the league a year after the Suns, invested far more heavily in player welfare and retention strategies. The Giants hired footy welfare couple Craig and Melissa Lambert from the Brisbane Lions and moved all of the club's elite young talent into houses in a gated community at Breakfast Point in Sydney at a cost of about $400,000.

In contrast, teenage Suns players were sent out to live with random host families around the Gold Coast.

'They were dealt the same hand as the Gold Coast in a more difficult market and made it work,' an industry figure said of GWS.

The investment paid massive dividends as the group built bonds and friendships that would help stave off recruiting raids from rival clubs, culminating in a grand final appearance in 2019.

Another strategic error at the Suns was the inexperience of the club's key leaders. None of the group, made up of McKenna, Auld, football manager Marcus Ashcroft or captain Ablett had ever served in such lofty and critical positions, while the inaugural president, John Witheriff, a local businessman, did not have an AFL industry background. All were appointed by an AFL executive without any club experience of their own.

Auld had won the race to the Suns' top job over Geelong chief financial officer Stuart Fox, who would go on to become CEO at Hawthorn during its 2013–15 triple premiership run before being installed as chief executive officer of the Melbourne Cricket Club.

Under the Suns' initial business model it was also not intended for Marcus Ashcroft to be installed as general manager of football, but he emerged as the cheaper option

The Suns were grossly under-resourced and yet still focused on cost savings in the early years which never gave the football department a chance. Despite this, the savings must have impressed Auld's masters back at AFL headquarters, who later moved him back to Melbourne in a key executive post liaising with all eighteen clubs.

But the most damning failure of the Suns in its foundation years was the meagre club facilities. For the first seven years, players, coaches and staff were forced to operate out of portable tin sheds next door to Carrara Stadium.

'People don't realise how archaic the facilities were and what players have had to endure. It is just incredible,' the Suns' second senior coach, Rodney Eade, bemoaned near the end of his tenure in 2017. 'No air-conditioning in the gym when it's 35 degrees and 90 per cent humidity, insects and rats.'[9]

In its first nine seasons, the Suns never finished higher than twelfth on the ladder as a string of the best talent it had drafted walked out the door to sign with Melbourne clubs. Three key players in Richmond's 2019 premiership – Tom Lynch, Dion Prestia and Josh Caddy – all defected from the Gold Coast.

The club's plight reached crisis point under its third senior coach, Stuart Dew, in 2019 when the AFL agreed to shower its expansion baby with another bout of generous draft and list concessions – on top of total AFL funding for 2019 of $27.5 million. The Suns lost eighteen-straight matches to finish the season.

But the bailout package, compromising three more years of national drafts, did not come with a hint of an apology from the AFL. McLachlan outright rejected suggestions that he or his administration had made strategic errors establishing the Suns and should share the blame for the club's decade of misery.

'No I don't,' he declared, pointing to a serious shoulder injury suffered by Gary Ablett during the 2014 season. 'They never got another run at it, and seemingly to me, had huge runs of bad luck,' McLachlan said.

'You had to have a chuckle at that,' foundation Suns player Campbell Brown responded. 'There's more to footy clubs than one player hurting his shoulder, let's be honest.'

Accepting responsibility for failures isn't a part of the AFL's DNA.

As Jeff Kennett summed up: 'The AFL never admit publicly that they've made a mistake – never – and it's because they are answerable to no one but themselves.'

# CHAPTER 13

# 'Mafia dons'

SYDNEY SWANS CHAIRMAN RICHARD COLLESS WAS AT HIS Mosman home overlooking Middle Harbour when Mike Fitzpatrick's name flashed up on his iPhone.

Colless's Swans had just pulled off one of the most audacious recruiting coups in Australian Rules history, luring superstar Hawthorn free-agent Lance 'Buddy' Franklin away from Victoria on a monster nine-year, $10 million deal. Franklin was considered a certainty to sign at the Giants and news of the Swans' stunning play landed like a bombshell.

It was Wednesday, 2 October 2013 and Colless, at the time footy's longest-serving club chairman, suspected Fitzpatrick was calling to congratulate him on a job well done.

A distinguished businessman and company director, Colless had been the inaugural chairman of the West Coast Eagles in Perth in 1987, tipping in $1 million of his own money to help set up the club, before moving to Sydney and being drafted onto the Swans board in 1993.

He became club chairman a year later and played a key role in turning the Swans, arguably the AFL's most important franchise, from strugglers to premiership powerhouse.

Ross Oakley, chief executive of the league from 1986 to 1996, would rank Colless as the second most important football figure of his era behind foundation commissioner Graeme Samuel. The AFL's vision for a thriving national competition simply could not have been achieved without the sustained success of a team entrenched in rugby league heartland.

Known disparagingly as 'aerial ping pong' in the northern states, the AFL needed to corner the crucial market of Sydney if it was to continue its march.

In 2014 and beyond, Franklin was the player the Swans believed could return the AFL to the front and back pages of the New South Wales newspapers, just as the Hall of Fame forward and goals record-holder Tony Lockett had done in the mid-1990s.

But Fitzpatrick wasn't calling to pass on his congratulations.

Colless took the call in the vicinity of his wife, Susie. 'There was no warm-up, no introduction – the opening pleasantries were the "F" bomb and the "C" bomb,' Colless recalled. 'I must admit I was taken aback. It went on for about ten minutes and it was basically just a torrent of abuse. It got to a point where he said to me, and I'm paraphrasing: "If any of this gets out to the press – this conversation – I'll know where it came from and you watch out." To which I think I said: "Mike – get fucked."[1]

'I have never been so offended and I said if you ever speak like this again to me you are the one that will have something to consider. I said, "Mike, you are the chairman of the AFL, which rightly or wrongly is regarded as the leading sports governing body in Australia, and you're acting like you're a Mafia Don."'

Twenty years earlier, Fitzpatrick's expletive-laden outburst would not have been tolerated, but times had changed. This was the kind of heavy-handed behaviour that had become commonplace under the divide and conquer method of the modern AFL.

Colless attempted to explain to Fitzpatrick how his club had signed Franklin fairly and squarely under the AFL's own rules, but the league's most senior official was having none of it.

'I said: "Tell me what we've done wrong?" He said: "That's not the fucking point. Don't get fucking smart with me. You knew what we wanted to do and you came to us with your bloody COLA [cost-of-living allowance], and I told you I'd support you on COLA and then you raced away and did this deal."'

The cost-of-living allowance was a special payment system introduced by the commission several years before to help Sydney-based AFL players cope with the Harbour City's exorbitant property prices in relation to other Australian cities. Worth about $900,000 a season on top of the salary cap in 2013, it had long been a point of contention among southern state clubs.

'He [Fitzpatrick] said, "And you know I fucking well supported COLA – well I'm not doing that now." I thought well that's really mature,' Colless said.

'I said, "Mike this is bizarre, you're making this some kind of conspiracy." And my wife said what was amusing for her was that whenever I said "But Mike" he kept talking over me. I also said to him: "Mike the truth is if I wanted to pursue this, the guilty party is not the Swans or Lance Franklin or GWS or [Franklin's manager] Liam Pickering, it's the AFL."

The AFL broke at least three of its rules in relation to this. It dealt consistently with the player outside the prescribed area. You had that window and then it closed. You kept dealing with the player or manager during that period.

'Secondly, you were in a position to top up the amount of money that was coming from the club through a third-party arrangement, and that was merely you transferring funds from one of your sponsors to GWS or to Franklin.

'And the third was that you would allow GWS to trade with Hawthorn and I think that was designed to make it easier for Hawthorn to get some young players, which again is illegal.

'But it was like talking to a brick wall.'

When the story about Fitzpatrick's expletive-laden outburst broke in August 2015, the AFL did not deny that the conversation between Fitzpatrick and the Swans chairman had taken place, it only clarified that Colless's suggestion the league had tried to interfere with the Franklin deal was incorrect.

'The AFL wishes to state for the record it completely rejects allegations ... the AFL had sought to circumvent its own rules ... regarding player Lance Franklin,' the league said. '[The AFL] was not involved in any dealings that player Franklin and his management may have had with any other club in the competition ... under the free agency rules, before the player made his final decision to accept an offer from the Sydney Swans.'[2]

A stunned Collingwood president Eddie McGuire declared the Fitzpatrick–Colless conversation 'the most explosive a confrontation as I've ever seen at the AFL'. McGuire declared, 'He [Colless] has accused the AFL of systematically cheating the salary cap, the trade rules, the free agency rules [and] collusion behind the scenes. It's staggering. I read it last night ... I couldn't go to sleep.'[3]

'One, I couldn't believe the vitriol that is obviously raging between the two, but then I couldn't believe the content. This is what I've been screaming about for years and it's always been thrown back as "whingeing McGuire" and all that sort of stuff. Now it's laid bare.

'I'm going to actually keep my powder dry for twenty hours about this, before we come out and have a big chat. I have to speak to people today seriously about all this type of thing. These allegations are fundamental to the rules of the AFL.'

But McGuire did not take the matter further.

No one ever does.

Ron Joseph, an AFL life member who served as a club boss at North Melbourne and the Swans for more than forty years, said the industry silence in the wake of the Colless revelations proved clubs under the rule of Demetriou and McLachlan had simply become 'too frightened to speak up'.

'The only person who will stand up and argue these issues today is Jeff Kennett. Eddie McGuire will stand up for the first five minutes, but then he'll have lunch with the AFL.'[4]

It's a policy that served McGuire well. The powerful Collingwood president escaped sanction over a series of shocking public gaffes during his two-decade reign at the club, most notably an incident in July 2013 when he said on his breakfast radio program that Indigenous player Adam Goodes should be used to promote the musical *King Kong*.

McGuire quipped, 'Get Adam Goodes down for it, do you reckon? You know with the ape thing, the whole thing, I'm just saying the pumping him up and mucking around and all that sort of stuff.'

It triggered nationwide condemnation, especially given Goodes had already been racially vilified, but within hours of the incident Demetriou declared that the league wouldn't be punishing McGuire. 'He's punishing himself this morning, I've got no doubt,' Demetriou said. 'It's unfortunate, and I'm glad he's apologised quickly.'[5]

Player agent Peter Jess, who steered Indigenous AFL star Nicky Winmar through a stellar career marred by racist taunts, said the league's failure to act was shameful, but not surprising.

'In Europe or America, McGuire would have been excluded from all management positions in the sport for saying that and all of his commercial relationships with the league would have been terminated – but in the Melbourne bubble that ignores his recidivist behaviours, he was sent to an education program that lasted two hours and was rewarded by being named Chef de Mission for the AFL's International tour of Ireland in 2014,' Jess said. 'It's little wonder with that attitude from the AFL that Adam Goodes still hasn't walked back into the game.'[6]

McGuire's power and political influence was on show in 2008 when Collingwood contentiously took control of the historic Olympic Park headquarters in Swan Street, Melbourne. McGuire was also a director of Athletics Australia, the governing body of Olympic Park tenant Athletics Victoria, which was shifted against its will to a new $50 million facility at Albert Park.

'There is no doubt we live in a football town in Melbourne, but you've got to question how fifty professional footballers can have the power to move an Olympic venue that has been here for more than fifty years,' Athletics Victoria CEO Nick Honey said at the time.[7]

Athletics legend Ron Clarke, who set three world records at the Olympic Park track, was even more direct. 'What's he [Eddie] going to do next to protect the sport? He's obviously got a conflict of interest but I'm not going to tell him what to do,' Clarke said.

But McGuire's AFL industry mates were always there to protect him when push came to shove.

In a newspaper column in 2014, after Demetriou had announced his decision to retire, journalist Caroline Wilson suggested it was McGuire who had become 'the most powerful man in football'.

'The good news for the AFL is that its near-certain new chief, Gillon McLachlan, comes heavily recommended by McGuire,' Wilson said. 'It is true that most clubs back McLachlan, but having McGuire onside is the trump card.'[8]

McGuire finally came unstuck in February 2021 after the leaking of a secret report that found there had been 'systemic racism within the Collingwood Football Club'. The damning 35-page 'Do Better' report had been commissioned by McGuire's board following a series of claims made by 2010 premiership player Héritier Lumumba, but was kept under wraps. The independent report had found that Collingwood's response to repeated incidents of racism in its ranks 'has been at best ineffective, or at worst exacerbated the impact'.

Its release was a major embarrassment for the club, and yet at a hastily convened press conference that afternoon McGuire got it horribly wrong (again) by claiming it was a 'historic and proud day'. Another firestorm involving the Magpies president had been lit and this time not even his most powerful Melbourne mates could save him.

McLachlan said he had asked McGuire to clarify his use of the word 'proud' but danced around questions about whether his position had become untenable. 'I know, from the conversation I had with Ed, that he's committed to taking the club forward and to implementing the recommendations,' the league boss said. 'This has never been about an individual. It needs to be a whole of club approach and, to be frank, a whole of industry approach to deliver on it.'

Victorian Premier Daniel Andrews defended McGuire on two occasions. 'You don't run from problems, you work your guts out to try and fix them,' Andrews said when asked if McGuire needed to stand down. 'The Eddie McGuire that I know is equal to that task, and I can tell you in my discussions with him, he is very, very committed to doing that work.'

But within hours of that statement, McGuire had resigned. Amid mounting pressure from concerned club sponsors and a deeply divided Collingwood board, McGuire sniffed the wind and quit, claiming he had become 'a lightning rod for vitriol'. But in truth, he had been run out of his own club.

Incredibly, and despite coming on the very same day a New South Wales casino inquiry report said there were 'very serious doubts' over Crown Resorts' suitability to run a casino in Sydney if he remained on its board, it was Demetriou (in a rare foray back into football politics) who led the tributes for McGuire.

The former AFL boss agreed to an interview on Melbourne's SEN radio (so long as questions about his Crown Resorts issues weren't asked) and lauded McGuire for his 'profound impact' on the game. He declared that McGuire's resignation was a 'sad' and 'unfortunate' ending, said he did not 'subscribe to the theory' that Collingwood was a 'racist football club' and added that he felt the 'Do Better' report needed to have a 'lot more detail' in it. 'He has been a big change merchant, a big advocate for the game, a big positive for the game. Notwithstanding that he's had issues, but everyone does ... it's human nature,' Demetriou said.[9]

\*\*\*

After his retirement in 2017, Fitzpatrick defended his conduct in the Colless phone call. 'I think you should, every now and then, put a marker down,' he said, revealing it was far from spontaneous. 'It's fair to say I was angry. But it wasn't done just off the top of my head. I was going to tell him, and I thought about it, and I thought about what I'd say.'[10]

Fitzpatrick claimed his spray was based purely on the league's anger at the Swans' alleged misuse of COLA, but Sydney chiefs are adamant Buddy Franklin's decision to turn his back on an offer from the AFL's second expansion club, Greater Western Sydney, was a motivating factor. The humiliation of the Suns experiment had pricked the ego of the administration.

A subsequent AFL 'investigation' naturally cleared the Swans of any wrongdoing in the Franklin play, but retribution came anyway. The Swans were stripped of their COLA allowance before being hit with an even more unfathomable punishment: an unprecedented two-year ban on accessing any other players through trades or free agency.

'That was an absolute disgrace,' former AFL commissioner and retired Western Australian Anti-Corruption Commission chief Terry O'Connor, QC, said of the Franklin episode. 'The breathtaking hypocrisy of the AFL for sanctioning clubs and players for indiscretions and breaches of the rules, and then when it suited them, they involved themselves in endeavouring to place a free agent at GWS. As a former commissioner, I found that to be unbelievable.'[11]

O'Connor, who lived in Perth, revealed he confronted AFL commissioner Richard Goyder about the decision to remove the COLA and to ban Sydney from trades.

'I said to Richard Goyder, "What are you doing there?" And he said, "Oh, we wanted to save them from themselves."

I mean what absolute complete and utter bullshit. I said, "Well what about the Western Bulldogs? They've just acquired Tom Boyd for $1 million a year and their position is hardly strong. Why aren't you doing something about them?" "Oh, well they're different." Yeah, of course they're different – they haven't turned around and buggered up your plan to put Franklin in western Sydney.

'The way Fitzpatrick spoke to Richard Colless was typical of the way the AFL deals with people with whom they disagree and is a terrible indictment on them. It is intolerable.'

O'Connor was involved in the deliberations to introduce COLA during his days on the commission. 'COLA was introduced because the cost of living in Sydney is so much greater than other capital cities. It was not something introduced without thought,' he said. 'We received expert advice that the cost of living in Sydney was significantly higher than elsewhere in Australia. The policy was based on that expert advice.

'It is disappointing that the commission did not have the courage to stand up to the clubs given the cost of living pressures are probably greater now than when the COLA was introduced.'

Colless said the removal of COLA was an easy thing for the commission to do because no one in Melbourne was going to object to it. 'What is critically important to understand is that in late 2013 I had separate meetings with Andrew Demetriou and Fitzpatrick,' Colless said. 'In both cases there were at least six people in the room representing the AFL and Sydney. And both of them said categorically that COLA wasn't at risk – it was reasonable and there is no undue pressure from the other clubs to remove it. For Fitzpatrick to subsequently come out and endeavour to position himself as "COLA had only survived because of him" is simply not true.[12]

'The whole point with COLA was it was an AFL initiative based on considerable analysis of housing affordability – both ownership and rental – which showed unequivocally that the costs in Sydney far exceeded those in Melbourne which in turn far exceeded those elsewhere in the country. So, for the AFL to remove it without any discussion given the enormous amount of time and effort that had gone into creating it was very hard to comprehend.

'The other thing that was not only surprising but bitterly disappointing was that a significant number of commissioners, some who'd been involved in the creation of it, didn't realise how it worked. It was strictly pro-rataed, in other words each player's package was increased by a fixed percentage,' Colless explained.

'The myth that the AFL never sought to correct was that this was money that could be stockpiled to acquire the likes of Franklin and [Kurt] Tippett. It was a continuation of a theme that the Swans had been continually propped up by the AFL.'

Colless added: 'What really disappointed me, and still does, is not one representative of the other seventeen clubs issued any public statement of support for Sydney's position.'

Fitzpatrick retired as commission chairman in April 2017 and was replaced by Goyder. Fitzpatrick's reign saw the creation of two new clubs and the introduction of the AFL Women's competition. In 2019 he was recognised as an Officer of the Order of Australia for 'distinguished service to Australian Rules football through executive roles, to business, and to medical research'.

But Fitzpatrick was also a chairman who gave free rein to the AFL executive and did not curtail the behaviour that defined the Demetriou era.

His intervention in the Essendon drugs scandal reinforced the complete lack of independence in the AFL's disciplinary processes.

But it was his decision to pick up the phone and excoriate Colless, a long-time servant of the game, and oversee the stripping of COLA and enforcement of a trade ban on the Swans that most alarmed the football industry.

'It was done vindictively, it was done brutally,' Colless said. 'And the trade ban, as far as I am concerned, is the greatest act of bastardry that I have ever observed or experienced in my time in football. It was symptomatic of the complete lack of respect that the AFL had for the clubs and the complete disregard for their own rules when things didn't play out the way they wanted them to.

'To this day, no one has said that Sydney actually did something wrong in securing Lance Franklin via free agency. In reality the AFL probably broke four or five of their own rules – and if a club had done it, they probably would have been fined millions of dollars and lost multiple draft picks.'

Reflecting on the Fitzpatrick phone call, Colless said: 'The repeated threats that if this got into the public domain there would be consequences, I found more than anything absolutely astonishing.

'With the passage of time the one word that I would use to describe the incident is "pathetic".'

Colless had been whacked in plain sight and barely an industry colleague said a word.

## CHAPTER 14

# Spin kings

Australia's bold bid to host soccer's World Cup kindled a wave of patriotic spirit.

Aussie A-listers Nicole Kidman, Hugh Jackman, Elle Macpherson and Mark Webber fronted a global campaign launched by Football Federation Australia (FFA) chairman Frank Lowy at Parliament House in Canberra in June 2009. 'This is an extraordinary opportunity for us to showcase Australia to the world,' a beaming prime minister Kevin Rudd declared.

The bid was in full swing when a member of the AFL's media unit hooked up for coffee with a Fairfax investigative journalist in early 2010.

An AFL strategist had just completed an internal briefing paper into the likely impacts of a FIFA World Cup staged on Australian soil and his research included insights into two controversial European lobbyists – Peter Hargitay and Fedor Radmann – hired by FFA to help secure the globe's biggest sporting event. The pair, it was later revealed, stood to receive up to $11.37 million in fees and bonuses if Australia's bid was successful, payments which had not been disclosed to the government.

According to an insider, the information passed on to the Fairfax reporter by the AFL set in train an award-winning investigation that would help derail the FFA's $47 million taxpayer-funded World Cup bid.

'*The Age* had no real interest in the story until they were tipped off,' the insider said. 'There was a lot of ill-feeling between the two codes at the time over access to stadiums like the MCG and Docklands Stadium and they [the FFA] had strong suspicions that the AFL might have been putting some stuff out there. The Fairfax stories certainly did a lot of damage to the bid.'

But the insider said the AFL's backroom attempts to sabotage Australia's World Cup plans were standard operating procedure of the media team that sits on the second floor of the AFL's Docklands headquarters. 'It's about protecting and promoting the brand, managing the CEO's image and minimising the damage when inevitable incidents occur,' the insider said.

One incident successfully kept under wraps took place before a Melbourne–Brisbane Lions exhibition match in Shanghai in 2010 when a player was seen attempting to solicit prostitutes on the streets, illegal in China.

A delegation of senior AFL figures, including commissioners and executives, were on the trip but chose not to act. Journalists on the junket heard whispers of the incident and started asking questions but the AFL managed to kill a potentially damaging story.

What started out as a one-man communications operation under ex-football journalist Ian McDonald in the late 1980s (a post also filled for a while by legendary *Herald Sun* chief football writer Mike Sheahan) grew to become a department of its own under Demetriou's reign.

Junior media staffers take care of the mundane football and promotional announcements, while more senior figures are responsible for messaging and crisis management. Elizabeth Lukin and ex–*Herald Sun* police rounds reporter Brian Walsh have filled the top communications posts for more than a decade between them. Walsh was a loyal servant under Demetriou and returned to headquarters in late 2019 to assist McLachlan after a season of public relations disasters.

Fan unrest reached flashpoint in June 2019 over a heavy-handed crackdown on barracking at the AFL-owned Docklands Stadium. Supporters were seen being plucked from their seats during TV broadcasts and warned to tone down their behaviour, while security guards wearing jackets emblazoned with the words 'Behavioural Awareness Officers' roamed the stands.

Nat Edwards, an AFL employed journalist, inflamed the debate when she gave a radio interview the day after a game between Essendon and Hawthorn, saying supporters in her section of the stadium felt like they were being 'spied on'. 'I was on level three and it was very awkward,' Edwards said. 'Security was staring down anyone who became animated and several fans were warned for just barracking.'[1]

Edwards was called in at AFL House and admonished for daring to speak out, but the supporter backlash was a runaway train. A fan at a Richmond match was evicted and banned for three matches for calling an umpire a 'green maggot' before a supporter known only as 'Frankie' blew the security crisis wide open.

'Frankie' was in the outer during a Saturday afternoon match between his beloved Carlton and Brisbane when he was removed from Docklands Stadium for calling out in the direction of umpire Mathew Nicholls as he came off the ground for the half-time break.

'It's hard to umpire with one hand tied behind your back you bald-headed flog,' Frankie, a bald man, said to the equally follically challenged Nicholls.

Frankie was escorted to the rear of the stadium and detained for twenty minutes until a member of the AFL integrity unit arrived to take his details.

Jacqui Reed, a 3AW boundary rider, witnessed the incident and recounted the eviction on air, fuelling public unease about the heavy-handed treatment of fans.

When asked about the episode on 3AW radio the following Friday, McLachlan added a new layer to the story, claiming 'Frankie' had run 'across two bays of seats' in an aggressive and intimidating manner to abuse umpire Nicholls.

'I don't reckon it was just because of those words,' McLachlan claimed. 'Mathew Nicholls is a very experienced umpire, I got the notes about it, I followed it up, he said it was the most intimidated he's been in his hundreds of games of football.'

*The Age* newspaper, citing an AFL source, ran with the story, claiming 'Frankie' was 'evicted for spooking [the] umpire by running, screaming, waving his arms'.[2]

The only problem was, it was completely made up.

'Frankie' had never left his seat on level one. The 'running like a mad man' story was a fabrication aimed at justifying the actions taken against him as the security crisis engulfed the game. 'Frankie' engaged lawyers and demanded a retraction. Fallout from the incident had led him to take stress leave from work, but apologies for blatant vilification aren't part of the brief at AFL House.

A sheepish McLachlan would only say 'that was my advice at the time', although in an email to 'Frankie's' lawyers, the AFL vowed never to repeat the claim he had 'run at the umpire and leant over the umpire's race'.[3]

'The AFL notes those objections and does not intend to repeat those statements,' league lawyer Stephen Meade, McLachlan's old Uni Blues teammate, said in the email.

'No, I haven't apologised,' McLachlan said the next day. 'I think we're done. There are people ejected all the time from the football, if he feels it was unjust he should take appropriate action, and he's done that.'

The case appeared closed until a new twist emerged. McLachlan had not been in Australia when he made the claims on 3AW about 'Frankie' running across two bays of seats but was, in fact, living it up on a secret Hawaiian holiday.

A story on *The Age* website just after midday on Monday, 17 June 2019 claimed McLachlan had 'summoned the venue's chief executive Michael Green to his office' that morning to discuss the crackdown on fan behaviour, but the paper had been misled.[4] McLachlan and his wife, Laura, were not in Melbourne but at the Pacific paradise attending a fiftieth birthday bash for the son of trucking billionaire Lindsay Fox.

Wounded and embarrassed by the league's handling of the security crisis, McLachlan turned to Walsh to again take charge of the AFL's corporate affairs.

Walsh had left the AFL in October 2011 to head up communications for the National Australia Bank before being poached to head up Bastion Reputation Management, an entity of marketing and advisory company Bastion Group. Bastion's board members included retired AFL boss Andrew Demetriou and Gillon McLachlan's brother, Hamish.[5]

Ex–AFL government relations staffer Phil Martin also worked at Bastion as did the company's chairman Jim Watts, the former St Kilda chief executive who served briefly as a member of Demetriou's AFL executive team as general manager of corporate development and industry relations.

A newly appointed chief executive at one cash-strapped Melbourne-based club expressed surprise at the size of a contract his predecessor had agreed to with Bastion for consulting services.

In 2015, Demetriou emerged as chairman of Cox Architecture's 'board of management', the design firm behind major redevelopments at the Adelaide Oval, SCG, MCG and Perth's Optus Stadium.

Another company, where Demetriou was chairman – BKD Executive Leaders – listed its 'recent clients' as the AFL, Greater Western Sydney, Crocmedia (a media company with close commercial links to the AFL) and, ironically, given Demetriou's role in the Bombers drugs saga, the Essendon Football Club.

In October 2020, Port Adelaide chairman David Koch confirmed his club had used BKD in helping select Matthew Richardson, an internal candidate, as its new chief executive officer. 'As a board we didn't ever want to be accused of making the easy decision so we got Andrew Demetriou's sports executive recruitment firm to scour the market and put Matthew through the wringer,' Koch said. 'The end result was Andrew concluded we had the best person right here already.'

BKD's two other directors were North Melbourne chairman Ben Buckley and former Essendon football boss Rob Kerr, who had worked under Demetriou during his days at the AFL Players' Association. In March 2020, Kerr was unveiled as chief executive of the AFL Umpires Association. In November 2020, Buckley announced that he had appointed Demetriou's old friend Dr Harry Unglik – co-creator of the AFL's illicit drugs policy – to the North Melbourne board.

Walsh's replacement at the AFL in 2012 was veteran Melbourne PR man James Tonkin, but he was never embraced by the AFL's top brass. 'I think they prefer people who are fiercely protective of the organisation,' one league staffer said of Tonkin's brief stint.

Another senior AFL media figure is Patrick Keane, a former AAP cricket writer who joined the league in April 1999. 'Keane is a lifer – he knows where all the bodies are buried and everything that is going on,' one league insider said.

Until he was transferred to the office of the chief executive in early 2019, Keane was the first point of contact for almost two decades for journalists covering the AFL beat and, according to one colleague, he seemed to take great pride in his reputation. His aggression was encouraged, but behind his back, AFL executives snigger at Keane's penchant for saving his pennies and bringing a packed lunch to work.

Controlling the message (usually with the assistance of compliant journalists and broadcasters) is an AFL art form.

And often it gets personal.

Ben Hart was the public affairs manager for the AFL Players' Association (AFLPA) in 2011 when the union faced off against league chiefs during a bitter round of collective bargaining agreement negotiations. The AFL suspected Hart, a former journalist and chief of staff to Victorian environment minister Gavin Jennings, of being the driver behind the association's successful media strategy. As the AFLPA began gaining traction and public support in its bid for a fixed percentage of the league's revenues, an agitated Demetriou began publicly targeting Hart. Most football fans would never have heard of him, but Demetriou made repeated (and usually belittling) references to Hart as the weeks rolled on in a bid to unsettle the AFLPA negotiating team.

'Coming from politics, I was shocked at how much control the AFL expected to have over the whole industry, its intolerance of dissent and the lengths they went to in order to ensure that competing agendas were minimised or eliminated,' Hart reflected. 'Demetriou quickly identified me as a troublemaker, simply because I was being effective in presenting the players' claims around things like pay and retirement support in a positive light in the media. He clearly sought to intimidate me publicly through his regular media spots.

'My understanding is that the AFL pressured AFLPA management to have me sacked. In what other world would a company feel it could demand the union sack their media guy, just because he was doing his job too well?

'I left my brief stint in that world feeling it was a toxic closed shop, a world of backroom deals and opaque patronage, where no one ever dared criticise the Dear Leader, and the only agenda was the head office agenda.'[6]

\*\*\*

The AFL's 'media management' sometimes extends to its own.

Each morning AFL-related news clippings are emailed to the AFL commissioners and selected senior staff, and often stories critical of the AFL's own conduct are omitted.

An AFL spinner will always be by the CEO's side for appearances before the press, but in-depth question and answer sessions are rare. Ross Oakley chose to spruik his message in a weekly slot on Neil Mitchell's top-rating 3AW morning drive show, a tradition adopted by his successors Wayne Jackson, Demetriou and McLachlan.

The media unit is responsible for speechwriting, press announcements and media briefings – on and off the record. But one senior AFL figure said it would be 'unfair' to blame the media unit for damaging leaks during scandals like the Essendon drugs investigation or the Melbourne tanking affair.

'There's a lot of media-savvy people who work at AFL House,' he said.

'They have their own "go to" journalists, they know the right people to talk to, and can run their own agenda.'

And those who dared probe and question or shine a light into dark corners were cut down at the knees, as one respected veteran broadcaster found out.

Tim Lane called his first VFL game for the ABC in August 1979. A pitch-perfect tone that builds to a crescendo and an uncanny ability to find the right words at the right time has made Lane a legend of the broadcasting craft across football, cricket and track and field. He also has a nose for news.

Towards the end of the 2010 AFL season Lane's interest was piqued when he read a story in *The Age* about rising Sydney Swans star Kieren Jack. The son of legendary rugby league player Garry Jack, Kieren had told journalist Emma Quayle how his journey to the rival code had almost been derailed before it started after his registration papers for the 2005 national draft went missing in the post. Jack revealed a special dispensation had been awarded to him by the league, clearing the path for him to be selected by Sydney with the last pick in the rookie draft.

The snippet came soon after the AFL's bold recruitment of NRL stars Israel Folau to play for its fledgling New South Wales expansion side, Greater Western Sydney, and Karmichael Hunt for the Gold Coast Suns.

'It made me wonder whether Kieren Jack was the lightbulb moment, when the AFL realised the marketing value of having someone from the rugby codes as a poster boy for the AFL,' Lane said.[7]

Were the papers really lost in the post or was it all part of a cunning plan to ensure the son of an NRL champ would run out for an AFL team in rugby league heartland?

Lane spent several months pursuing his hunch, joining forces with *Sydney Morning Herald* columnist Roy Masters, who had coached Garry Jack at the Western Suburbs Magpies in 1981. Masters spoke to Jack Sr who allegedly told him, 'they smothered it by saying it was lost in the mail'.

The waters were muddied further by the emergence of an interview Kieren Jack had given to *Daily Telegraph* sports writer Todd Balym in September 2010.

'I didn't know much about the draft and didn't know you had to nominate ...' Jack told Balym. 'I was pretty lucky in the end. I might not be standing here if we didn't get permission off the AFL.'

On 11 December 2011, Lane published a news story and an analysis piece in *The Age* casting doubt over the legitimacy of Jack's passage to the Swans.

Eleven days later, almost on the eve of Christmas, the AFL announced its integrity department had investigated the circumstances behind Jack's drafting and 'found insufficient evidence to establish any breach of the AFL rules'.

The AFL said Jack Jr had signed a statutory declaration on the eve of the rookie draft regarding his lost paperwork and recommended that the matter be closed.

Unconvinced, Lane published another column on 24 December declaring the AFL all-clear couldn't be taken seriously. 'No one with any understanding of this matter could be convinced by what was released on Thursday,' Lane wrote. 'As if to show there's nothing it can't do, the league has now delivered a white Christmas; a Festive Season snow-job.'[8]

Lane made contact with the AFL the next January seeking further answers before being hit with a legal letter demanding he apologise or be sued for defamation.

*The Age* was not Lane's primary employer, and an apology ran at the bottom of his next column, but there would be a heavier price to pay.

Lane had been a member of the Australian Football Hall of Fame selection panel since 2003. It was a prestigious committee, charged with nominating players, coaches, umpires and administrators from all states and territories worthy of elevation. Lane had also hosted the annual black-tie dinner that unveiled inductees at Crown Casino's Palladium ballroom since 2005. He completed both duties in the year after his Kieren Jack exposé but was removed from the selection committee and stripped of hosting duties in favour of Fox Footy's Gerard Whateley in 2013.

Lane, the longest-serving commentator in the game, was given a couple of reasons for his sacking.

One was that the AFL wanted the event to have a stronger TV presence and Fox Footy wanted one of their own, Whateley, to drive it. The other reason related to a question Lane had directed to Glenn Archer during the 2012 dinner, which elicited an awkward response about the Wayne Carey sex scandal that had rocked North Melbourne on the eve of the 2002 season.

But unlike other ex–Hall of Fame committee members, Lane was never invited back to future dinners.

'How could I not feel it as retribution?' Lane mused.

Like so many before, and after, for daring to shine a light in inconvenient places, Lane had become *persona non grata*.

Late in the 2016 season, in the final months of Mike Fitzpatrick's chairmanship of the commission, Lane discussed the entirety of this matter with him. Fitzpatrick responded to the meeting four days later by text, indicating he had spoken with McLachlan to 'straighten out' the Hall of Fame invitation issue.

At the time of writing, well over three years later, no invitation has arrived. Lane consoles himself with the thought that perhaps it's been sent each year but got lost in the mail.

\*\*\*

In December 2012 – a few months before the handing down of the Melbourne tanking findings and the emergence of the Essendon drugs saga – the AFL was rocked by a salary cap cheating scandal at the Adelaide Crows.

The story surrounded a secret agreement struck between Crows chiefs and star forward Kurt Tippett during a meeting at the Kurrawa Surf Club in Broadbeach, Queensland, in September 2009.

Desperate to avoid losing Tippett to the newly formed and cashed-up Gold Coast Suns, Crows chief executive Steven Trigg and club football boss John Reid flew to the Sunshine state to make him an offer he couldn't refuse.

Tippett was offered a $1.8 million three-year contract – $400,000 in the first year and $700,000 in years two and three – plus two secret side deals, which were not disclosed in copies of Tippett's contract submitted to the AFL.

The first was a commitment, against league rules, agreeing to trade Tippett to a club of his choice for a second-round draft pick at the end of the contract. The second, and most damning, was an agreement to underwrite payments of $200,000 in independent third-party deals on top of the $1.8 million.

The real contract, complete with instructions to keep it a secret from the AFL, was kept in an office at Crows headquarters in Adelaide.

It was as brazen as cheating can get – draft tampering and salary cap rorting rolled into one – and exposed three years later when the Sydney Swans, seeking to recruit Tippett, became aware of the agreement for him to be traded for a second-round draft pick.

The league investigated, charges were laid against Trigg, Reid, Tippett and others, and a closed hearing was held by members of the AFL Commission in December 2012.

Tippett's lawyer, David Galbally, QC, said it was 'a complete shemozzle'.[9]

His first concern was that the Crows and the AFL had employed the same law firm, Minter Ellison, to deal with the matter. Minter Ellison's Melbourne office represented the AFL and its Adelaide branch the Crows.

At one stage Trigg was also going to be represented by Minter Ellison, before engaging another law firm.

Galbally also pushed unsuccessfully for Demetriou to withdraw himself from the commission hearing because the AFL CEO had held conversations about the Tippett arrangement with Crows chairman Rob Chapman, who had immediately alerted Demetriou to the problem once becoming aware of it.

Tippett was fined $50,000 and banned for eleven matches, Trigg was fined $50,000 and suspended for six months and Adelaide was fined $300,000 and lost selections across two national drafts.

The penalties were lenient compared to those heaped on Carlton a decade earlier for salary cap rorts.

'It is not a valid comparison,' Demetriou said a few days later. '[At Carlton] it was systemic and prolonged.'[10]

He was right but Galbally said his lasting impression of the case was that 'Trigg was a favoured administrator and so the AFL wanted to keep him in the game.'

Trigg, an experienced chief executive, and Tippett, a young player who later said his trust in his club had backfired, received almost identical punishments.

On 5 December 2012, in an 'exclusive' interview with journalist Patrick Smith, Demetriou announced that the AFL intended to open future hearings to the media in a bid to give greater clarity around commission decisions.

'In retrospect, I wish the inquiry had been open,' Demetriou told Smith.

'There has been a thought within the AFL that we do not need to hold open inquiries, but I think that is not there now. We have nothing to hide. I believe we'll have open inquiries in the future.'

It never happened. And was never going to.

The Melbourne tanking affair, the Essendon drugs 'hearing' and all subsequent AFL integrity investigations were dealt with in exactly the same way. Behind closed doors.

The promise of open hearings was AFL media spin from the top shelf. Feed the chooks. Move along.

But a twist to the Tippett case was the AFL's decision to charge and suspend Reid for twelve months even though he had retired and was no longer contracted to a club as an official.

The precedent had been set but was not followed less than a year later when Dean Robinson, who had resigned from his position at Essendon, escaped AFL charges for bringing the game into disrepute, despite being continually named as a co-conspirator along with Stephen Dank in ASADA's interim report.

\*\*\*

The AFL's desperation to control the messaging hit peak mode in 2012 when the league unveiled its own in-house digital platform, AFL Media.

With a workforce of more than one hundred ensconced at league headquarters, AFL Media was designed to curb the dominance of traditional platforms and become 'an independent credible news organisation'. It was also designed as a stalking horse for future TV rights negotiations, giving potential bidders the impression the AFL could one day produce its own broadcasts and sell them off directly to online subscribers.

For fans wanting updates on results and injuries or game-day analysis, AFL Media was a premium service. But when the news centred on more difficult off-field subjects or the conduct of the AFL itself, it often fell short, through no fault of its journalists.

The website's 'independence' was exposed in 2014 when lawyers representing its editorial workers took the AFL to the Fair Work Commission seeking the right to collectively bargain. In its submissions, the AFL claimed the staff were not actually journalists but 'working in sports administration'.

Senior AFL Media journalist Mitch Cleary found this out for himself in August 2020 when he was stood down by league chiefs for revealing the wife of Richmond captain Trent Cotchin had visited a Gold Coast day spa against strict AFL quarantine hub rules. It was a legitimate yarn, but the AFL had given an undertaking to clubs (which Cleary didn't know about) not to name family members involved in quarantine breaches.

'If I was a workplace lawyer the question I would be focusing on is did Cleary think he was a journalist or did he think he was an employee of the AFL,' broadcaster Gerard Whateley said. 'That's just a straight-out betrayal of journalism.'[11]

Further evidence of a lack of focus on reporting news without bias was clear in February 2020. An award-winning story revealing footy great Graham 'Polly' Farmer had become the first Australian Rules player diagnosed post-death with the devastating neurological disease chronic traumatic encephalopathy – linked to repeated head knocks playing football – was picked up within hours by every major news website in the country except one – AFL Media.

\*\*\*

Sacked as St Kilda coach in late 2006, Grant Thomas made a new name for himself as an expert commentator for *The Age* newspaper, SEN radio and Channel 9's popular Monday night football program, *Footy Classified*.

An unflinching Thomas called it as he saw it, and was not afraid to criticise the AFL when issues arose. It was refreshing to hear raw honesty and footy fans loved it.

In early 2009, SEN station boss Barry Quick called Thomas to congratulate him on his contributions, telling him he was SEN's 'number one football talent'. He was driving discussions and ratings.

But league officials had lodged repeated complaints about Thomas's questioning of the AFL's decision-making and leadership, and on many occasions the umpiring department and its umpires. SEN became concerned its rights to broadcast AFL matches would not be renewed.

A week later, Quick called Thomas and asked if he could come and see him.

'I thought he was going to bring me a nice bottle of wine but instead he said, "Mate, I'm sorry, we've got some financial constraints, we've got to terminate your contract,"' Thomas said. 'I burst out laughing and said, "What do you mean, we're only seven weeks into the season and you've got to pay me for the next thirty-five." He said, "Yeah, we are paying you out."'[12]

The AFL denied any involvement in the Thomas sacking but the explanation provided by station management didn't pass the pub test.

Thomas's media career ended a few years later when he resigned from *Footy Classified* after he was informed by Channel 9 producers about further complaints and threats of litigation against Channel 9 from Demetriou. Nine was not an AFL rights holder but still felt the pressure from head office.[13]

'Demetriou threatened legal action against me and I said let him do it,' Thomas said. 'He said he'd accept an apology and I refused, so they made [co-host] Garry Lyon apologise for me.

'In the end, I said to the guys, "Why are you paying me so much money to be hoodwinked into saying what you want me to say? Whenever I say something that I want to say we seem to get a bit of publicity out of it and people actually agree with it. Why don't you just pay a puppet $15,000 and tell him what to say?"'

Most major Australian media organisations rely heavily on AFL content and Demetriou and McLachlan always understood the power it afforded them.

Journalists who question the league or investigate hidden recesses of their empire are derided and ostracised.

In early September 2013, Demetriou taunted *The Australian*'s Chip Le Grand on two Melbourne radio stations after he had reported that the league was set to drop its charges against Essendon club doctor Bruce Reid for his part in the supplements scandal.

Reid had refused to accept a penalty in the farcical 'hearings' held at AFL House the previous month and lodged a Supreme Court writ that would have forced league figures to front a public courtroom.

When asked about the report on ABC radio Demetriou said: 'I have no knowledge of that, you'd have to ask Homer'.[14] It was a reference to Le Grand's birth name, Homer Eugene Le Grand.

Demetriou described the story as 'another piece of garbage written by Chip Le Grand, who didn't bother to ring us up for a comment yesterday … He's been wrong throughout the whole Essendon saga, he's wrong again and he ought to pick up the phone and ring someone at the AFL and get a comment rather than writing garbage.'

Sadly for Demetriou, the story was 100 per cent correct.

The AFL dropped all charges against Reid days later in return for the Supreme Court proceedings being discontinued. It was no surprise. The AFL's head of integrity had sworn an affidavit in the proceedings and Reid's lawyers had indicated that he would be required for cross-examination. Magically, the charges disappeared.

As for the attack on his birth name, Le Grand quipped that he had not been bullied about that 'since grade four at Hampton primary school'.

\*\*\*

Threats and intimidation are par for the course working the AFL beat.

At a corporate golf event in March 2016, player agent Craig 'Ned' Kelly told two *Herald Sun* journalists in the clubhouse of Melbourne's Capital Golf Club that he planned to wrap a golf club around the head of the newspaper's chief football writer, Mark Robinson, if he saw him.

Kelly had clearly taken a dislike to something Robinson had written.

A few years earlier, Kelly – a member of Collingwood's 1990 premiership team – caused a stir of his own by expressing interest in one day divesting his business interests and taking on the Magpies presidency.

'Yeah – at some stage I'd love to do that,' Kelly said in a TV interview.[15]

'At the appropriate family time ... and if the people within Collingwood footy club see it as a benefit, I'd love to go back and do my dues, because I owe it plenty.'

But the man who occupied the position, Eddie McGuire, was fiercely protective of his patch. The boy from Broadie, whose appetite for a yarn as a Channel 10 news hound in the 1980s was insatiable, had become the media mogul from Toorak. His private company, McGuire Media, had made a fortune cashing in on AFL-related enterprises and so when I contacted him for a comment on the Kelly interview in July 2010, he switched into attack mode.

'Don't start destabilising my club. I'll give you the fucking tip right now, if you blokes start digging and carrying on and making things up I'll fucking shred youse,' McGuire barked. 'Okay? So if you blokes start fucking making things up or try to destabilise my club in any way, shape or fucking form, heaven fuckin' help you, okay?

'Don't make things up. You heard what he said last night. He said he had an ambition one day to contribute to the Collingwood Football Club as many people do. Full stop.

'If you reckon there's a story in that good luck, but I'll fucking tear you a new one because it's bullshit, you know that. Ned's a mate of mine, there's no fucking challenge or any of that bullshit going on. So don't even try to make things up, cos you'll embarrass yourself ...

'You are writing a lot of beat-up stories about Collingwood. You can write whatever you like, mate, but I'm telling you that you'll be judged on what you write. Just as dear old Caro [Caroline Wilson] found out ...

'You'll get absolutely cut off at the pass. You'll get ex-communicated – and not just you but the entire newspaper.'[16]

Seems Eddie Everywhere had been watching a few too many episodes of *The Sopranos*.

\*\*\*

Melbourne's *Herald Sun* newspaper and coverage of all things AFL go hand in hand.

Since the merger of the Rupert Murdoch owned *Herald* and the *Sun News-Pictorial* in 1990, the *Herald Sun* and football have been a match made in heaven.

The room at AFL House where most major announcements are delivered by league bosses is named in honour of the paper's legendary chief football reporter, Mike Sheahan, who retired in the months before the Essendon drugs debacle exploded. His replacement was Mark Robinson, a passionate and hard-nosed newspaper man with a knack for mixing just as easily with the man on the street as the suits from the big end of town.

Robinson got his start at the *Bendigo Advertiser* in country Victoria and worked his way to the top of Australian sports journalism thanks to an uncompromising drive to pursue the hardest news. He was unswayed by spin.

Robinson also knew Essendon coach James Hird, having ghost-written his column for many years at the *Herald Sun* during Hird's Brownlow Medal–winning playing days. When the drugs scandal broke, Robinson had enough contacts inside and outside of Essendon to get a head start on the biggest story the game has ever known.

By April 2013, Robinson had become aware of the AFL's desperate manoeuvres in late January and early February that year to convince Essendon chairman David Evans to 'self-report' the club to ASADA. Robinson found out about the crisis meeting at Evans' home the night before the club 'self-reported' where Demetriou had allegedly called Evans and confirmed that it was the Bombers being investigated for the use of performance-enhancing drugs.

The newspaper's big break came in mid-July when it obtained an extract from a witness's secret testimony given to ASADA investigators detailing Demetriou's telephone call to Evans.

Demetriou savagely berated Robinson when he called the AFL boss the day before the story was published seeking comment. He vehemently denied any wrongdoing.

The day the story ran, Demetriou declared to Neil Mitchell on 3AW that he could not have tipped off the Essendon chairman because he didn't know the name of the club being investigated.

Sections of the football media dismissed the 'tip-off' story but it had exposed the truth behind the AFL's interference in the process and its backroom attempts to achieve outcomes in its own self-interest.

Robinson had recorded his conversation with Demetriou on his dictaphone and played it to his chief-of-staff, Shaun Phillips, ahead of the story's publication. Demetriou found out about the tape and accused Robinson of playing it around town. He demanded an investigation, which took place and found nothing, but it was agreed the expletive-riddled tape would be destroyed.[17]

It was a classic Demetriou diversionary tactic aimed at shifting the focus from his own conduct to someone else's.

Time after time during the Essendon saga (and every other saga) stories beneficial to the AFL's position would surface when the league was being criticised or was under pressure.

The AFL is a master at manipulating the media cycle and there is no shortage of journalists, broadcasters, past players, administrators and industry stakeholders willing to form a Praetorian Guard around them.

# CHAPTER 15

# Inside job

Luke Beveridge smelt a rat.

The Western Bulldogs had kicked the first three goals of their do-or-die elimination final, but something wasn't right.

It was Saturday, 12 September 2015 and Beveridge's Bulldogs were facing off against an inspired Adelaide Crows team coached by Scott Camporeale under the bright lights of the MCG. Camporeale had taken the reins at the Crows in tragic circumstances just a few weeks earlier after the senseless death of their coach Phil Walsh.

As the opening stanza wore on, a Dogs assistant coach voiced his surprise from the back of the box at Adelaide's anticipation of their forward-line tactics.

It was an epic final that went down to the wire before Crows skipper Taylor Walker ran down the wing and lasered a long, match-winning pass across his body to teammate Charlie Cameron. Adelaide would prevail by seven points to set up a semi-final clash against Hawthorn. For the Dogs, it was season over.

On the morning after the match, Crows defender Kyle Cheney caught up for breakfast with his former Hawthorn teammate Ben Stratton at a Melbourne café. Cheney had played at the Hawks in 2014 and remained close to several players at the club.

As the pair chatted, Stratton was taken aback when Cheney told him that before the match, Western Bulldogs player Michael Talia had passed on 'game-sensitive information' to his brother, star Adelaide defender Daniel Talia. While Daniel played in the crucial knockout final, Michael had been left out of the Western Bulldogs team.

Troubled by what he had heard, Stratton sounded out Hawthorn teammate Josh Gibson for advice. Gibson, Cheney and Stratton had all been coached by Beveridge during his days as an assistant under Hawthorn senior coach Alastair Clarkson. All three had a deep respect for Beveridge, a master motivator who would go on to coach the Dogs to a drought-breaking flag in 2016.

Gibson, fully appreciating the seriousness of what he was doing, phoned Beveridge the next day to tip him off about the Cheney–Stratton conversation.

It was no laughing matter.

Beveridge immediately contacted Bulldogs president Peter Gordon, a formidable lawyer and businessman. Gordon, like Beveridge, was alarmed, but expressed caution. These were potentially devastating allegations, and if the AFL were to be alerted, more information was required.

The next day, Tuesday, 15 September, Michael Talia was called into a meeting room at the club's Whitten Oval headquarters and grilled by Gordon and Bulldogs chief executive David Stevenson.

According to documents that surfaced ten months later, Talia admitted at that meeting that he had spoken to his brother on the day before the game, and sent him two text messages. The documents asserted that he admitted discussing his brother's likely match-up with Bulldogs forward Jake Stringer.[1]

He also agreed that if Daniel Talia had told his teammates about an 'unusual role' that Dogs forward Tory Dickson would play in the match, it was possible his brother had learnt the information from him during a phone call the previous Friday. But he denied 'transmitting any confidential information' and denied telling Daniel he was annoyed at being excluded from the team.

Bulldogs football officials caught wind of the explosive allegations when Michael Talia was told not to attend a meeting of all players before their departure for their off-season break. Incredulous at what he was hearing, Dogs assistant coach Steve King fired off a text message to Crows backline coach Darren Milburn – an old teammate at Geelong.

According to testimony provided by King, he asked Milburn: 'What's Michael gone and done?' King said Milburn replied: 'Not much' ... or 'Not all that much.'

Documents revealed that the Dogs later argued Milburn's response showed he understood immediately that the 'Michael' to which the text referred was Michael Talia, and that it related to allegations of leaking.

Milburn would later dispute King's version of events, claiming that King had referred specifically to Michael Talia in his text.

An enduring mateship was sorely tested.

The content of the messages has never been confirmed, because both assistant coaches were later accused of deleting them – an act the Dogs said had probably been done 'collusively' when the pair learnt an AFL investigation was likely to be launched.

The decision to allegedly wipe those messages was ultimately slammed by the Dogs as obstructing the investigation, but their very existence would still form a key part of the Bulldogs' submission that the Dogs–Crows final had been compromised.

The day after the texts were exchanged, a deeply concerned Beveridge got on the phone to Stratton to test what Gibson had said. Beveridge told AFL investigators that Stratton had confirmed what Gibson had relayed about the Talia brothers.

Shortly after, Beveridge received a call from Cheney.

The Dogs coach told investigators a contrite Cheney told him he was 'fearful about his position' at the Crows 'if any complaint went ahead' and he 'felt bad about being involved in the leak'. Beveridge advised Cheney to report the matter to Adelaide football boss David Noble, assuring him he had done nothing wrong. Cheney acted on the advice – but Noble told investigators that Cheney had told him that the allegations of leaking were 'all false'.

Then came another twist.

Bulldogs list manager Jason McCartney told the club about a conversation he had that morning, Wednesday, 16 September, with the father of Crows defender Jake Lever. According to McCartney, Al Lever told him about a second Adelaide player who was aware of and felt uncomfortable about Daniel Talia's revelations. His son, Jake, had been an emergency for the final.

On Thursday, 17 September, Beveridge called Cheney back. The Dogs coach relayed the Lever conversation and assured him he was now not the only Adelaide player to express concern. Beveridge would later tell investigators that Cheney thanked him for the call and had not backed down from his initial claims.

Five days later, interrupting their list management and player trade plays, the Western Bulldogs formally asked the AFL to investigate.

The crux of the explosive allegations levelled against Michael and Daniel Talia was that the outcome of an AFL final had been compromised by the leaked inside information.

It was tantamount to a scandal, but when the story broke on the night of the AFL's All-Australian dinner on 22 September 2015, journalists were quietly briefed by league media staffers that it was all a storm in a teacup.

Few details of the actual allegations were made public, but the theory being promoted by the league was that the Bulldogs had grossly overreacted in requesting a formal investigation.

Michael Talia's manager, player agent Liam Pickering, declared that he was certain the brothers would be cleared by the AFL's integrity department.

'It's totally unfair on Michael,' Pickering said. 'I think there's absolutely nothing to see here. In fact I don't think that, I know that.'[2]

Tensions boiled over at the Brownlow Medal dinner on 28 September when Beveridge and journalist Damian Barrett had a verbal altercation in the men's bathroom at Crown Casino. Barrett's reporting and commentary on the story had been favourable towards the Talias and critical of the Bulldogs.

The Crows and the Talia brothers had always maintained their innocence and two months later were cleared by the AFL integrity unit.

The explanation given after a 63-day probe was that Cheney had sparked the investigation after playing a 'practical joke' on Beveridge. It seemed implausible – and certainly was never funny – but given what was publicly known at the time, and what journalists were privately being told, the case appeared closed.

But eight months after the 'nothing to see here' sign went up, a cache of documents detailing explosive undisclosed claims about the Talia investigation emerged.

The documents included a letter and submission from the Western Bulldogs to the AFL, exposing their fury at the league's handling of the probe and its exoneration of the brothers. 'There is clearly sufficient basis for the AFL to find that there was an improper communication of confidential information,' Dogs president Peter Gordon asserted to the league in the damning submission.

The documents revealed witness testimony that stated Michael Talia was 'angry and resentful that he had been excluded from the WBFC team for the final' before talking to his brother. It also detailed the previously unknown 'independent corroboration' involving King, Milburn, McCartney and Jake and Al Lever.

The Dogs were scathing of the AFL for accepting the explanations of players at the centre of the scandal rather than the views of Beveridge and McCartney. Beveridge, the club said, was prepared to go 'on oath' about his conversations with Cheney. The Bulldogs dismissed the 'practical joke' explanation outright, as an 'invention'. The AFL should be concerned that Cheney had been 'participating in a cover-up', the Bulldogs said, adding: 'His behaviour is disgraceful and inappropriate.'

It was also revealed an AFL investigator had told Dogs chiefs that he 'thought nothing of it' after Michael Talia claimed to have lost his phone and Daniel deleted texts – actions the Dogs described as 'matters for deep concern and suspicion' and potential civil or criminal acts.

In a letter sent to the AFL on 14 October 2015, Gordon declared that the club had lost faith in the integrity unit's ability to carry out the Talia investigation. Then, in a 12 November submission, Gordon wrote: 'WBFC does not accept the truthfulness of the Talias' explanation for the loss of their phone records they have alleged. That both brothers would lose access to evidence in all the circumstances described simply does not pass the smell test.'

The documents raised serious concerns about yet another AFL 'investigation', but by the time they were aired in October 2016 much had changed in the once tortured world of the Western Bulldogs.

In one of footy's greatest fairy tales, Beveridge's men won four straight finals to claim the club's first premiership in sixty-two long years. Beveridge displayed his class seconds before raising the cup by inviting injured Dogs skipper Bob Murphy onto the dais and placing his premiership medal around his neck. Murphy, a heart and soul Bulldog, had missed out on playing but was given a glorious moment by a coach who fully understood the essence of football.

Relations between the Western Bulldogs and the AFL appeared to mend quickly. In late 2016, Gordon emerged as key negotiator in talks surrounding the future of Docklands Stadium; a deal that would ultimately secure its five tenant clubs, including the Dogs, vastly improved gate returns.

The following year, the Bulldogs were granted their wish to play home matches in Ballarat and were picked to take on North Melbourne in footy's first ever Good Friday clash.

But the Talia affair has never sat well with Gordon, who rated it the most troubling experience in his thirty years in football. 'I look back on this, five years on, and remain bewildered and angered,' Gordon said. 'Cheney never explained why, if it was all a joke, he had the two very serious "admission conversations" with Luke Beveridge that he did and why he waited almost a month before he volunteered the joke explanation. Nor has anyone ever explained how "the joke" was funny.

'No one ever asked Ben Stratton if it seemed like a joke when Cheney told him. Or Josh Gibson. Darren Milburn apparently alleges Steven King had actually asked him, "What's Michael Talia gone and done?" But that's no explanation. It acknowledges their exchange took place but doesn't explain Milburn's response of "not all that much".

'If Milburn had no clue about why King was asking him about Michael Talia, why would he respond "not all that much" and not "WTF are you talking about?" No explanation for Lever. No explanation for Michael's crucial admission to me. No explanation for the failure of the AFL's integrity unit to attempt to recover the lost and the deleted text and phone messages between the two brothers.

'We later learnt that at the same time as the AFL integrity unit was electing not to recover these phone records, it was actively recovering deleted text messages in the Lachie Whitfield investigation ... so the AFL knew they could be recovered and how to do it ... if it wanted to.

'I've never believed about this matter, that Michael Talia acted with a premeditated intent to corrupt a game result,' Gordon mused. 'I think he spoke to his brother impulsively with a kind of hurt and immature petulance after learning he had been dropped from the team. He made a mistake. But there was nothing impulsive or emotional about the AFL's soft-pedalling of the integrity investigation.'

The Talia affair opened Gordon's eyes to something else that troubled him.

'I have one other reflection about this matter. It's hard for a club to call out an integrity breach sometimes. It's hard to be a whistleblower. Especially in circumstances like this. I will add that it's particularly unrewarding for a president or director who is an unpaid volunteer to walk into the lion's den like this. When we did so, we immediately became a target for an aggressive and hostile football media which derided our concerns and our actions.

'I remember one opinion piece by Caroline Wilson as especially malicious and vitriolic,' he said. 'Wilson had not spoken to me for the piece but it was clear [to me] she had been briefed by the AFL, as well as by Adelaide Football Club executives and Michael Talia's camp. Even more curiously, her article came out a matter of hours after I had told the AFL's integrity unit that I regarded its investigation as more ethically challenged than Talia's original actions.

'I don't have any doubt that, having decided how they wanted to dispose of this complaint, several senior people in the AFL management team also decided that it would be necessary or at least helpful to publicly position me and the club as sore losers, obsessive and, as only Caroline Wilson would put it, a laughing stock,' Gordon said.

'Another journalist closely aligned to the AFL would concede to me a few months later that he knew of not a single journalist or experienced AFL industry person who did not believe that events had transpired in the Talia affair exactly as the Bulldogs had alleged. But none of those who launched public attacks on the Bulldogs ever publicly recanted.

'I think the AFL ought to reflect deeply on what business its public relations people and executive team have turning the media guns on club people who are telling an inconvenient truth.'[3]

A similar pattern would emerge during almost every AFL integrity unit investigation, where selected journalists appeared to have a direct line to league insiders or investigators. Strategic leaks allowed the AFL to shape and manipulate the public narrative that it wanted.

The Talia brothers scandal goes to the heart of the AFL's hypocrisy on integrity.

League chiefs had been presented with overwhelming (and independently collaborated) evidence that a footy final had been compromised by the leaking of inside information, yet worked desperately for weeks to dismiss it.

Why?

Simply, the commercial ramifications of an adverse finding against the Talias and Adelaide Crows would have been too damaging for head office to even contemplate. Lucrative gambling licences would have been put at risk and the integrity of the 2015 finals exposed.

So an alternative outcome was concocted; and under the bus went Gordon, a lawyer who had served his football club with distinction across two terms, and Beveridge, whose whole coaching philosophy was built on integrity.

Someone always has to pay a price in the name of the empire; or as Richard Colless explained it: 'The playbook is either ignore or joke about it or if it heats up, privately threaten whoever is mounting any sort of challenge.'[4]

## CHAPTER 16

# Kelly gang

GRAEME 'GUBBY' ALLAN WAS THREATENING TO GO ROGUE.

It was October 2016, and the veteran club football boss was at the centre of an investigation into claims he had helped Greater Western Sydney young gun Lachie Whitfield hide from drug testers.

Whitfield, a star junior and the number one overall selection in the 2012 national draft, had contacted Allan in a distressed state in May the previous year looking for help. He had been using illicit drugs and was feuding with his girlfriend. Allan immediately arranged for Whitfield to spend the night at the home of the club's welfare manager, Craig Lambert.

For twelve months, the AFL investigation into Whitfield, Allan and Lambert went nowhere.

A member of the public had tipped off ASADA about Whitfield's stay at the Lamberts' home but there was no urgency – or more likely no desire – by the league to punish its own fledgling expansion club.

It sat in the bulging bottom drawer at AFL House until the

night of Monday, 29 August 2016 – three days after Allan was sensationally parachuted into the top job in Collingwood's football department over demoted Magpies footy boss Neil Balme.

Allan had defected from the Giants to the Pies several months earlier to take charge of its women's football and netball programs, but it was an open secret that he would end up replacing Balme at the end of the season.

As soon as it happened, journalists at competing newspapers were tipped off about the dormant Whitfield investigation, which roared back to life.

If the motive of the leaker was to wipe out Allan and his freshly inked four-year deal at the Magpies, it certainly worked. Allan, Lambert and Whitfield were thrust into a fresh football scandal; but the AFL, too, had some explaining to do.

Why had their so-called 'investigation' into Whitfield's sleepover at the Lamberts' home sat idle for sixteen months? And why wasn't Collingwood alerted to the allegations by the league before it had hired Allan if the investigation was still active?

The scandal reached fever pitch in October 2016 when Allan hired top dispute resolution lawyer Leon Zwier to lead his defence against pending AFL charges – the same 'Mr Fix-It' Melbourne had turned to in the ASADA matter.

Zwier didn't come cheap, but his engagement sent a clear signal to the AFL that Allan intended to fiercely contest the claims he had deliberately hidden Whitfield away so he could avoid an illicit drugs test. The Allan camp let it be known that they were prepared to go to court and test the credibility of Whitfield's ex-girlfriend, who had sounded the alarm, and the reliability of information gathered by the AFL integrity department.

Lambert, too, had lawyered up and so the AFL got to work doing what it did best: beating people into submission and avoiding a public hearing.

Lambert, a former star player with Richmond and Brisbane, was a pivotal figure in the establishment of an Australian Rules club in rugby league heartland and is a respected football person, but he was of no further use or concern to the AFL. Once the matter was settled he was suspended for a year and banished from the game. He would end up selling photocopiers.

Allan was a different kettle of fish.

Across a three-decade career in football administration, 'Gubby' knew where many of footy's bodies were buried. Some he'd buried himself. His backroom manoeuvrings in helping establish Greater Western Sydney were embarrassingly exposed in 2011 after it was revealed he had secretly employed the roof-tiler father of star recruit Tom Scully on a six-year contract worth $680,000 to help lure his son away from the Melbourne Demons.[1]

GWS was forced to include Phil Scully's wages in its salary cap after the AFL conceded his hiring as a recruiter was directly related to his son's decision to quit the Demons. It was a grubby deal that angered rival clubs but, incredibly, after the story broke Demetriou publicly lauded it.

'It's a stroke of genius from Graeme Allan, that he's managed to attract one of the finest young talents and also attract his father, who's a recruiting manager,' Demetriou declared. 'It's within the rules, it's in the salary cap, it's legitimate. We are a family code and it's good to keep fathers and sons together, I think.'[2]

But documents revealed Scully Sr had been offered his contract in November 2010 – twelve months before his son 'officially' walked out on Melbourne.

Allan was not a man the AFL wanted on the outside of the tent.

He was fighting hard in the Whitfield saga until suddenly, on the eve of the 2016 national draft, the AFL announced that the matter had been resolved.

Allan, Lambert and Whitfield had all accepted sanctions for conduct prejudicial to the interests of the AFL.

Allan and Lambert copped twelve-month bans and Whitfield was suspended for six months.

But what had happened? Why did Allan lay down his weapons just weeks after vowing to go nuclear?

Five months later, in March 2017, powerful AFL player agent Craig Kelly confirmed that Allan would spend part of his football exile working and studying in Manhattan. Kelly admitted that he had helped Allan, then aged sixty-two, to enrol in two business management short courses at the prestigious New York University Stern School of Business. The suspended football boss would also be given a desk at the Times Square headquarters of Kelly's global management company, TLA Worldwide, while working alongside the firm's Major League Baseball agents.

Kelly insisted the arrangement had been struck out of friendship and was in no way linked to Allan's decision to accept a suspension in the Whitfield case. Allan had been Collingwood's football boss in 1990 when Kelly was a member of the club's drought-breaking premiership under coach Leigh Matthews.

'He's paying his own way,' Kelly declared. 'He got himself into the courses, we just networked him in to New York. I've known Gubby for a long time and he's told me he wants to further develop and improve himself.'[3]

For all his sins, Allan was back consulting for North Melbourne in 2018 before landing a football advisory gig with the AFL's blessing at St Kilda.

He'd played his cards beautifully.

\*\*\*

Craig Kelly was still playing at Collingwood, working part-time in the club's marketing and sales area, when the call that changed his life came through in 1995.

The AFL had just established its own in-house player marketing and promotions business aimed at heading off a venture called Club 10 led by pioneering football agent Ricky Nixon, and needed someone to run it.

Long-time league lawyer Jeff Browne said Kelly came recommended for the job by none other than Collingwood's then football manager, Graeme 'Gubby' Allan.

'I was asked to set that up. I asked around about who we could get to run it,' Browne recalled. 'Gubby recommended Craig Kelly. I met with Craig and recommended Craig and the AFL then accepted Craig.'[4]

Kelly's AFL-backed project was named Pro Squad and set the defender on the road to player management domination. In 1996, Kelly joined forces with Olympic swimmer Rob Woodhouse and created a new sports management entity, Elite Sports Properties (ESP).

The pair hit the jackpot for the first time in the early 2000s after selling the business for $17.5 million to a buyer who soon went bankrupt – buying it back 'Kerry Packer–Alan Bond style' for just $2 million.

ESP became a market force, signing many of the AFL's best players. It began securing lucrative AFL contracts, including an official memorabilia licence, and would go on to manage major money-spinning football functions such as the AFL Grand Final eve luncheon at Crown Casino, the Grand Final week live site and the Footy Festival at Yarra Park, the Brownlow Medal after-party and the VIP September Club where corporates are wined and dined during and after the premiership decider at the MCG.

Even commemorative premiership beer cans are whacked on bottle-shop shelves with the help of the firm, which was bought out by US company TLA Worldwide in 2015 in a deal worth up to $25.5 million; with Kelly staying at the helm. TLA has described itself as the AFL's 'PR agency of choice'.

Kelly's close relationship with AFL head office has long rankled rival player managers and sports marketing firms eager to do business with the AFL. These other agencies complain about a lack of transparent tendering.

The AFL has a procurement manager and a procurement policy but some deals are still done the old-fashioned way.

'Ned [Kelly] is great at what he does, and may well be the right person to run all of them, but there's just no transparent bidding process,' one rival industry figure said. 'If it [the AFL] was a public company or a government department they would have to go through a rigid process.'

When McLachlan celebrated his fortieth birthday in late 2013 with a cowboys-and-Indians themed party at his rural retreat at Birregurra, 40 kilometres northwest of Lorne, Kelly was front and centre.

A long-time mate of the AFL boss-to-be, Kelly arranged for dozens of expensive London plane trees to be purchased at $255 a pop to line the drive of the McLachlan property. He hit up a who's who of the Melbourne football establishment to help pay for them as well as a string of top AFL executives:

Darren Birch, Andrew Dillon, Simon Lethlean and Richard Simkiss.

It was a window into the Kelly–McLachlan clique.

'Those plane trees are a testament to the boys' club that rule our game,' one industry figure said.[5]

The rises of McLachlan and Kelly were inexorably linked.

Both hailed from South Australia and shared a love of horses and the land. McLachlan's younger brother Hamish sat briefly on the board of ESP and worked for several years in the company's events department, helping establish its polo division. Hamish was also a key player and principal shareholder behind the failed AFL Hall of Fame and Sensation venture in Swanston Street, Melbourne, which closed after just three months in October 2004 with debts of up to $3 million.

A Federal Court judge slammed it at the time as being 'hopelessly insolvent'.[6] Creditors were promised between nine and twelve cents in the dollar after administrators KordaMentha were called in to mop up the mess.

The disastrous Hall of Fame project was tendered out by the league to the Spyglass Management Group, a consortium led by South Australian businessman Ian Gray, a close friend of then-AFL boss Wayne Jackson.[7]

It later emerged Gillon McLachlan had his own financial link to the Hall of Fame as a shareholder of Hush Productions, a business that was contracted to supply media services to the project. Hush Productions was run by Demetriou's one-time housemate and Hawthorn teammate, Robert Dickson, who was tragically killed in a car accident in South Africa in 2009.

McLachlan said that he had off-loaded his stake in Hush Productions on the advice of Demetriou before the Hall of Fame opened its doors in August 2004. 'This is a minute interest in a company which didn't make any money,' McLachlan said at the time. 'I don't believe I have done anything that is in any way conflicted with my position at the AFL.'[8]

He said that he had sold his stake in the company to sports consultants Ben Crowe and Glenn Lovett, whose firm had engaged strategist Andrew Catterall before he joined the AFL in 2004.

The AFL was forced to assume joint ownership of the flopped Hall of Fame venture and carried Spyglass on its own books for years.

As Gillon climbed to the top of Australian sport, Hamish made his own name in a Channel 7 football commentary role, hosting the Brownlow Medal and fronting on-ground presentations during blockbuster games such as Anzac Day and the AFL Grand Final.

Another rising star to cut his teeth under Kelly at ESP in those early days was Richard Simkiss, who would become the AFL's commercial operations manager before being sacked in 2017 over an inappropriate sexual relationship with a female staffer.

On the day McLachlan was unveiled as Demetriou's replacement in April 2014, Kelly slipped quietly into the back of a packed press conference at AFL House, beaming with pride.

The ties that bind them are everywhere.

Former Olympic swimmer Nicole Livingstone, the woman chosen to head up the AFL Women's competition after McLachlan established it in 2017, was a foundation client of ESP.

Kelly's Collingwood premiership teammate and old housemate Michael Christian was appointed as the AFL match review officer a month after Livingstone's appointment.

AFL general manager of commercial, Kylie Rogers, is another close friend of Kelly's and her husband is a former

Old Xaverians Club XVIII and under-19s coach. Kelly played for Old Xavs as did Lethlean and AFL legal counsel Andrew Dillon.

When the Essendon drugs inferno erupted, Kelly's go-to man for a legal crisis, criminal lawyer Tony Hargreaves, emerged as the Bombers' trusted legal counsel before curiously going on to represent the thirty-four players on behalf of the AFL players' union in their fight to clear their name.

Hundreds of AFL players and some of the biggest-name coaches such as Nathan Buckley, Chris Scott, Adam Simpson, Leon Cameron, Simon Goodwin and Stuart Dew are clients of Kelly's company.

Movers and shakers in the football media including Garry Lyon, Luke Darcy, Anthony Hudson, Mark Ricciuto, Jonathan Brown, Matthew Lloyd, Dwayne Russell and Hamish McLachlan are also in the TLA camp.

Another of Kelly's former Collingwood teammates, Gary Pert, has been a staple of the AFL industry. Pushed out as chief executive of the Magpies after a decade-long stint in 2017, Pert emerged as a surprise selection to take charge of Melbourne two years later. His wife Andi has also worked as a consultant to the AFL on women's leadership.

In early 2020, the AFL announced that long-time Kelly client Brad Scott, a two-time premiership player at Brisbane and coach of North Melbourne until parting ways with the club in May 2019, had landed a job as the league's competition evolution manager before being named head of AFL Victoria after the COVID-19 reshuffle.

Later that year, ex-TLA player manager Dan Richardson, fresh from being axed as Essendon's football boss, landed on his feet after being appointed the AFL's Head of Umpiring.

Kelly walks a fine line between championing his clients' interests and those of his AFL mates. The conflict was on show at a meeting of player agents and AFL Players' Association (AFLPA) heads held to discuss the progress of pay negotiations with the league at Victoria Park in Abbotsford in 2016.

Kelly stunned some of his fellow managers when he stood up and urged the players' union to reach a deal with the AFL without the threat of a strike.

'Being a farmer from way back, I am fundamentally opposed to a strike,' Kelly explained to me at the time. 'I believe with the right conversations and the right information being shared openly, we should be able to get an outcome for the clubs, the players and the AFL.'[9]

Pressed on his company's close ties to head office, Kelly said: 'We are commercially close to the AFL, but so are the players, so is every club and so is the AFLPA. What we've got to understand is that we are not like the United States. We are a small market and we all need to work together to support our corporate partners, grow the game and the players must be recognised in that pie.

'And if anyone wants to have a look at the amount of money that we [TLA] have generated and provided to players and the AFL, in growing activities and events that didn't exist ten or fifteen years ago, then by all means come and sit down and I'll show you the numbers.

'This organisation has contributed as much as it has been paid over the journey.'

When I spoke to retired AFL commissioner Bill Kelty about Kelly's close links to head office for the writing of this book, he said simply: 'People make money. It's not a friendly society. The AFL makes a lot of money for people because that's what happens in life.

'There are some processes that could be improved. They're not perfect, but it's one of the most successful sporting organisations in the world, isn't it?'[10]

\*\*\*

Kelly has been able to marginalise the influence of many rival player agents, including veteran manager Peter Jess.

At his peak in the late 1980s and early 1990s, Jess represented 140 AFL players, about a third of the competition. His cousin Jimmy 'The Ghost' Jess was a star for powerhouse club Richmond.

'I managed Jim and after I finalised his deals, I picked up about fifteen of his Tigers teammates and then it exploded across the league because I was getting them the best deals,' Jess said. 'I was shifting them and moving them and I would tell the league that the players were just like workers. They must have all the same corporate benefits: long-service leave, superannuation, workers compensation, insurance and a fair wage system based on the total earnings of the competition.'[11]

Inevitably, Jess started butting heads with the AFL administration because of his hardline stance on 'wage justice'.

'They were obsessed with American football,' Jess said. 'They wanted to turn the league into a franchise model like they have in the United States, so they created all these satellite teams in Sydney and Brisbane without the infrastructure for the club or the players.

'I had players sleeping in cars when they first went up to Sydney and Brisbane. They'd ring me and say they've got no money, because the club couldn't afford to pay them. It was an absolute disgrace.'

By the late 1990s, Jess said the AFL began pressuring clubs to cut ties with him. 'They were actively directing clubs not to deal with me,' he said. 'Player management was never my core business, but it showed me how devoid of any corporate morals the AFL had become.'

Jess said Kelly became 'the chosen one' after he was picked to take on Ricky Nixon.

'Kelly's group became a functionary of the AFL itself, with a wide range of commercial activities being delivered without tender,' Jess said. 'The commercial boundaries between his company and the AFL were so blurred that his organisation appeared to be a branch office of the league.'

Jess revealed losing one of his last big-name clients to TLA – Essendon star Jobe Watson – just weeks after he won the 2012 Brownlow Medal.

'He was poached on the basis that Kelly had a special relationship with the AFL and its sponsors,' Jess said.

A few weeks before Watson's defection, Richmond star Trent Cotchin also cut ties with his long-time manager, Anthony McConville, to join the Kelly stable.

The AFL's supremacy cannot be maintained alone. It relies heavily on a loyal band of industry enablers, and in McLachlan's mate Craig Kelly, there have been few greater beneficiaries.[12]

## CHAPTER 17

# 'The AFL I want to lead'

GILLON MCLACHLAN'S EYES DARTED ACROSS A PACKED MIKE Sheahan Media Centre at league headquarters. It was as though he was looking for someone amid the sea of bright lights and assembled journalists, TV crews and photographers.

He took his seat alone at the front of the room and began reading from a statement to confirm the sackings that stunned and divided the football world.

'The AFL that I want to lead is a professional organisation based on integrity, respect, care for each other, and responsibility,' the AFL chief executive declared. 'We are committed to a process of change, and I am confident that change is being seen and felt across our industry. Last night, I accepted the resignation of general manager of football, Simon Lethlean, and general manager commercial, Richard Simkiss. This has occurred following issues that have fully come to light over the past few days. They were quite separate matters, but have caused distress and concern to a number of people.'

It was Friday, 14 July 2017 and, finally, the cat was out of the bag.

Lethlean and Simkiss, two married executives from McLachlan's inner sanctum, had been fired for 'inappropriate' sexual relationships with younger female AFL office workers.

It had been a taxing week for McLachlan, a friend of both men, as it dawned on him that he had no other option but to sack them.

The AFL boss spoke about values and a changing landscape in football around respect and responsibility; but deep down he was seething. In a private address to his staff, McLachlan threatened to hunt down those who had leaked to the press and helped expose the Lethlean and Simkiss affairs.[1]

There's always a fine line between public commentary and private beliefs.

'He called everyone together and said he was going to find the leak,' a witness said. 'He let us have it and left that meeting with tears in his eyes. Everyone was shocked. We were like, "What the fuck just happened?" We got our arses handed to us on a plate. There would have been 250 people in the room and maybe 249 who had no idea what he was talking about.'

As details of the AFL affairs saga seeped out, many questioned what right, if any, the AFL had to terminate the employment of two men engaging in consensual sexual relationships with adult co-workers.

'People have affairs, that's life,' workplace lawyer Josh Bornstein said.

'We can have our own views about married people having affairs, but they should not be grounds for loss of employment, unless there is harassment or stalking or bullying involved.'[2]

But like many of the scandals that have engulfed the AFL since the Demetriou days, this became a bigger story because of the cover-up.

And while McLachlan had claimed the sackings were the result of information that had only just 'come to light', the reality was far different.

Senior league officials had known about the ticking time bomb in their ranks for months – and worked actively to smother it.

Danny Weidler, a Sydney-based Channel 9 journalist, was the first to be duped by the AFL's cover-up machine. Weidler, a reporter whose usual focus was NRL, had tried and failed for days to get a straight answer out of someone at AFL headquarters. Yarns of the Australian Rules variety didn't usually interest him, but this one did.

It was March 2017 and a rugby contact had told him about a workplace issue at the AFL's Sydney offices in Moore Park across the road from the Sydney Cricket Ground. The story related to AFL football operations manager Simon Lethlean and an alleged affair he was having with AFL NSW worker Maddi Blomberg. Lethlean was married with children and Blomberg was the partner of rugby union star Kurtley Beale. It was a messy situation and Weidler wanted to go directly to Lethlean to put the allegations to him.

On the morning of Friday, 10 March, he phoned AFL media manager Patrick Keane and said he was looking into an issue involving Lethlean.[3]

Keane provided Weidler with contact details for Lethlean and his personal assistant, Vicki Lloyd.

At 12.40 p.m., Weidler texted Keane telling him that his email to Lloyd had bounced back. 'Can you text me the correct email – thanks,' Weidler wrote.

Five minutes later, Weidler sent another email to Lloyd using the correct address. 'Hi ... Can Simon please call me regarding a story I'm preparing ... It relates to a relationship he is having,' he wrote.

At 2.27 p.m. it was Keane – not Lloyd – who responded, telling Weidler by text that his email had been received. 'I can't answer when/what form Simon may come back to you but letting you know it [has] been received,' Keane wrote.

'Thanks mate, I can provide more details if needed,' Weidler replied.

The following morning at 6.53 a.m., Weidler detailed the allegations to Lethlean in an email.

'Hi Simon ... I was hoping you could provide specific answers to these questions: 1. Did you know Maddi was Kurtley Beale's partner when you were having an affair with her? 2. Did you know someone from your workplace had alerted him? 3. Is it correct your last contact with Maddi was in Double Bay in Sydney a few weeks ago? 4. Did you tell Maddi you would not leave your wife for her? 5. Do you think it's appropriate that you remain in a position of power in the AFL women's game?

'I'm happy to discuss all of these points with you and the story this morning. I'm available to talk at 9.45am if you are free. Thanks Danny Weidler.'

Minutes later, Weidler informed Keane.

'Hi mate ... I've sent specific questions through to Simon on ... Just wanted to confirm ... that he has received my email.'

Having heard nothing, Weidler texted Keane again, asking: 'Who is the best person to put some questions to re Simon? I am wanting to know what impact this will have ... given his heavy involvement in the women's game – I'd like to get someone on the record please. Thanks.'

But neither Keane, Lloyd nor Lethlean ever responded.

Weidler ran a small snippet without names in his weekly *Sydney Morning Herald* column and moved on.

The politics of aerial ping pong were not for him.

\*\*\*

Eighteen weeks after Weidler got frozen out, *Herald Sun* journalist Stephen Drill got a call from a whistleblower detailing the same information.

He was told Lethlean had been having an affair with a younger AFL NSW employee, which had prompted concerns among other staff.

Drill hit the phones and copped the same cold treatment.

On 6 June, he sent a list of questions to league media executive Elizabeth Lukin regarding the Lethlean affair, and received no response. On 6 July, he asked further questions but, again, received no response. On 10 July, Drill published a story on page three headlined 'AFL affair ruckus' detailing a relationship between 'a senior Australian Football League manager and a young female employee' that had been 'outed by insiders concerned over head office's treatment of women'.[4]

Drill wrote: 'Details of the controversial relationship have been leaked, amid claims of a cover-up ... AFL insiders concerned about the affair between the manager and employee have leaked text messages revealing her anguish and confusion over the relationship.'

No names were mentioned but it sent tremors through AFL House.

Lethlean's affair was known to some at league headquarters, but so was another sexual relationship involving another married league executive, Richard Simkiss, and a young female lawyer.

The second affair complicated the AFL's internal handling of the story – and then Drill became aware of it. On 13 July, he sent new questions to Lukin about the second affair involving Simkiss, the league's commercial manager, and the game was up.

On 14 July, McLachlan announced that he had accepted the resignations of both Lethlean and Simkiss.

'There's always accountability for every action and I'm not going to talk about all the ins and outs, all I know is there were facts that came to light this week that no one could step around,' McLachlan said. 'I had some visibility over information but not everything, I certainly had bits and pieces. I discharged my responsibilities as chief executive officer to the best of my abilities, referred information I had to HR and I was comfortable where things were.'

But the emergence of Weidler's emails and SMS messages, several months after Lethlean and Simkiss were sacked, proved senior league figures had been aware of at least one of the affairs four months before they acted.

So who knew what at AFL House? And when did they know it? How high up the food chain did Weidler's unanswered questions go? What action was taken with regards to the allegations put to Keane, Lloyd and Lethlean by Weidler? Was the AFL's human resources team notified? Was an investigation of any kind launched? Was McLachlan made aware of the allegations raised by Weidler? And what about the commission? When were they first told?

The AFL, so publicly committed to transparency and good corporate practice, declined to answer any of those questions. It shut up shop and hoped the Weidler revelations, which surfaced amid the hype of the 2017 Melbourne Cup Carnival, would get lost in the wash. Lethlean had been promoted to the position of AFL football operations manager on 2 March – just eight days before Weidler's initial inquiries. There was no appetite to follow it up.

Even when Drill's story broke on 10 July, without either Simkiss or Lethlean being named, league spin doctors went into damage control, briefing journalists and senior footy figures that there was nothing in it. Hardly the actions of an organisation 'committed to a process of change'.

Lethlean and Simkiss paid a heavy price, but it's more than likely that if the league had responded to Weidler when he first came knocking, one or both would have kept their job.

The cover-up cost them both.

McLachlan was close to both executives, particularly Lethlean, a state representative teammate in the Victorian Amateur Football League years earlier, and made it clear that both would be welcomed back into the game when the time was right.

Simkiss landed a new job just six months later, working for his friend Craig Hutchison at Crocmedia. He had opened doors for Hutchison at the AFL and now the favour was being returned.

Crocmedia, which helped the AFL secure a lucrative sponsorship deal with McDonald's, later bought from the AFL the rights to produce the *AFL Record* for all matches (a deal worth $8.1 million) and also controls the industry's lucrative radio rights. The radio rights went out to tender, but the sale of the footy record did not.

Hutchison's cosy arrangements with the AFL were embarrassingly exposed in September 2019 when he was embroiled in a footy finals ticket gouging probe. A sports ticketing business run by Hutchison was caught selling overpriced tickets to finals matches in breach of Victorian government laws.

In October 2017, Carlton, with the support of the AFL, made a mess of a plan to install Lethlean as Blues chief executive officer over the top of Steven Trigg. Carlton's courting of Lethlean was an open secret but not all Blues directors were convinced he was the right man for the job. He was left in the lurch and had to settle for a lesser role running football at St Kilda, bringing the affairs scandal to an end.

*** 

Amid much fanfare in April 2015, McLachlan was appointed a founding member of the Victorian Male Champions of Change, a group convened by equal opportunity and human rights commissioner Kate Jenkins.

He was among nineteen high-profile men recruited from the corporate and political sectors to promote gender equality in the workplace. Among them was former Victorian premier John Cain, a genuine champion of women's rights, who famously forced Melbourne's elite private sporting clubs on public land, including the Melbourne Cricket Club and Victoria Racing Club, to accept women as full members in the 1980s.

'They are committed to ... gender equality, because it's the right thing to do and because it makes business sense,' Jenkins declared at the Victorian Male Champions of Change unveiling.[5]

Yet those who have worked at AFL headquarters during the McLachlan era question the league's commitment to the advancement of women's rights.

'It's an absolute boys' club that he runs and it's not right that they project some kind of image that he cleaned the place up after Andrew left,' one insider said. 'It's no better. The vast majority of women are still treated like shit and are paid way less than their male counterparts.'

I spoke to more than a dozen current and former staff, including ex-executives, who detailed grievances regarding what they described as an 'unsafe' AFL workplace environment – aided and abetted by a 'complicit' human resources department and a hierarchy unwilling to address it.

Many said they were forced to leave AFL House, because they either felt betrayed and unprotected or grew sick of the behaviour. A former female staffer, who said it had been her 'dream' to work at the AFL, recounted an incident in mid-2016 when her enraged sales manager boss marched her into the Colin Carter meeting room on the ground floor of AFL House and shut the door behind them.

'He stood in front of the door holding the handle,' the woman said. 'He wouldn't allow me to leave. He was angry. Ranting. Out of control, possibly alcohol-affected. He yelled and swore and told me I had no right to tell him what he can and can't do. His face was red, veins protruded and he was spitting his words. I was intimidated. My heart was thumping, hands shaking and sweating ... I asked him four times to please let me out of the room. I kept telling him I felt scared and feared him. I can remember it all so vividly. It ruined me. I couldn't breathe.'

After 'about fifteen minutes' the woman said the manager opened the door and allowed her to go.

'I immediately ran back to my desk and a colleague saw me in distress and her first words were, "What's he done now?" She took me to a nearby meeting room trying to console me. She contacted human resources. A report was laid. One of many I was told against him. From there we undertook a series of mediation sessions with the head of HR.'

But rather than supporting her, the woman said the incident was brushed aside and the male superior went unpunished. She received no offer of counselling and became ill with stress and anxiety. The male manager had previously thrown a pen at her head and pursued her into the carpark under AFL House, yelling in anger, she said.

'I felt completely cornered and unsupported,' the woman said. 'I was told he had apologised and what more did I expect. I so much loved and enjoyed my role and colleagues and external contacts, but his constant bullying and taking credit for my work and achievements took a mental and physical toll.

'When I handed in my resignation, I cried and cried. I didn't want to leave and the sole reason I was, was to get away from my boss. I told her [a senior HR manager] I had studied all my life and got two degrees to work in the AFL industry and she just said, "You know, there are a million other jobs out there." At that point she shut her diary and walked off.

'I had only approached her in confidence and hope of some solidarity. To no avail. She didn't even document anything.'

In another shocking episode, a female staffer sexually assaulted by a male manager at a 2017 work function was abandoned by the AFL less than a year later and forced to resign when her request for more flexible work hours was rejected.

The woman said she felt compelled to tell her story in the hope that other workers would be better protected.

'I went there for a few drinks and to have a laugh and a boogie on the dance floor,' she said. 'I was just standing at a circular table – a stand-up lean-on table – talking to a friend who was on the opposite side and he just shoved his hand up my skirt.

'My eyes went wide in panic. I just moved sideways, excused myself and walked off. He had come and stood directly next to me. He went up my skirt to the side of my right leg. Fairly

high. It would have been in line with … you know … You
never forget where a creep touches you. I was terrified. I went
home straight after. It was disturbing.'

Human resources investigated and the attacker resigned
before securing employment with another major sports
organisation.

But within a year of the assault, the man's victim was also
forced out after her request for more flexible work hours to
deal with a family issue was flatly refused. 'That is the fault of
the AFL,' the woman said. 'They don't care about who they
step on. That's why they get everyone to sign a non-disclosure
agreement on the way out.'

Another young woman recalled how a senior AFL manager
had accosted her 'physically' while off his face at a work
function, but did not want to give any more detail for fear of
being identified and punished.

A former executive who has worked across several industries
said the culture was the worst they had experienced.

'There's a lot of smoke because there's fire. It's just male
entitlement. And so I fought it really hard,' they said.

'Great women – really good, talented, capable women –
have left the AFL in droves over the years,' said another senior
staff member.

In 2015, the AFL signed off on a financial settlement with a
senior female employee who colleagues say was the victim of a
systematic campaign of bullying and white-anting by two male
executives. Her ordeal came to a head in an early-afternoon
meeting held in a room on the ground floor of AFL House
overlooking Harbour Esplanade attended by four executives
and two senior managers.

The woman left the building visibly distressed, and never
returned.

Farewelling one of the two male executives in a speech in October 2020, McLachlan jokingly admitted he was the 'angriest guy' he had met, but praised him for enhancing the organisation's culture.[6]

'[Name deleted] was about my first hire. I remember at the time thinking, "I don't know, I think he's really competent, but he's potentially the angriest guy that I've ever met,"' McLachlan said. 'It turned out both were true. At times the angriest guy I've ever met but incredibly competent – huge legacy in terms of outcomes for the AFL.

'Just an impact around the building as well as the outcomes. There's a legacy in all of that. The merit of the story, when I thought about [name deleted] – [is] it marries up the executional tenacity and the ability to get stuff done with his contribution to fun and irreverence and culture, which I think is the core of our building.'

A previous senior leader within the AFL said that the AFL's leadership 'perpetuated the misconduct by condoning it in silence'.

'They are equally culpable when they stand by and watch that kind of behaviour,' the figure said. 'Until the AFL executive and commission acknowledge there is a systemic culture issue and take ownership of it with a genuine resolve to drive change, then nothing changes. The buck stops at the top.

'It's a dereliction of leadership on Gill's part not to have addressed [name deleted] way before now and that is because of his friendship with him.'

In almost every instance, the victims said the human resources department had enabled the behaviour.

One woman said she left the AFL more furious with HR than her attacker. 'HR completely threw me under the bus,' the ex-staffer said. 'I was in pieces after I left. They absolutely destroyed me and made me feel incompetent and like a failure. All I needed was basic understanding and support.

'It was intimidating enough to try to confront the bullying of an executive, only to be hung out to dry by senior HR staff in a meeting they had supposedly set up for me to voice my complaint. The culture is just so toxic.'

A senior male manager who lost his job during the McLachlan era said of the AFL human resources department: 'It's the greatest misnomer of all time, take the human bit out of it.'

A former member of the AFL HR team said: 'I've waited for this day to be honest. I've got a lot to say but whether or not I want to talk about it is a different story. We always joke "Oh, that's chapter 26, that's chapter 15." You'd never have to work again if you published our book. I've got to really think about it because I could blow this shit right up. But I've got really good friends who still work there.'

Another AFL staffer described witnessing an executive handing out cocaine at a 2018 Brownlow Medal after-party at the Albion Rooftop bar in South Melbourne.

'He pulled out a small plastic bag of cocaine from his pocket and passed it to two young women, who took it to the bathrooms,' the staffer recounted. 'The group he had shared it with were in and out of the bathroom all night – all getting higher and higher – it was blatantly obvious.

'One young AFL staff member was affected so badly she had to go home from the ill effects of the drug.'

A second league employee said of the incident: 'I was in the bathroom when they were doing that. I was in and out and thought, "What is going on in here?"'

In late 2016, another AFL manager mistakenly sent a WhatsApp message boasting about the purchase of several bags of cocaine to a dozen of his travel companions on a study trip to New York and Miami. It was the talk of the industry.

A one-time member of McLachlan's senior team said 'the biggest issue that the AFL has is that they don't regenerate executives like normal businesses should, and so you build a culture that is dysfunctional'.

'It's absolutely destructive nepotism,' the ex-staffer said. 'It becomes like a family and people are unable to make objective decisions because there are such deep friendships gained from so many years of being together. They've lost their ability to be able to make the right judgement. They have been together way too long.'

\*\*\*

The AFL said it had made a moral judgement in forcing Simkiss and Lethlean out in 2017 (even though the Weidler messages proved it had not acted for months), but in the months to follow league bosses became aware of another affair between a senior married male employee (whose wife was pregnant) and a younger female staff member. But he did not lose his job, and was later promoted.

Morality, it seems, is a relative concept.

'They only act when it's in the paper,' one AFL figure said.

Another office relationship began around the same time between general manager of finance and broadcasting Travis Auld – a senior member of McLachlan's executive team – and a younger human resources staffer, which raised eyebrows throughout the industry.

Auld's wife and children were living in Queensland (where they had shifted during his stint as chief executive of the Gold

Coast Suns) and while the marriage had been in trouble it was far from over.

In 2018, the woman reported to Auld after he became the human resources department's acting general manager while her previous manager took maternity leave. 'They would flirt in the office. Everybody knew they were an item. She was his direct report,' one whistleblower said.

The office affairs reached farcical proportions when Auld and the woman began investigating the other relationship after numerous complaints from staff.

'They [the other couple] would have been well aware of Travis's relationship at the time, as was the rest of the business, which made the choice for one illicit couple to be investigating another all the more curious,' the whistleblower said. 'But the view was that if another two stories came out of men having affairs with subordinates it would have rocked the industry. So they covered them up.'

On one occasion, a member of Auld's team was directed to negotiate arrangements with his girlfriend. 'She was expected to talk to her about it [her workplace issues]. She said, "You're banging my boss – I'm not talking to you,"' the whistleblower said.

It wasn't until late 2019 that McLachlan finally acknowledged Auld and the woman were in a relationship.

'Gill got up at the Mad Monday drinks and announced that Travis and [the woman] were in a relationship and making it all official even though it had been an open secret in the office for about two years,' they said. 'Staff were cringing at how the whole thing was an attempt at rewriting history. But how come Travis is allowed to declare his relationship years after it started? The answer is because by then [his girlfriend] was back reporting to [someone else].' The woman quietly departed the AFL in April 2021.

\*\*\*

While comparable in many ways, McLachlan lacks the decisiveness of Demetriou. The pair are as ruthless as each other but reach outcomes through different means. McLachlan doesn't indulge in face-to-face confrontation if he can avoid it. A favourite default position when confronted with an uncomfortable topic is to say he has 'no visibility' over the issue.

McLachlan's handling of the booing saga that hounded Sydney champion Adam Goodes out of the game was typical of the decision-making by committee that would come to define his leadership. It wasn't until after Goodes had walked away from football a broken man at the end of 2015 that McLachlan addressed his own failures in the saga.

'By the time Adam retired, he had been subject to a level of crowd booing and behaviour that none of our players should ever face,' McLachlan wrote in a statement buried in the 2015 AFL annual report.[7] 'As a game, we should have acted sooner and I am sorry we acted too slowly.'

The belated apology was in stark contrast to comments he had made months earlier: 'I can't tell the supporters how to behave. Our game has always been an outlet for people to express themselves ... I just have great confidence in their ability to work through this issue, to have their views but then ultimately respect the wishes of the players, the clubs and the industry that Adam be given an environment to come back and play.'[8]

A senior AFL figure said he had 'no doubt' Demetriou would have tackled the Goodes booing episode 'on instinct' and called it out at the time, while McLachlan got caught up seeking the views of 'too many people'.

The deliberate and sustained booing of Goodes at grounds around the country had become evident early in the 2015 season. At an AFL Indigenous Advisory Council meeting midway through the year attended by two commissioners, the group's chair Paul Briggs and league diversity manager Jason Mifsud advised the league to be proactive and publicly condemn the booing.

But it never happened.

Briggs and Mifsud presented an Indigenous strategy document at an AFL Commission meeting later that year and not a single question was asked about the Goodes issue.

When the Goodes saga surfaced again in 2019 with the release of a damning documentary, the AFL again apologised, but bemused club chiefs by insisting the carefully drafted apology statement be attributed not just to head office but all eighteen clubs.

Many had called out the Goodes treatment at the time, while Sydney certainly had nothing to apologise for.

Retired Aboriginal and Torres Strait Islander Social Justice Commissioner Mick Gooda, who led the Royal Commission into the protection and detention of children in the Northern Territory and an AFL contingent invited to address the United Nations Human Rights Council in 2011, said McLachlan should have been removed as AFL boss because of his failings in the Goodes case.

'I had a friend on the AFL Commission who told me at the time that people were blaming Adam for it – that he had brought it on himself,' Gooda said. 'They were saying exactly what the rednecks were saying. Where has Gillon McLachlan been here? What, put a bloody apology in an annual report six months later? That's how important they thought it was. They all just sat back and let it happen.

'They could have done something really profound, but they didn't do anything. They were like rabbits in the headlights. They didn't know how to deal with it. They never called everyone together to say, "Well what do we do here?" That's what they were thinking at the time – that he brought it on himself. [And] Mike Fitzpatrick was a bloody Rhodes Scholar, that tells you something.'[9]

Indigenous players account for about 11 per cent of the AFL's 850 players but are grossly under-represented in coaching and administration.

On the eve of Indigenous Round in 2015, AFL staffer Chris Johnson, a triple premiership player at the Brisbane Lions, lost his job as an Indigenous talent manager as a result of AFL cost-cutting measures. Johnson was earning less than $100,000 in a role aimed at helping Indigenous youngsters from across the country fulfil their AFL dreams and learn to cope with the demands of professional sport. It was an appalling decision that flew in the face of the AFL's commitment to reconciliation.

'On any measure it was a pitiful decision to let him go and would not have happened on Demetriou's watch,' one of Johnson's colleagues said.

In November 2018 it was revealed repeated emails and phone calls to AFL staff regarding ongoing funding for AFL Indigenous Broadcasting, which beams games into Australia's most remote communities via the National Indigenous Radio Service, had gone unanswered.[10] The league had been encouraging the service to enter into a partnership with Craig Hutchison's company, Crocmedia, controller of the AFL radio rights.

While the AFL trumpets its commitment to Indigenous Australians, Aboriginal leaders were shocked to discover in mid-2020 that the league had been operating without a Reconciliation Action Plan (RAP) – an organisation's formal commitment to be more inclusive of Aboriginal and Torres Strait Islander people. It was revealed the league's inaugural RAP had expired four years earlier and had not been updated.

'I'm gobsmacked,' Aboriginal broadcaster and 2019 Football Woman of the Year Shelley Ware said of the revelation.[11] 'I just can't believe it. My mind can't grasp it. I have one at my [kids'] school. How is this even possible?'

\*\*\*

McLachlan's desire to obtain industry approval for his administration's decisions drove the formation of an AFL 'competition committee' in 2018.

Made up of hand-picked club presidents, chief executives, football managers, coaches and players, the committee was designed to implement changes around the competition's rules and structure for endorsement by the commission.

One of its early recommendations was for the introduction of an 18-metre goal square, twice the length of the traditional square, which was widely derided and rejected.

As long-time Western Bulldogs president Peter Gordon pointed out about the competition committee, there is 'no basis for it in the rules'.

'I was sitting around the AFL table in 1993 when the modern iteration of the AFL Commission was set up – and there was no provision for an industry governance committee in those discussions or in the AFL Articles of Association,' Gordon said. 'If it had been suggested back then that the CEO and footy manager could hand-pick those presidents and industry people with whom they wanted to consult on every issue, and the rest of the clubs ... "well, we'll see you every now and then" ... it would have got short shrift.

'It's been an executive fiat by the AFL CEO and his general manager of football operations.'[12]

Foundation commissioner Dick Seddon questioned McLachlan's 'true passion' for the Australian Rules game. 'The jury is still out on Gillon, although he is continuing on with the Demetriou policies he inherited, a number of which I believe should be scrapped or at best altered,' Seddon said. 'He has shown no sign of doing that. Maybe one could question whether he has a true passion for AFL football and a true appreciation of the various stakeholders.'[13]

But Gordon, who served two terms at the Dogs, rates McLachlan on an 'overall assessment' as 'the best CEO of the AFL/VFL in the thirty years since I first became a president'.

'Whenever his time comes, and whatever great achievements he can look at, the one that stands out is that he has been the one true champion of creating a national competition for women,' Gordon said.

Another industry figure said McLachlan would 'take a stand when he needs to but doesn't do it from a place of conviction'.

'He has a divide and conquer style of leadership and is happy to create tension and friction among his executives and then play the peacemaker,' the figure said. 'But he also has a pathological desire to be liked and to be popular, whereas Andrew didn't care less what people thought of him.'

The AFL's commitment to respect and responsibility was tested again in April 2018 when Fremantle coach Ross Lyon was embroiled in a sexual harassment storm.

It emerged a young Dockers office worker had received a secret six-figure payout from the club over an incident at a Fremantle Christmas party at a Perth bar several years earlier. Lyon was accused of making indecent and suggestive comments to the woman, who quit her job soon after. She was about two months pregnant at the time, with Lyon accused of telling her in front of witnesses that he liked her 'budding boobs'.[14]

An AFL integrity department investigation found no sanctions were required, despite the payment of 'hush money'.

Friends close to the victim said she had been warned not to talk and been left 'completely humiliated' by the AFL's handling of the probe.

Even more shamefully, journalists working on the story were briefed by club or league sources about how the woman had 'usually worn casual clothes around the club but on the night had dressed up'.[15] Like it mattered what she was wearing.

'If you did an investigation and found nothing, you would have to be dumb, blind and deaf,' a source close to the victim said. 'It was a pretend investigation. They want to protect themselves and the club.'

When asked about the concept of 'hush money', McLachlan would only say: 'The core part of the [respect and responsibility] policy is actually resolving the issue. It is part of the policy for it to be confidential, and there is a wide series of options available for getting resolution.'[16]

But the ethics of confidentiality clauses in sexual harassment cases is a matter of great controversy and they are banned in some parts of the world.

Barely a few months passed before the AFL's handling of another integrity 'investigation' was publicly ridiculed.

The probe centred on a toxic pre-season camp held by the Adelaide Crows in Queensland in January 2018 where players were subjected to extreme mental, physical and cultural abuse.

The 'cult-like' bonding session had been designed to push a grand final team one step further, but instead backfired spectacularly, fracturing the playing group and pitting many against club management. Claims of what had transpired included players being blindfolded, tied to trees, driven around in blackened buses and subjected to deeply personal taunts.

Yet in late 2018, the AFL announced it had cleared the Crows of wrongdoing and concluded that there had been 'no breach of industry rules'. Why?

Top South Australian commercial lawyer Greg Griffin said the answer was buried away in an amendment made to the Adelaide Crows' constitution four years earlier, which gave the AFL effective control of the board, making it the club's ultimate authority.

'It makes a nonsense of the suggestion that the AFL can conduct an independent inquiry into the operations of the club,' Griffin said. 'The AFL is inherently unlikely to come out and publish a report that concludes that the club's conduct has exposed it and hence the AFL to a legal liability. It was never going to happen. The process was completely deficient in terms of corporate governance.'[17]

Two years later, after journalists reported fresh details of the Crows camp already known to the AFL, South Australia's SafeWork authority announced it had launched its own investigation.

When interviewed by the AFL Commission in 2014 for the top job won by McLachlan, Geelong chief executive Brian Cook delivered some home truths to the game's governing body, which did not endear him to some in the room. On reflection, they are a stark reminder of what could have been.

'I would have done it differently to Andrew and Gill,' Cook later said. 'I would have been really strong on getting all the major stakeholders to agree to a common purpose and common values. And identify what is our competitive advantage over other sports and really work on it. I think if the AFL had done that over the past twenty years in a really meaningful way, they wouldn't simply be a very good organisation, which they are, they would be a great organisation.'[18]

\*\*\*

The power afforded to the AFL's top dogs opens many doors, a fringe benefit exposed spectacularly in August 2018 when McLachlan found himself at the centre of a scandal all of his own making.

Documents leaked by a whistleblower from within the Department of Immigration in Canberra revealed how then home affairs minister Peter Dutton had intervened to save a French au pair from deportation after McLachlan had alerted him to the issue.[19]

The French woman had been detained at Adelaide airport in October 2015 and had her tourist visa cancelled amid suspicions she was intending to stay and work in Australia. The au pair had worked for relatives of McLachlan's in South Australia, who went to the league chief seeking his assistance.

In a blatant misuse of AFL resources, McLachlan then contacted his head of government relations, Jude Donnelly, who made inquiries of Dutton's office about the detained au pair. The woman's deportation was swiftly overturned in exchange for a three-month tourist visa.

A Senate investigation into the au pair scandal revealed McLachlan had previously asked Donnelly to contact prime minister Tony Abbott's office in 2014 to check on the visa status of an Argentinian polo player.

McLachlan was left embarrassed by the revelations but faced no censure from the AFL Commission.

Top lawyer Leon Zwier – the same man who represented 'Gubby' Allan in the Lachie Whitfield scandal and the Demons in the ASADA probe – was engaged to help McLachlan navigate his way through the crisis.

Zwier's 'Mr Fix-It' skills prevailed again.

When asked if he had received special treatment because of his lofty position, McLachlan said: 'No. That's a question for someone else, but I don't think so … I get asked to help people all the time. I was asked to facilitate a contact and that's what I did.'[20]

End of story. Move along.

***

One of McLachlan's biggest wins in the hot seat of Australia's favourite sport came in April 2018 when the Victorian government agreed to spend $225 million of taxpayer funds to upgrade the AFL-owned Docklands Stadium.

It was a monster deal that would bolster the bank accounts of the stadium's five tenant clubs and in turn guarantee the MCG hosting rights for the AFL Grand Final until 2057.

McLachlan was front and centre at Treasurer Tim Pallas's post-budget briefing lunch at the Park Hyatt hotel in East Melbourne where the deal was being detailed when the shrill of a race call interrupted proceedings.

As business leaders rubbernecked in search of the offender, it was a red-faced McLachlan seen scrambling for the mute button on his phone after checking out the early action at Warrnambool.

The Docklands deal was a magnificent arrangement for Victorian clubs but angered interstate teams who were not consulted on the decision to lock in the MCG as home of the premiership decider for another thirty years.

'The AFL can hold itself up as a genuinely national competition as much as it wants to but sooner or later it will expose itself as what it is and always has been – the Victorian Football League in disguise,' *West Australian* journalist Mark Duffield wrote at the time.[21]

The AFL under McLachlan's stewardship maintained its place as the most dominant sporting code in Australia, even through the COVID-19 crisis.

The creation of the AFL Women's national competition in 2017, while long overdue, added a new dimension, but hit troubled waters two years later when a breakaway group of players engaged workers' rights law firm Maurice Blackburn citing deep dissatisfaction at the players' union's handling of the pay and conditions negotiation with the AFL.

McLachlan (or his successor) will soon be tested on the issue of pay equity.

The league's costly experiment with AFLX – a hybrid fast-food version of the game – was a flop; the extent of concussions being suffered by players is a growing concern; and the future of Tasmanian football and funding for Australian Rules at the grassroots level require urgent attention.

'The AFL has a significant income and I am concerned that the great bulk of that money is being spent on the AFL competition and the AFL bureaucracy and that the grassroots aren't being given enough,' ex-AFL commissioner Terry O'Connor said.[22]

The former Eagles president said it was farcical that clubs had been given their own academies to compete with academies in the developing states after 'kicking up a fuss because the Sydney academy had unearthed one very good player in Isaac Heeney,' O'Connor said. 'What people forget is that in New South Wales and Queensland, AFL is the third or fourth most popular winter sport. Thus for young athletes thinking of playing a football code, our game is not front of mind. In the southern states the opposite is the case. For young men in these states, AFL is the first choice.

'The academies in New South Wales and Queensland were designed to search out and attract to our game young athletes who could learn about, play and enjoy our game. It was really designed to bolster the local competitions; the view being that if we were to obtain a reasonable flow of draftees for the senior competition we needed strong and vibrant local competitions.'

\*\*\*

The AFL trumpets itself as a community leader but remains one of the biggest beneficiaries of the contentious gambling industry.

After handing over to McLachlan in 2014, Demetriou joined the board of directors of James Packer's Crown Resorts, whose subsidiary, CrownBet (later rebranded BetEasy), won an $8-million-a-year contract as the AFL's official wagering partner.

At the company's annual general meeting in October 2019, Demetriou declared that 'the values of the AFL are not too distant from the values of Crown'. He said: 'I think our commitment to the community reminds me a lot of what the AFL does.'[23] The league quietly extended its arrangement with BetEasy in early 2020.

'Whilst the AFL have had great success promoting the game, the greatest failing was their immorality in doing sponsorship deals with corporate bookmakers such as BetEasy,' long-time gambling reform crusader Tim Costello said. 'It was deeply disappointing that Andrew Demetriou joined the Crown Resorts board shortly after leaving the AFL, as well as the BetEasy board. When I asked him about his re-standing as a director at the Crown AGM in 2019 and cited the social damage of Crown, he defended the Crown business as being essentially the same as the AFL – an entertainment business.

'This shocked me. Crown's business model depends on gambling. The business model of football did not require gambling and certainly doesn't require BetEasy ads that normalise and mainstream betting and football for our kids. We have a generation of children who now think of AFL in odds.'[24]

Demetriou's stint as a Crown Resorts independent director came spectacularly unstuck in October 2020 after his performance in the witness box during an inquiry into the company's fitness to hold a gaming New South Wales casino licence.

'There are no formal requirements to become director of a top 100 ASX-listed company,' journalist Sarah Danckert wrote after his two-day grilling. 'But there's an expectation that directors have a deep understanding of corporate governance, or at least know the definition of an independent director. Demetriou's evidence raises many questions about his grip on both.'[25]

The former league boss was also grilled over his legal issues surrounding another Melbourne-based company, Acquire Learning, a vocational group which collapsed in 2017 owing creditors almost $145 million.

Demetriou had earned $900,000 a year in an advisory role to the company, but liquidators, who sued his family trust in a bid to claw back payments made to him while he was involved in the business, questioned in the Supreme Court whether he was in fact a 'shadow director'. No determination was ever made.

Acquire was fined $4.5 million by the Australian Competition and Consumer Commission after a Federal Court judge ruled it had taken advantage of vulnerable students and 'rorted' a government scheme.

'Its activities resembled those of an unscrupulous fly by night operation rather than those of a prominent and market leading provider of student recruitment services, as it describes itself,' Justice Bernard Murphy said.[26]

When former Supreme Court judge Patricia Bergin handed down her scathing 750-page report into Crown Resorts culture and governance failings in February 2021, she dedicated nineteen pages to Demetriou and his 'quite bizarre' and 'unedifying performance' in the witness box. Bergin concluded that a regulatory body 'would be justified in lacking confidence in placing reliance upon Mr Demetriou in the future'.[27]

While she focused on his use of written notes in giving evidence (and his repeated denials of having done so) Bergin was also critical of his lack of knowledge about gambling junkets, his lack of money laundering training, his 'shock' at the arrest of Crown employees in China (in part 'because he did not know that the company had employees in China' – despite being a member of Crown's risk management committee) and his 'rather fawning' commitment in an email to James Packer to serving the best interests of Crown 'and most importantly, you'. Bergin also said Demetriou had 'embarked on a most unimpressive mission' in trying to play down the extent of the money laundering issues at Crown.

Within hours of the report's tabling, Philip Crawford, the chairman of the New South Wales Independent Liquor and Gaming Authority, led calls for the former AFL boss (and others) to resign if the company wanted to hold a casino licence at Barangaroo in the future, but for several days he refused to go.

Under a headline in *The Australian* saying, 'We won't go', business writer Damon Kitney stated: 'It is understood Mr Demetriou believes he has done nothing wrong and is being unfairly condemned for taking notes with him when he appeared before the ILGA inquiry.'

But eventually Demetriou bowed to the inevitable and resigned.

In a column in the *Australian Financial Review*, Myriam Robin reminded Demetriou how years earlier at the height of the Essendon drugs saga he had declared of club figures who felt hard done by in the joint AFL–ASADA investigation: 'Organisations ... are always bigger than the individual. You should always put the interests of the whole first and foremost'.[28]

'It is evidently a sentiment he holds for others more than himself,' Robin said. 'He undermined any such high-minded sentiments by leaving, not with good grace, but with a promise to "defend my reputation at every opportunity" against the "unfair and unjust" report. Presumably that means Demetriou will keep the issues raised in said report alive and in the public eye whenever given the opportunity. So much for the organisational good.'

Costello and federal senator Nick Xenophon met with McLachlan in December 2015 to discuss the AFL's heavy reliance on the gambling dollar.

'He was happy that AFL clubs were getting out of pokies, but he was unmoved about our request for the AFL to get out of gambling,' Costello recalled of the meeting. 'He loves his punting and owned race horses with ex-Channel 7 CEO Tim Worner, but I wondered whether his obstinacy was more to do with his AFL performance bonus being linked to sports betting sponsorship.'

The AFL's love affair with corporate bookies is contradictory to its public stance on poker machines. After becoming AFL chairman in 2017, Richard Goyder declared that he 'hated' pokies and that the 'custodians of the game' needed to tackle the reliance of the competition's clubs on the industry.

The majority of Melbourne teams have since cut ties with the pokies sector, while profits from sports betting continue to pour in to headquarters.

'They have no principles,' billionaire Carlton powerbroker and poker machine king Bruce Mathieson said of the AFL. 'If it lines their own pockets, it's a different thing, but then they come and play God elsewhere. It's like saying you can drink whisky, but you can't drink gin or brandy. If you believe in a cause and you live by the rules, then fair enough, but if you don't, then you're just a hypocrite.

'The league right across the board is just a complete, bloody boys' club,' Mathieson said. 'And they run it to suit themselves, it's as simple as that. Everyone feeds off it. No one upsets anyone because they won't get an invitation to this function or that function. "You scratch my back, I'll scratch your back." Everyone wants to be a part of the club.

'You tell me how many people the league employs and the cost of running that league compared to a private business? It's just a joke – and if you don't go along with them, you are blackballed.'[29]

\*\*\*

McLachlan was destined to take charge of the AFL empire since the day Wayne Jackson plucked him from the strategy division of consulting firm Andersen Consulting in 2000. An opportunity arose to run the rival NRL in 2012 but he was always the commission's chosen one to succeed Demetriou.

The introduction of AFLW, the Docklands Stadium funding deal and navigation of the COVID-19-plagued 2020 season will be his likely legacy. There is more light and shade with McLachlan than his predecessor. He's harder to define.

A ruthless deal-maker on the one hand but someone who compulsively wants to be liked on the other.

# CHAPTER 18

# The reckoning

PETER GORDON'S MOBILE PHONE PINGED AT 6.14 A.M. ON Friday, 13 March 2020.

It was a text message from AFL chief executive Gillon McLachlan, up and about before the break of dawn canvassing views on Australia's escalating COVID-19 outbreak.

Speculation had swirled that the Melbourne Formula One Grand Prix at Albert Park was about to be abandoned and with the footy season scheduled to kick off at the MCG just six days later, McLachlan sensed trouble.

He asked Gordon, president of the Western Bulldogs and a man in whose judgement he trusted, for his 'instincts' on what to do about the AFL season start.

'I would suspend crowds for the first month and reserve the decision to extend that depending on the trajectory of virus incidence. Happy to discuss. All the best,' Gordon fired back.[1]

A couple of hours later, after the pair had held a lengthy discussion on the phone, Gordon sent the AFL chief another SMS. 'Seems to me the public health priority is to flatten the growth curve. In that context, wonder if we shouldn't also be concerned about crowds of several thousand at the weekend's AFLW games, and remaining weeks,' the Dogs boss wrote.

The enormity of the global coronavirus crisis had crept up slowly on McLachlan.

Just two weeks earlier, in an interview with a Melbourne football journalist in his office at AFL House, he had expressed confidence in the AFL's ability to withstand its economic impact.

Even the AFL's chief medical officer, Dr Peter Harcourt, appeared oblivious to the gathering storm. On 11 March, Harcourt was still insisting on taking a planned ten-day trip to Europe.

'You shouldn't ask questions like that. I can't get over being asked,' Harcourt said angrily when quizzed by a journalist about his travel plans.[2]

The league was even holding out on whether to cancel a match between St Kilda and Port Adelaide scheduled for 31 May at Jiangwan Stadium in Shanghai, China.

But Gordon knew plenty about the ravages of respiratory illness. His antenna on the seriousness of the COVID-19 virus had been up for weeks.

In 1985, as a 27-year-old rising star litigator out of Braybrook in Melbourne's inner-west, Gordon secured Australia's first successful asbestos cancer damages verdict. He would lead another two thousand successful asbestos claims and also the world's first trial against a blood bank for Australians suffering medically acquired HIV – like COVID-19, another invisible viral enemy.

By 2 p.m. on 13 March, McLachlan and the league commission had adopted Gordon's view and taken the unprecedented step of banning fans from attending the first few rounds of AFL matches across the country.

Footy's coronavirus catastrophe had begun.

Three days later, without consultation with the powerful players' union, McLachlan announced that the season would be cut from twenty-two rounds to seventeen as a contingency in the event that multiple weeks were lost.

But even then, as the days ticked down to the 19 March season opener between arch rivals Richmond and Carlton at the MCG, Gordon had become increasingly uneasy about the prospect of AFL games being played at all.

On the eve of the match, he found himself on a telephone hook-up with McLachlan and Collingwood counterpart Eddie McGuire.

'Gill was canvassing views and I told him mine. My feeling was that we should cancel and not play round one,' Gordon said.[3] 'You have to remember, at that point, no one knew whether Melbourne and Sydney were going to be like the reports from Italy with people dying in corridors in hospitals because all the beds were taken.

'[But] Ed's feeling was that we should play on and I felt Gill was really torn about it. He was obviously also talking to the commission and a whole lot of people. I thought I made a pretty convincing case that would hold the day but then Ed launched into this incredible five-minute speech. He said that for Australians in times of trouble there's always been footy. He told stories about the Great Depression and about World War I.

'You could tell he was getting emotional as he was saying it. So was I. He was saying people are looking to us at this time; to football; and we have to give them something to hold onto.

'I remember thinking to myself, "I wish someone had recorded this", because honestly, it was one of the best speeches I have ever heard ... and it was to an audience of two.'

McGuire has always had the ear of the AFL's top dogs.

Weeks earlier, at his weekend rental perched on the cliffs of Portsea on Victoria's Mornington Peninsula, McGuire and McLachlan had cooked up a plan to play a fundraising State of Origin clash to help raise money for bushfire relief.

McLachlan's in-laws owned the holiday home next door and the Magpies president took delight in explaining how the concept had been thrashed out after the AFL supremo casually wandered into his backyard with a chicken sandwich hanging from his mouth in the early days of January 2020.

But while McGuire's 'speech' to Gordon and McLachlan won the day and the AFL pushed ahead with the opening round, the plan wouldn't survive the week.

On Sunday, 22 March, at half-time during the Hawthorn–Brisbane match in Melbourne, a weary McLachlan fronted an emergency press conference in Melbourne and announced that the season would be suspended indefinitely because of the growing COVID-19 crisis.

'To say that this is the most serious threat to our game in one hundred years is an understatement. It is unprecedented in its impact,' McLachlan said. 'As a community and as a code we all need to take the unprecedented and required actions to get through this together.'

For all its brawn, the league's cash reserves and a $60 million future fund could not sustain the competition without the staging of matches. About 80 per cent of all industry staff were stood down without pay indefinitely and the game's 850 players were sent home, saddled with weights and makeshift gym equipment and told to keep fit in the hope that the season could be reignited once the first wave of the virus passed. Onlookers expressed surprise at the speed with which the nation's biggest sporting juggernaut had crumbled.

But if anything, McLachlan thrives in crisis management.

One of his opening moves was to form a coronavirus 'war cabinet' to help steer the competition's survival plan. He selected Gordon and McGuire as well as Sydney Swans chairman Andrew Pridham and Hawthorn president Jeff Kennett to sit on the AFL rescue team.

As one club boss put it, it made more sense to have some of the game's biggest personalities throwing rocks from inside rather than the outside.

'It's been odd for me because when Jeff was first premier of Victoria in 1992 ... I was one of the hundred thousand people marching up Bourke Street shouting abuse at Parliament House and demonstrating over the cuts he was making all over Victoria,' Gordon said of the committee's eclectic mix. 'If you'd told me then that twenty-eight years later, I'd be in a cabinet with him, supervising decisions about multi-million-dollar cuts, and job losses ... me with my background, I'd have told you you were insane.

'We've had our differences, Jeff and I, but I have learnt to listen to and respect his views.'

Unsurprisingly, it was McGuire who made the most noise in the early days of McLachlan's 'war cabinet'. On 18 March, the Collingwood boss revealed that the league had wasted no time in reaching out to the Victorian and federal governments for help.

McGuire, whose brother Frank is the Labor member for the Melbourne seat of Broadmeadows, revealed on his weekly *Footy Classified* TV analysis show that discussions between AFL heavyweights and Premier Daniel Andrews were already well advanced on obtaining a 'massive line of credit' to save the game from a financial wipeout.

'I spoke with the Premier of Victoria Daniel Andrews who is well aware of the economic impact on Victoria if clubs were to fold or to have to sack so many people,' McGuire said. 'The football industry feeds a lot of people in this town and right around the country. He is talking with Gill McLachlan at the moment as well as [AFL executive] Ray Gunston and Richard Goyder, the chairman of the AFL Commission, about how they can help football survive.

'There won't be a handout because the state of Victoria has to look after itself. The state government will not be giving out a handout, but there are other machinations that can come into play where there might be a line of credit to help save the AFL and get through.'[4]

Victorian Opposition leader Michael O'Brien didn't like the smell of it.

'Daniel Andrews should not be giving preferential treatment to the AFL for a financial bailout,' O'Brien said.

A substantial line of credit was eventually secured from two banks without government support, but the league's cosy relationship with governments had again been paraded for all to see.

\*\*\*

The first flashpoint of footy's COVID-19 shutdown came in a dispute over player pay.

The average player salary had hit $395,000 in 2019, but with revenues drying up overnight, the AFL declared it simply couldn't continue to pay its players' wages in full.

Tense negotiations over a wages cut between McLachlan and AFL Players' Association (AFLPA) chief Paul Marsh dragged on for days. The players volunteered pay cuts of 50 per cent until the season restart, but the league wanted savage reductions of about 80 per cent.

Anger spilled over when veteran player agent Peter Jess dared suggest that the pay cut being forced on players should be matched by McLachlan's executive team. All twelve AFL executives were retained at AFL House after the industry-wide stand-downs on pay cuts of just 20 per cent which saw their own average wages drop from $880,000 to $704,000.

Bemused staff in Kylie Rogers' commercial department rolled their eyes when she emerged from a meeting after being informed of her wage cut and muttered audibly 'there goes the reno'.

But Jess said if it was good enough for the players to take an 80 per cent cut, it was good enough for the AFL administration and all senior club staff.

'If it's one in, it's all in. That's the Australian way – when you don't dud your mates,' Jess said. 'It's not the fault of the players that this has happened. The whole risk burden should be shared across the whole football portfolio. There is absolutely no reason that the executive should be a group by themselves.'[5]

The league reacted angrily, claiming McLachlan had agreed to match the player pay cuts, although details of the pledge weren't publicly disclosed.

A compromise was reached on 27 March, which saw player wages cut by 70 per cent, returning to 50 per cent once the 2020 season resumed.

'Never let a good crisis go to waste,' Sir Winston Churchill once said and it was Jeff Kennett, the former Victorian premier and long-time critic of the AFL's governance system, who first sensed an opening for reform. Although a member of the AFL's 'war cabinet', the Hawthorn boss immediately understood the opportunity the COVID-19 crisis had presented.

In a letter to the other seventeen club presidents in early April 2020, Kennett rallied support to force the AFL to open up its books and commit to fuller financial disclosure to the clubs. The letter was duly leaked in an attempt to embarrass Kennett, but the first shot had been fired in the push for change.

The AFLPA was next to go.

In an email to all 850 players in June, AFLPA boss Paul Marsh revealed he would be seeking full access to the league's financial records before agreeing to talks over proposed player pay cuts in 2021 and beyond.

With a wages deal locked in until the end of 2022, the AFLPA had the upper hand at the negotiating table for the first time in its history.

'We need complete transparency from the AFL ahead of the review and any consideration for change to the collective bargaining agreement can only be done once we understand the actual impact of COVID-19 on the industry,' Marsh said.[6]

It would take months to prise out the information, but by September 2020, the AFL had surrendered pages of previously undisclosed financial data to the clubs and the AFLPA.

The once impenetrable AFL empire was vulnerable and under attack.

\*\*\*

The 2020 competition had been put on ice for eighty-two days as the first wave of the coronavirus crisis swept Australia before the season was restarted on Thursday, 11 June.

But as preparations for the resumption commenced, doors that had once swung open for the AFL started slamming in their face. Strict border restrictions imposed in South Australia and Western Australia curtailed the league's ambitions.

The two Perth clubs, West Coast and Fremantle, were forced to relocate to 'hubs' in south-east Queensland, while

South Australian authorities flatly rejected an AFL request to give Adelaide and Port Adelaide players special quarantine exemptions to fly in and out of the state for matches.

In mid-May, three weeks before the proposed season restart, a South Australian COVID-19 committee fired off a damning letter to McLachlan. 'On public health advice, the committee has resolved that any economic and social benefits to be gained by allowing modification or exemptions to SA quarantine requirements for AFL players and staff were not outweighed by the public health risk,' the committee said.[7]

Another storm erupted in April when the AFLPA briefed its members on the prospect of players being quarantined for up to twenty weeks in interstate hubs in a desperate bid to keep the season going.

McGuire savaged the AFLPA for fear mongering. 'This is the adults table this time. We are not talking about football, we are in the middle of a pandemic,' McGuire said. 'I mean that is so extreme. That is Armageddon. There has been massive stress in families over this and it's not even on the table.'[8]

But as rival states started pulling down the shutters when the second wave of the COVID crisis gripped Victoria in late June and early July, that is exactly what transpired.

On 1 July, dozens of players and club officials living in coronavirus hot spots in Melbourne's northern suburbs were given less than twelve hours to move out of their homes to ensure they were permitted to play matches interstate.

Days later, in a desperate bid to keep the season alive and the money rolling in, all ten Victorian clubs were evacuated from the state and housed in special COVID-19 bubble 'hubs' in New South Wales, Queensland and Western Australia at a cost of about $3 million a week.

The alternative price to pay was unfathomable.

Some players, understandably, initially baulked at the prospect of spending weeks and even months on the road, away from their families as the coronavirus raged.

'One of the parts I struggle with is, who says my job is more important than her job?' Adelaide Crows star Rory Sloane wondered of leaving his wife Belinda and six-month-old son, Sonny, behind.

'He's got five hundred thousand reasons why his job is more important than her job,' McGuire declared on national TV in another foot-in-mouth moment.

The AFL's authority in the nation's corridors of power had been diminished in an instant. And the league, so used to getting its way with governments and local authorities, was faced with a daily scramble just to ensure matches were played.

In late July, after the AFL and North Melbourne went on a media drive all but declaring that matches were set to return to Hobart and Launceston, the Tasmanian government shot it out of the sky.

'We will not do anything that we believe will put the health of Tasmanians at risk and so, to be frank, in terms of the AFL, that is the least of my considerations,' Premier Peter Gutwein said.

The Launceston *Examiner* put it best. 'So it turns out the AFL isn't the highest authority within Tasmania after all. Who knew? Certainly nobody in AFL House,' the newspaper declared.[9] 'Apparently there's some self-important body going around calling itself "the Tasmanian Government" that seems to think it has some sort of power of veto over important decisions ...

'It may be tantamount to treason in this footy-mad country, but, for the time being at least, the Tasmanian Premier appears to be making policy decisions based on the health of Tasmanians rather than the finances of AFL clubs.'

*The Examiner* had called out one of the AFL's tried and tested media strategies.

'First they come up with a manifesto that ignores any established criteria; then, they allow a local media to break the story to guarantee maximum publicity; next, they announce it formally complete with the proviso that it requires local authority approval; and finally they sit back and wait for the local authority to provide said approval,' the newspaper said.

'For legal reasons it would be unwise to use the word blackmail, but it would be difficult to think of a clearer example of trying to force Tasmania's hand.'

Ultimately, it was the Queensland Labor government – months out from a state election – that would come to the AFL's rescue, agreeing to stage the majority of the season's matches, including the grand final, at Brisbane's Gabba ground in exchange for an undisclosed financial windfall.

Anger erupted in early September when more than four hundred AFL officials, families and stakeholders jetted into the Gold Coast, spending fourteen days quarantining at a five-star resort, while the Queensland border remained closed to patients in northern New South Wales seeking medical treatments.

McGuire, among those granted special access into the Sunshine State, slammed the criticism as the 'politics of envy', but within days of his release from the quarantine resort, the Collingwood boss was photographed at the Pink Flamingo nightclub on the Gold Coast. He claimed straight-faced that it was a reconnaissance mission for how the Victorian hospitality industry might operate under loosened COVID-19 restrictions.

'I do a few different things in my life, including being on the board of Visit Victoria, and ... speak extensively to people in the restaurant and hospitality industry about how we get

Victoria going again,' McGuire explained after the photograph leaked. '[That is] part of what I was looking at the other night and how it all works.'[10]

The politics of envy or the politics of entitlement?

\*\*\*

Modern AFL administrators spent little time worrying about the nation's rival winter football code, the NRL. Smaller TV rights and sponsorships, inferior player wages and a steady flow of behavioural scandals engulfing rugby league stars gave AFL chiefs good cause to believe in their superiority.

But the appointment of New South Wales horse racing administrator Peter V'landys to the head of the Australian Rugby League Commission in September 2019 was a game changer.

An enterprising, straight-shooting, can-do leader, V'landys was a competitor of the likes the AFL had never encountered.

As the AFL set in train an ultra-cautious return-to-play strategy in step with the thinking of Victorian Premier Daniel Andrews, V'landys and the NRL went public with an ambitious plan to relaunch the rugby league season on 28 May 2020.

It caught the AFL off guard and prompted several of McLachlan's 'war cabinet' members to publicly ridicule V'landys and accuse him of social irresponsibility.

'I haven't seen anything that's impressed me with the NRL at the moment,' McGuire sneered in early May.

'Down here, he's irrelevant,' Kennett said of V'landys. 'He could walk down the street in Melbourne and no one would recognise him.'

But as the 28 May NRL return date drew closer, it was clear that rugby league had outplayed its biggest rival.

'I'm used to that sort of rhetoric from Victoria, it's nothing new for me,' a vindicated V'landys said. 'We set ourselves a challenge and a target date. Everyone has got behind it in the rugby league world and if we achieve it, it's an achievement by the game itself.'

Achieve it they did, posting record TV ratings in a two-week window free of AFL matches, prompting Richmond coach Damien Hardwick to declare that he wished the AFL had followed V'landys' 'aspirational-type leadership' in setting a return date.

At the TV rights negotiating table, too, V'landys played a more pragmatic game than the AFL Commission's high-powered broadcasting subcommittee made up of chairman Richard Goyder, former News Corp boss Kim Williams, Paul Bassat, Robin Bishop and McLachlan.

Goyder, in stark contrast to V'landys, was rarely seen or heard throughout the COVID-19 crisis, leaving the day-to-day talking and heavy-lifting to McLachlan and his executive team. Living in Perth and chairing Qantas and Woodside Petroleum put a lot on Goyder's plate – and in the eyes of some club bosses, too much.

V'landys immediately understood the new realities of the media landscape, ravaged by a fall in advertising dollars, and renegotiated his code's TV rights accordingly, announcing an extended deal with Foxtel running until the end of 2027 just hours before the 28 May kick-off.

But McLachlan dug in his heels. The AFL's trademark conservatism – and supreme confidence that it would remain the nation's No. 1 sport – had not been lost. The league had been severely wounded, but its DNA remained the same.

McLachlan would wait until the end of the year before extending the AFL's pay-TV deal.

\*\*\*

The league's untapped riches had dried up overnight.

In the early days of the crisis, McGuire expressed fears of a potential 'run on the clubs' by supporters seeking refunds on their 2020 memberships, but it did not transpire.

Of the competition's 739,000 paid-up members with game entry rights, less than five per cent demanded all their money back because of the COVID-19 shutdown.

Still, accusations of a 'rort' were raised in June after it was revealed fans were being induced to claim tax deductions on their membership payments. The scheme involving the Australian Sports Foundation was devised to discourage supporters from cashing out subscriptions worth more than $250 million across the competition.

Melbourne University taxation specialist professor Ann O'Connell called it out for what it was. Ordinary Australians struggling in the COVID-19 crisis, she said, should not have been propping up the hugely profitable AFL competition.

'It is clear that it was never intended that any membership payments to AFL clubs would be tax deductible,' Professor O'Connell said. 'Given that so many in our community are financially distressed, is it really a good time for the AFL to be asking taxpayers to foot the bill?'[11]

Trouble for the AFL was also coming from within.

Angered over their treatment during the lengthy stand-down period, disgruntled AFL staff turned to the unions in a bid to save their jobs. The United Services Union (USU) in New South Wales and the Victorian branch of the Australian Services Union started signing up staff who had been told they would be required to reapply for their positions.

'The AFL claims a commitment to social justice and equality, but they are failing to uphold those values with their treatment of the loyal staff who work tirelessly behind the scenes,' USU general secretary Graeme Kelly said in August.

Leaked internal documents detailed the league's plan to slash hundreds of jobs and streamline its bureaucracy to create what it declared would be a 'leaner, faster, stronger and more focused' head office.

'We will have a leaner structure with less roles,' the document said. 'Many roles will be impacted based on changes to what programs, products and services we continue, do differently or stop. While we will keep some specialist roles there will be more generalist roles, with multiple responsibilities.'[12]

Staff agonising about their futures were surprised when McLachlan popped up on their computer screens and outlined the jobs-cutting process via video link. He was in the front seat of his Toyota four-wheel drive because he'd had to seek higher ground for better reception because of internet problems at his farm near Birregurra in country Victoria.

The dispute turned ugly when Sydney-based umpiring manager Pierce Field contacted hundreds of stood-down colleagues by email offering union support. Field was given a directive to cease using AFL group emails, prompting the USU to threaten action at the Fair Work Commission.

Despite the mass stand-downs, the league point-blank refused to disclose – even to the clubs – how many staff it had on its books. It wasn't until a leaked organisational chart surfaced that it was revealed the AFL workforce had climbed to a staggering 795 – almost one worker for every player – by the time the COVID-19 crisis hit.

About two hundred rank-and-file AFL staff were ultimately made redundant, while club football departments were also

decimated after the league enforced a $6.2 million soft cap
for 2021 (down from $9.7 million), resulting in the axing
of hundreds more workers, including assistant coaches and
medical staff.

The clubland cuts of about 35 per cent (enforced at the
height of the crisis) were followed months later – after the
storm had passed – by a far friendlier deal between the AFL
and the AFL Players' Association, which effectively saw player
wages fall by just 3.5 per cent in 2021.

In August, the league made noises to suggest that its own
executive team was also going to be significantly reduced, but it
didn't exactly transpire. Longstanding executive Darren Birch
did take a redundancy package and Ray Gunston shifted to an
advisory role, however the inner sanctum emerged relatively
unscathed.

COVID-19 had wiped two-decades of smugness off the
AFL administration's face.

The harsh new economic reality meant the commercial
riches and government handouts that had fuelled an empire
would be harder to come by.

And in stripping back to survive, they realised, too, that
they could operate just as effectively with far less excess and
far less staff. It was a recognition that the business model
could not be sustained.

'What it all showed was that the AFL had pissed all those
mountains of money up against the wall in the good times,'
one key stakeholder said, 'and they'll never see that money
again – but they have actually acknowledged that they can
function quite well on a different level.

'It's been a disgrace really. You hear all these people saying,
"Well done, Gill." But the bottom line is – why did it all go on
for so long?'

The AFL machine had been put on its heels, but its behaviours had not changed, as demonstrated by the arrival of a 400-strong caravan of officials and stakeholders in Queensland shacked up in a five-star hotel. In their own minds, they were still the Masters of the Universe, even if that universe had been diminished.

Only a push for reform from within the football industry would stop them from a gradual recovery and a return to more of the same.

The first major sign of an appetite for change came when Hawthorn president Jeff Kennett abandoned plans to retire at the end of the 2020 season, partly to help navigate his Hawks to safety, but also with an eye towards ushering in reform of the AFL administration.

Then, at a meeting between the eighteen club presidents and McLachlan and Goyder in mid-October, Sydney Swans chairman Andrew Pridham boldly spoke up and suggested the league needed to consider a structural review of the entire competition, including the commission system put in place after the 1993 Crawford report.

It was the result of months of backroom discussions.

'This should be seen as an opportunity, not a threat,' Pridham explained. 'We have a crisis. Let's see how we can best reset to thrive.'[13]

Multiple clubs indicated support, but Collingwood was not among them. McGuire, a long-time linchpin of football's boys' club system (who had always walked both sides of the street between club and league), was non-committal.

He was facing his own problems amid calls for a clean-out of Collingwood's board and was forced to resign the presidency in February 2021 after the leaking of a damning report into racism at the club. However, the Magpies did join a group of the game's richest clubs, including West Coast, Richmond, Hawthorn and Essendon in talks aimed at convincing the AFL to guarantee annual distributions, post-COVID-19, for all clubs equivalent to the full salary cap – and not just to the competition's cash-strapped teams.

The castle walls of AFL House were being breached, but would it gather momentum or just peter out?

\*\*\*

Kennett wasn't joking when he said McLachlan and his executive team deserved medals for their efforts in finding a way to keep the 2020 season rolling and the money coming in.

McLachlan, the league told journalists, had worked eighteen-hour days for seventy straight days at the height of the crisis – all in strict isolation.

'I think his leadership has been outstanding,' Brisbane Lions chief executive Greg Swann said of McLachlan after the season restart. 'He's covered off everything. He's across the medical protocols, the return to play, he met with coaches, CEOs, footy managers, presidents, broadcasters, all state governments, health ministers, medical officers, whoever needed to be spoken to ... he ran the show.

'His legacy is the survival of the game, without trying to make it too dramatic.'[14]

Revenues across the AFL competition would fall by about $500 million because of the pandemic, but in October McLachlan announced that 'we're going to come out [with] aggregate industry losses that'll be under $100 million'. The net result was made prettier by savage cost cuts, job losses and wages savings made in lieu of monstrous government-funded JobKeeper payments to stood-down club and league staff, and players.

Veteran commissioner Bill Kelty said the AFL's deliverance of the 2020 season was 'one of the greatest sports management feats of the century'.

'First of all, you've got to keep the players clear of COVID-19 – that was just an incredible achievement,' Kelty said. 'Secondly, you've got the position of reorganisation. The players had to give up being with their families and friends. The clubs have had to be incredibly flexible and the AFL did a truly remarkable job. It was superb.'[15]

On the eve of the grand final, McGuire suggested, 'Gill McLachlan should almost get an Order of Australia for his services to the community.'

But, in the end, it was the 850 AFL players, the clubs and their families (who sacrificed so much) who saved the game.

By agreeing to spend months living out of COVID-19 hubs across the country, sometimes playing two games in a week, the players helped the league to complete a condensed seventeen-round home-and-away season and a four-week finals campaign, culminating with Richmond's win over Geelong at the Gabba in the first night grand final on Saturday, 24 October.

Games played without crowds during the bleak winter months were a stark reminder, too, that it was the fan in the stand that mattered most, not the suits who had ruled with an iron fist for so long.

The coronavirus crisis, as devastating as it was, might ultimately help change Australian Rules football for the better – but only if reform results in greater transparency and accountability, better governance and less cronyism, and a more equitable distribution of the wealth of the game.

# CHAPTER 19

# What to do

AUSTRALIAN RULES FOOTBALL IS A PHENOMENON OF THE Lucky Country.

Invented as a winter pursuit to keep off-season cricketers fit, it became the people's game soon after the first recognised match between Melbourne Grammar School and Scotch College played at Richmond Paddock, a stone's throw from the current site of the MCG, in 1858.

Clubs sprung up across the colony and crowds flocked to watch, so instead of following the rest of the world into rugby union, rugby league or soccer, Australia's southern states embraced their own, home-made, football code.

It became a way of life.

The story of two-time Brownlow Medal winner Ivor Warne-Smith, who served in World War I and was a champion player of the Melbourne Football Club in the late 1920s and early 1930s, encapsulates the game's link to the Australian character.

'Warne-Smith's Saturdays began before sunrise, shovelling coal at Spencer Street station,' his Sports Australia Hall of

Fame citation almost a century later said. 'After a five-hour shift, he would then head to Young and Jackson's hotel for a few quiet beers with work mates before strolling over to the MCG with his playing kit.'[1]

Warne-Smith went on to serve in World War II 'after appealing against a disbarment because of his age. Although in his forties, he saw active service as an infantryman in the Middle East and the Pacific. Upon return from the war, he became chairman of selectors at Melbourne in 1949, going on to work closely with champion coach Norm Smith.'

'Captain Blood' Jack Dyer, Ron Barassi, Teddy Whitten, Bob Skilton and 'Polly' Farmer would capture the imagination of generations of football fans.

But then the professional age hit, and Australian Rules hit crisis.

Insolvent clubs, Supreme Court challenges and the race for the creation of a national competition wreaked havoc in the late 1970s and early 1980s. A revamped central administration was required, and it was the VFL that got its act together first.

The early VFL commissioners made mistakes, but their intentions were mostly right. Friction between the clubs, who had ceded control, and their new masters was inevitable, but not impassable.

But with the riches that flowed into head office from the commercial boom of the early 2000s came power. Memberships, ratings and revenues told a story of a sport in rude health, but below the surface formed an organisation too willing to bend the rules and distort the truth for its own self-interests. A culture of arrogance crept in.

The AFL became a dictatorship under the leadership of Andrew Demetriou and chairmanship of Mike Fitzpatrick.

Gillon McLachlan was a child of the system, emerging as an equally ruthless, but less openly confrontational, leader in his own right.

Integrity was compromised, threats and intimidation became commonplace and the industry just learnt to accept it.

'The real problem is, they are never accountable,' one long-time club boss declared. 'There are never any checks and balances. We know the conflict of interest that took place with Ron Evans and Spotless going back three decades. We know about all the conflicts of interest and deals that have happened ever since. It's just a bottomless pit. There is layer upon layer of it – but they will reconcile it all by saying, "Well, that's just life. That takes place everywhere."

'And if you take your club hat off and say, "What were their strategic objectives?", how they went about it wasn't necessarily right, but they certainly achieved it for the greater good of the competition.

'I'm not as critical of Andrew Demetriou as others,' the former club boss continued. 'He was a bully and could be incredibly derogatory and was very much a control freak, but if you were prepared to work and accept that that's the way it was, it was very beneficial to clubs that were attempting to improve their performance.

'When we accepted that, "Okay, you're the boss – you're the masters and it's your domain, but we need to be rewarded for being subservient to you," then we were well and truly compensated for that subservient behaviour.

'Is that right? Probably not, but they would say they were doing it for the good of the cause.'

Former AFL executive Colin McLeod, who worked under Demetriou from 2004 to 2009, said Ron Evans had a mantra he would often remind league staff: 'We hold the game in trust on behalf of the community. We've inherited it, and our job is to pass it on in better shape.'[2]

But is that what happened under the leadership of the modern AFL?

Long-time club president and former Victorian premier Jeff Kennett doesn't think so.

'Other people might view me differently, but my whole mode of operation is about good governance; there is no substitute for good governance, whether that's, as we've now found out, in the churches, in the financial institutions or in aged care; it is a must,' Kennett said. 'And good governance not only means in the sense of how you operate, it also means, wherever you can, transparency.

'And the thing that always sits in the back of my mind, which the commission has obviously forgotten, is that they were set up to administer the code by the clubs, and therefore the clubs are the shareholders – but the shareholders are now treated as supernumeraries, and the shareholders are themselves divided, which the AFL can play off, by threatening where they allocate funds and resources.

'It always annoyed me that we didn't have twelve or sixteen or eighteen club presidents who would be united, on any particular issue. And I can't believe that some of the clubs report a profit – and yet they only do that because they get larger financial benefits from the AFL than others.'

Kennett argued: 'The model as was set up by the presidents when we moved from the VFL to the AFL has actually served the code very well; we are the leading sporting code in Australia by a million miles, so collectively the game has done a very good job, but a lot of that has been because of the efforts of the clubs, because they are the ones ultimately responsible for membership and supporters.

'The AFL Commission was always set up to be the guiding hand to administer the game and along the way, as in any organisation, you find some people are more flamboyant than others, some are less interested in governance and some are more set on enforcing their own views.

'So I don't think that the model is wrong – it's a question of whether the model can be more effective. Whether the model can be better.'[3]

The formation of the VFL Commission in 1984 and the subsequent Crawford report in 1993, leading to a reinforced commission system, were fundamental in the evolution of the game's administration. Kennett, and others, believe the time is right for another independent review.

'I mean if ever there was a time for someone independent to get in there and do an honest, proper review, it is now,' he said. 'And it should be publicly released so they're not just giving it to a mate. It has been for so long a boys' club.'

Kennett said the quality of the commission had weakened over the years.

'In days gone by the commission was made up of individuals who had greater interests and community standing and authority,' Kennett said. 'People like Kelty, Samuel and even Colin Carter ... they were very focused on what they were doing, but that said, as can often happen in organisations, the relationship between, in this case the chairman and the CEO is very important, and it was that combination that ran the AFL while Mike and Andrew were in charge.

'From my observation, that was something they almost did in tandem – they themselves controlled things.'

Respected Swans chairman Richard Colless called for a review of the AFL's governance system soon after retiring his post in 2015.

'I'm an AFL junkie, I'm passionate about the game and I just feel gutted about what I see,' Colless said. 'If the AFL was a public company, I don't think it would pass most tests. People are depressed, angry, disappointed but everyone is too gentlemanly to speak up.

'I think there needs to be a review of the AFL system as a whole. I don't think the AFL Commission, by and large, know what industry they're in. They actually run a football competition ... which involves an enormous amount of personal exertion and unpaid work.

'The AFL are besotted with brands and corporate speak.

'I think a lot of clubs and a lot of individuals are starting to get sick of the threats that have been made to them.'

In an interview conducted for the writing of this book, Colless said: 'I think after thirty-plus years it's timely for the AFL to review the concept of the independent commission and everything that flows from that.

'I don't mean because they're hopeless, I just think any business that gets so large and progressively loses accountability – and bad practices emerge and flourish – should do that.

'Do it branch and root. No restrictive terms of reference. No artificially short timeframe and see what emerges [because] where the commission is today is not what the founding fathers had in mind.'

Too much power, he said, was transferred from the commission to the executive after Fitzpatrick took over as chairman from Evans. 'Fitzpatrick was seen as a chairman from central casting – a Rhodes Scholar, a champion footballer, captain of a premiership team and he'd made a fortune – but I think he got caught out,' Colless said. 'Andrew played him off a break. His power grew profoundly and I think it took a lot of years for Fitzpatrick to realise what was going on – and by the time he did, the horse had bolted.

'I've got no desire to embark on an assassination of Fitzpatrick's character, but my overarching observation developed over a fair time with him at the helm is his singular lack of empathy.'

Robust debate was eliminated, Colless said, by the AFL's powers of intimidation.

'It's actually pretty difficult to mount a campaign, and the reality is the clubs have learnt that sometimes it's better to just keep your mouth shut,' he said. 'Why be a dead hero?'[4]

Western Australian Terry O'Connor, QC – a member of the AFL Commission from 1993 until 2001 – was the first and only commissioner to be voted off by the clubs. He was taken down in a power play led by Blues boss John Elliott and Melbourne president Joseph Gutnick amid suspicions he did not believe Victoria could sustain ten clubs.

'It wasn't the best, but as I said at the time, if the worst thing that happened in my life was a bunch of Melbourne clubs voting me off the commission, then God has been kind to me,' O'Connor said. 'It [the removal of Victorian clubs] was the opposite of my position.

'When I was on the commission I was appointed to chair a taskforce charged with developing a plan for the development of football in New South Wales. In that position I progressively came to the conclusion that developing markets about which I was passionate to the detriment of the heartland made no sense whatsoever – a conclusion reinforced by the problems created by the outcry in Sydney over the unsuccessful efforts to remove South Sydney from the NRL competition.'[5]

O'Connor monitored the governance of the AFL with great

interest and told me before his death in April 2020 it was time for the clubs to unite and demand a major review.

'I don't want to be critical about everything because in a lot of ways they have been very good – and that needs to be said – but I am concerned about some of the things they have done,' O'Connor said. 'The widespread perception that the AFL Commission is arrogant is not a good thing. It might be alleviated if the commission agreed to disclose financial accounts which people could understand rather than opaque accounts that don't provide any real information about where the money goes.

'Further, it is now more than twenty-five years since the Crawford report into the AFL Commission, which was initiated by the clubs. In my view, it is time for the clubs to demand another review given the AFL organisation is a much different beast than it was in 1992.'

As far back as 2001, O'Connor said he was concerned the commission had begun endorsing policy recommendations from the executive without adequate analysis. 'At times I felt the commission did not sufficiently discuss recommendations of the executive,' O'Connor said. 'The board sets the policy and the executive report on the implementation of that policy. That's the basic way it should work ... otherwise there's no point of the board. It's just window dressing.'

Few are better placed to reflect on the performance of the AFL administration than foundation VFL commissioner Graeme Samuel. He said he believed Demetriou and McLachlan had 'proved to be outstanding CEOs'.

'The AFL has been extremely fortunate to have them and that reflects itself in the professionalism of the operations of the organisation,' Samuel said. 'The AFL is unquestionably the most successful sporting competition and sporting business in this country.'[6]

But the former Australian Competition and Consumer Commission chairman questioned whether Fitzpatrick had been sufficiently 'engaged' as chairman during the Demetriou years.

'I doubt that some of those things about which questions have been raised would have occurred under the chairmanship of Richard Goyder,' Samuel said. 'Richard is a highly experienced, mature, sensible individual who really does know what is right and what is wrong. And that is not to be too disparaging of Mike, they are just different individuals.

'The CEO should be taking and receiving guidance that reflects maturity of judgement from the board and from the chair, and that may have been lacking. There was, perhaps, insufficient engagement by Fitzpatrick and thus the mature oversight and advice that Demetriou would have benefited from maybe wasn't as available as much as would have been ideal.'

Samuel said Australia's banking royal commission demonstrated the importance of governance in the corporate world.

'Whether it's a corporation or a business or a not-for-profit or a sporting organisation, so much comes down to leadership,' Samuel added. 'The tone starts at the top and it depends on your chairman and the CEO.'

On the league's handling of the Essendon drugs investigation, Samuel said: 'I thought it got out of control. To lose David Evans, to let the whole thing proceed the way it did.'

The secret intervention of Fitzpatrick and Melbourne financier John Wylie in the saga, he said, failed the 'extra rule' of governance. 'There are always rules about how you operate ... but there's an extra rule you should abide by; you will not do anything, any second of the day, that you'll be embarrassed to read about in the *Herald Sun*,' he said. 'It's the morning newspaper rule. The "should we" test, rather than "can we".'

Samuel's fellow foundation commissioner, Dick Seddon, is more critical of the game's administrative transformation.

Seddon said the 'pendulum has swung too far against the clubs. The power of the AFL Commission has become too great and should be wound back. And I think the commission and the AFL could do a lot better.

'Richard Goyder is a very successful businessman and very pleasant to meet at AFL social occasions, but I do not know anything about his football credentials. Andrew [Demetriou] was probably the best of all the executive commissioners, although I do not agree with some of his philosophies and the directions in which he has taken the AFL.

Seddon continued: 'I think the game has been ruined as a spectacle and I wish the AFL would stop fiddling with the rules – and I do not believe the AFL should be socially engineering society on trendy left-wing issues. They should stick to running a football competition.'[7]

A third foundation commissioner, businessman Peter Scanlon, praised the Demetriou–McLachlan partnership. 'I think a lot of what happened under Andrew was because of the combination,' Scanlon said. 'And if I can name it as that, I think they have done a fantastic job. It doesn't mean they haven't made mistakes but transparency has been good, I think, and they have been really diligent and made sure they've done their homework before making decisions.

'They have invested in markets [and] that takes courage because it's not easy to convince clubs to give up a few bob to invest elsewhere. You might argue was that too much? Not enough? And did it get spent the right way? But the courage to actually invest in those markets has been wonderful.

'And they have done a seriously good job in understanding and negotiating with media, because you can't negotiate with media anymore unless you really understand what is happening. You've got to understand how the media can make money out of the game, whether it's social media or apps or whatever it is.

'Their [commercial] contracts haven't looked that stale towards the end of them, which I think is quite impressive,' he said.

'I think Gillon is a rare talent. I'm a bit of a fan of his. He's very impressive and hopefully he is building up a Gill for Gill, because he needs someone. It's a fairly demanding job.'

As for Mike Fitzpatrick, Scanlon said: 'I thought he did a good job. An interesting cat. It's important in any organisation that the two people at the top both don't be the public spokesperson all the time. Mike allowed the space for Andrew to operate in and Andrew was pretty good in the public space.'[8]

Long-time commissioner Bill Kelty told me that if McLachlan or Demetriou hadn't chosen careers in football administration 'either of them could have been a premier'.

'They are just unbelievable,' he said. 'AFL football has more active members than any other organisation in Australia, including the unions, the churches and the political parties. The clubs are the most significant organisations in the country.

'The game itself is just fantastic. It's wonderful but it required people to say, "We're not going to try to change the game fundamentally, but I tell you what, we are going to make it really, really, really commercial – and impregnable."'

Fitzpatrick worked briefly for former premier John Cain's government as a senior adviser to the State Treasury Department in 1984.

'He was very good, Mike, but he became a zealot when he went to the AFL,' Cain told me before his passing in December 2019. 'I think they colonise everybody at the AFL to their way of thinking, like an imperial power handling the colonies in the seventeenth and eighteenth centuries.

'They convert and indoctrinate people to their will, and their will was to maximise income. They've got a huge bureaucracy in their own right, they pay themselves immense salaries; it's extraordinary, and what they did to the present government over the money to develop or tart up Docklands Stadium; to get $225 million [of taxpayer funds], despite the advice of a whole range of people, I just couldn't believe that.

'They have a remarkable skill at invading everybody around them, and getting them to bend to their will. And the money they throw around is quite extraordinary as we've seen with the Gold Coast Suns and the Giants.'

On the league's handling of scandals and integrity investigations, Cain said: 'When these incidents emerge they don't handle them very well. They display a culture in the administration for tolerance and settlement at any price. And the Essendon thing still hasn't been blotted from the discussion; it's still there, affecting them all these years on.'

Cain said he caught a glimpse of the AFL's immense power during negotiations with the MCG Trust.

'They were unforgiving. You couldn't cooperate,' he recalled. 'The best twelve games of the season became the basis of one of the revised agreements, and it seemed to me that they were always determined to try and diminish the role of the MCG and the MCC in the administration of their game.

'Mike Fitzpatrick used to argue, quite fiercely, that they deserved a bigger say because they brought the dominant content, which is true, it was a strong bargaining position ... but the people own the MCG, that's the key to it all; it's public land.'

The former premier said the 'capture of the game by the gambling industry was the best evidence of their clinging to money-making ventures'.

'And the gambling industry itself is being increasingly discredited,' he said.[9]

Legendary North Melbourne administrator Ron Joseph said the abuse of power by those in charge of the modern AFL disgusted him. 'Somewhere along the line the executive has become the be all and end all, and you really have to wonder about some of the decisions they have made,' Joseph said. 'They have been given too much authority and the clubs have been too weak to pull them back into line because the AFL virtually funds most of them. There's only a couple that jump up and down, otherwise they just say nothing.

'For as long as you've got an executive that is responsible to no one, which has been the case certainly since the Demetriou days, football is going to look back at a time when it got a lot of things wrong, which is now, and it's going to regret it down the track.

'Somebody has got to be brave enough to stand up and be counted. The first thing you have to break is that nexus because right now football is run by the divide and conquer law and the AFL do what they bloody well like.

'It makes me sad and angry and I'm at a stage of my life where I shouldn't get sad and angry about football.'[10]

David Galbally, QC, was there as a Collingwood board member when the game turned to a commission system in the 1980s and has witnessed first-hand the workings of its justice system.

'It was very clear that it was never the initial intention of the clubs to hand over all the power in running the competition – that they would maintain a say – but what has happened is that the commission has become its own body, and it regulates outside the specific interests of the clubs,' he said.

Galbally said the root cause of the AFL's behaviours was not difficult to identify. 'They just picked arrogant shits that decided they lived in a world of their own and believed they were more powerful than anyone else,' he said. 'It's arrogance and ego and power. If you want to do anything in Victoria, if you want to get to anybody in Victoria, the way to do it is through an AFL club.

'If you know a president, you know someone at the AFL, that's the way you can get to politicians, get to whatever you like. They all think it's the greatest thing since sliced bread.

'It's the power of Australian Rules football. And more particularly in Victoria than anywhere else.

'There were times on the journey through that I was disappointed and alarmed by the system.'[11]

Grant Thomas was a teammate of Demetriou and one of his harshest critics when coach of St Kilda. He's been portrayed as an anti-AFL man, but said he speaks out because he loves the game – not the 'mates' club' who have hijacked it.

'The whole thing just got morphed,' Thomas said. 'The clubs, and by virtue of that the members, used to own the game, but then the whole power base shifted.

'The model is probably the appropriate model ... but with the wrong people and the wrong values, you end up with a train wreck.

'What is the culture of the AFL? What are their values? Rules on the run, a mates' club, compromised partnerships and jobs for the boys become commonplace. There's a common joke around town about the huge lump under the carpet at AFL House because so much stuff gets swept under it.'

Thomas said the AFL had made an art form of empowering 'puppets and yes men' in senior positions at AFL headquarters and clubland. 'The AFL have been outstanding at making sure they've got the boys' club in order,' Thomas said. 'The amount of compromises they make in relation to commercial arrangements is just extraordinary. And we're still not out of the woods in regard to the threat from soccer and basketball. It's decision-making to perpetuate their position.'[12]

Jeff Browne was the league's legal adviser for almost two decades. He helped broker major AFL deals and wrote most of the game's rules and regulations. Browne is proud of the competition he helped build but recognised some worrying signs in the post-Evans era.

The AFL, he said, should have nothing to fear from another Crawford-style review. 'I could see this academic idealism creeping into the footy business,' Browne said. 'Even though I wasn't a football player, I was a football person, and we just needed to remind people about that ... to make sure we stayed popular.

'I do worry about it because I spent such an amount of my time involved in it. I worry that the management of the game is becoming too removed from the clubs. I don't think the clubs have much influence now, but clubs are very well run. They have good directors who are successful in other areas of their lives.'

Club bosses and commission members should meet on a quarterly basis, Browne said, to have 'open debates about all the issues. I think the commission would get a lot of interesting and very high quality feedback from the clubs. Reviews have always been helpful. There are clubs who feel that they are not being properly consulted and a good way to deal with that would be to have a review in relation to the clubs and the AFL and the power sharing and the information flow. That can only be a good thing and I don't see why anyone would oppose that.

'If the Crawford report was the last one, there is definitely time for one right now,' Browne said. 'If there is any angst that is building up in the clubs, then let them have their say.

'A review causes people to take a fresh look at what is going on and it gives everybody a chance to have their say. Out of the review they might talk about the structure of the commission and what sort of skills that group needs. And what sort of communication plan they need to adopt with the players' association and with the clubs, and how they should manage their capital. Should it be put into development teams or stadia and infrastructure or should more distributions be put into the clubs who need more money to survive?'[13]

Despite his club's experience in the Talia brothers saga, long-time Western Bulldogs president Peter Gordon is a defender of the overall performance of the AFL administration.

'No system or administration is ever perfect,' Gordon said. 'In my main career of the law, I've seen Australia's court system deliver howlers which, if they occurred in the goldfish bowl of AFL, would have had people marching in the streets with pitchforks. And yet, despite that, Australia's court system is one of the better court systems in the world. I think it is important to keep that in mind.

'I don't think the Talia investigation was the current AFL administration's finest hour, obviously,' Gordon said. 'But I was also a participant; so acknowledge that I'm not a disinterested commentator.

'This AFL administration [McLachlan's] is better than any other I've dealt with. In my first seven years as Bulldogs' president (1989–96), I saw my fair share of AFL chicanery.

'I think it's important to make the point that none of the issues, in either era in which I have been an AFL club president, which trouble me from a compliance or ethics point of view, go to a question of corruption for personal enrichment or advancement.

'There's been nothing like the sort of flat-out corruption for personal enrichment we've seen for example from FIFA officials during the same thirty-year period nor indeed, any of the sort of snouts-in-the-trough self-serving with which parts of the Olympic movement [Australia's included] have rewarded themselves during that time.

'Instead, I think the common thread of the issues which have troubled the AFL have been where AFL management over-reaches to micro-manage a result because it believes it can be trusted more than an independent process,' he explained. 'Either an external court or investigation or one of its own tribunals … to achieve the outcome which is in the best interests of the competition and its future.

'For example, over the years since I first became a club president in 1989, people have got the sense from time to time that certain tribunal outcomes on the eve of very big finals may have had the guiding hand of the AFL managing "the best outcome for the growth of the game". That's also my explanation for what miscarried in the AFL's Talia investigation.'

Of the contentious Essendon drugs saga, Gordon said: 'I don't believe there is any sustainable claim of serious ethical breach by the AFL Commission or senior management in the whole Essendon catastrophe … but whether there was or there wasn't ... I suspect we can at least agree that the AFL's actions reflected its view of the outcome it believed reflected the best outcome for the game ... including that Essendon's want of proper management and oversight be sanctioned, that the result at least reflect the lack of "guilty mind" on the part of the players, that a reckless approach to performance-enhancing drugs be condemned and that the process be dealt with as efficiently and as reasonably as possible.

'It seems to me that the AFL can at least be satisfied that, like democracy itself, it is the least worst of the major sporting competitions in Australia and around the world, for integrity.'

On the merits of an industry review, Gordon said club bosses need to be careful what they wish for.

'There are a number of things that are unsatisfactory and ought to be reviewed [about the AFL system], but I'm not going to empower a latter day version of David Crawford to come along and say, "I've looked at this industry. I'm an economic guru. We've got to shed the less profitable units. They're obsolete. Adios to [say] the Bulldogs and the Demons",' Gordon said. 'I'm not going to fall for that sort of three-card trick again.'

The terms of reference – guaranteeing the survival of clubs – would be critical before he supported it, he said.

Several other administrators interviewed for this book expressed concern about the 'emasculation' of the role of club presidents. Gordon shares this concern.

He has also spoken publicly about club boards effectively having to 'these days compete for the right to govern their clubs and their CEOs with AFL management. I think there are many in the senior echelons of the AFL who now see club boards and their presidents as merely tangential or incidental to the running of the modern game. But club boards are elected and the fact that they can be thrown out by rank-and-file members means they are the last vestige of control of the game by the people. So if they continue to be diminished and marginalised, in time you'll have eighteen AFL subsidiaries instead of clubs, and they will all look and act just the same, and something about the uniqueness and spirit of the game will die.'[14]

Colless had similar concerns: 'There is an enormous ceremonial component to running an AFL club which generally falls to the president and I think that has been progressively disregarded by the AFL.

'I am not asserting that the AFL Commission is incompetent or ineffectual; what I am asserting is that on balance they don't understand well enough how clubs operate and I think on occasions they forget that the strength of the AFL system is very much driven from the bottom up.'

But long-time AFL league commissioner Bill Kelty said the game's rude scoreboard of health told the only story that matters. 'Life is not about romance. Life is about the truth and the facts,' Kelty said. 'How many people attend the games? What are the players getting paid? How much is being generated in terms of revenues? How many people watch the games? What is the quality of the game? How many people are playing the game? Have any clubs disappeared?

'Every objective test says that our strategy is right and has worked. It has nothing to do with me, or Andrew or Ron or anyone. It's got to do with people – they are the facts – and when you look at the facts, the philosophy has worked.'

On Demetriou's methods of intimidation, Kelty said: 'We wanted somebody tougher and sometimes tough people are a bit tough. You can't complain. We got him in to do his job, and what job did he do? He got the biggest TV increase ever when he got Kerry Packer in. He changed the game for once and for all: the most significant set of commercial decisions in the history of the game – done by Andrew. Measure what has happened since – billions of dollars. It was the catalyst commercial deal.

'Then he goes to the MCC and says no, fuck you, you're not giving us enough money. We want better terms for our tenants. It's not good enough. Then he goes to the governments and says – start paying for these stadiums.

'All the things that lifted the AFL from a semi-professional body to a professional, commercial, arm's-length negotiator – are all associated with essentially two people – Andrew Demetriou and Gillon McLachlan. As a pair, they were terrific.

'Andrew is very, very tough. And that's what he got the job for. So all right, he's a bit tough on the media and offends some of the media and the journalists and they get really upset with him because he's a bit rude to some of you sometimes.'[15]

Kelty is right though, the scoreboard doesn't lie. The AFL is indisputably the nation's biggest and richest sport. But Kennett said those at the wheel would do well to remind themselves of the game's primary purpose.

'For so many people, after their family and place of employment, AFL football gives them the opportunity to vent their spleen in support or opposition,' he said. 'It allows them to speak to their CEO at the water cooler when they could never speak to them about anything else. It is, for so many people, the pressure cooker valve.

'I so remember going to a football match at [Princes Park in] Carlton when Hawthorn was playing Melbourne and I took [treasurer] Alan Stockdale along when we were in government,' Kennett recalled. 'Alan is a very docile sort of man, a very good man, but once the game started this little man blew up into a gorilla; he was yelling and screaming like a mad man, and then the moment the siren sounded at the end, he just shrank back into his own size.

'And that, for many people, is exactly what it's about. The wonderment of football, for which everyone who has ever been a part of it can take some credit, is that we can still go to games; one hundred thousand people, we can walk there safely, we can barrack, and win or lose, you walk away and people are just jovial.

'If you could somehow bottle that – and that spirit was the spirit of Australia – there would be no holding this country back at anything,' Kennett surmised.

'Football is generous, fun-loving and respectful ... and so why I am critical, as you always will be from time to time of certain individuals about the way certain things are done, is that the code is so terribly important for the mental well-being of so many people.'

***

Can the AFL be better?

The answer is clearly yes.

There are many avenues to reform.

### 1. *Independent review*

Much has changed since businessman David Crawford handed down his report into the AFL's administrative structure in March 1993. As Crawford himself wrote: 'Organisations should be dynamic and responsive to changes – hopefully to initiate but if not, to then be capable of responding to changed circumstances.'[16]

Too many respected football people and industry stakeholders have raised concerns about the AFL's governance systems in the years since. A warts-and-all review, not by management consultants or ethics advisers, but by independent people who know how the AFL system works, should be demanded by the clubs.

The terms of reference for the review should have strong input from the clubs, and the clubs should determine who conducts it – and its findings should be provided directly to the clubs as well as the commission.

## 2. *Executive accountability*
Making the powerful AFL executive more accountable to the commission it is supposed to report to should be the starting point for change.

Hands-on commissioners of the past like Graeme Samuel, Peter Scanlon, Dick Seddon, Terry O'Connor, Bill Kelty and Colin Carter were at the coal-face of important decision-making. They had oversight over what their executive was doing and why they were doing it.

But when Mike Fitzpatrick joined the AFL Commission in 2003, becoming its chair in 2007, he made clear he wanted to get out of the way and let the executives run the show.

Samuel is among those who question that approach, while O'Connor has said he identified signs of an overly dominant executive around 2001 when Ron Evans was still in the chair.

Fitzpatrick's replacement, Richard Goyder, lived in Perth and chaired two other prominent publicly listed companies, Qantas and Woodside Petroleum, while the majority of his fellow commissioners had little or no football experience – and almost all of them resided outside Victoria.

Some might say that is by design.

The commission must reclaim its authority.

### 3. *Commissioner selection*

As Richard Colless puts it: 'The grand bargain between the twelve VFL clubs and the newly created independent commission in late 1984 was that the clubs would lose their traditional day-to-day influence but at the end of each year have the opportunity, akin to shareholders in a public company, to vote for or against commissioners offering themselves for re-election.

'The thesis of the handover was that ultimately the commission would be accountable to the clubs in the way a public company is to its shareholders, but today the clubs are seen more as subsidiaries or satellites of the AFL, and it's a simple matter of fact that the AFL is accountable to nobody.'[17]

The solution would be to again give the clubs a genuine say in the make-up of the commission, potentially involving transparent elections.

'A sensible step would be for the clubs to appoint a nomination committee to recommend people who might be elected to the commission,' Terry O'Connor said. 'The commission should not be involved in this process.'

The game could only benefit from the elevation to the commission of bona fide football figures with a deep understanding of the industry and club operations such as Colless, Jeff Browne, Brian Cook, Peter Gordon, Leigh Matthews, Peggy O'Neal, Kevin Bartlett and Jeff Kennett.[18]

### 4. *Corporate governance charter*

Every year, in the final pages of its annual report, the AFL Commission pledges its commitment to good corporate governance.

'The AFL Commission acknowledges the importance of good corporate governance,' the citation says, 'which establishes accountability for the commission and management, and provides the policies and procedures for the equitable treatment of the 18 member clubs, recognition of the rights of other stakeholders and the commission's role as the custodian of Australian Football.'

The single-page statement includes vows to 'ensure ethical standards and appropriate behaviours are adhered to' and to 'have transparent reporting and communication with member clubs and other stakeholders'.

They are commitments that cannot be reconciled against the facts detailed in these pages.

Threats, leaks, bullying, manipulation, intimidation and character assassinations do not fit within the scope of those undertakings, while most clubs would scoff at the assurance of transparent reporting.

A requirement for commissioners to 'disclose all matters involving the AFL in which they have a material personal interest' is also stipulated. But the conflict of interest clause is too narrow, failing to capture Demetriou's business relationship with West Coast Eagles chairman Dalton Gooding during the club's illicit drugs crisis or his public commentary throughout the Essendon drugs investigation.

In regard to the commission's relationship with the executive, the statement asserts that 'the CEO is responsible for the day-to-day operations of the AFL and the implementation of the commission's strategies, in accordance with commission delegations, policies and procedures'.

The reality is the complete opposite. It is the AFL executive that is calling the shots on policies, strategies and procedures, not the commission.

The tail is wagging the dog and has done for almost two decades.

A more explicit corporate governance charter should be adopted by the AFL – and applied. Otherwise they are just meaningless words on a piece of paper.

## 5. *Financial transparency*

Transparency surrounding the league's expenditure is a significant issue. It is not satisfactory that clubs are denied access to relevant financial papers and the true costs of projects or executive wages and expenses.

'The thing that annoyed me intensely was the lack of detailed information that you got. It absolutely drove me mad,' Kennett declared. 'I would love to drill down onto what I see as the size of the AFL; the financial waste that is there.'

As shareholders, the clubs deserve to know where the game's money is being spent and should not fear seeking clarity (despite claims of commercial sensitivity). After all, the commission is supposed to be accountable to them.

Goyder's 2018 edict to place the salary of the AFL CEO back in the shadows seems contrary to good corporate governance. It should be reversed.

What have they got to hide?

## 6. *Proper tendering and procurement processes (and less cronyism)*

Jobs for the boys, an absence of probity in tendering, cronyism and nepotism narrow the scope of those who are permitted to enter and wield influence in the AFL universe.

The commission – on behalf of the clubs and stakeholders – should insist on more transparent processes around the awarding of commercial contracts and the recruitment of AFL staff.

## 7. Integrity investigations

The AFL's handling of major integrity probes requires immediate overhaul.

Footy fans are fed up with being treated like fools as they were in March 2013 when a straight-faced McLachlan turned towards the cameras and declared that he didn't 'know what the definition of tanking' was, even though his investigators had elicited full and frank confessions on a conspiracy to lose matches.

The AFL cooked up an alternative fantasy and asked us all to eat it.

Supreme Court Justice William Gillard was right when he recommended in his 2008 report that the league should establish an independent body to deal with serious misconduct allegations as a result of the West Coast Eagles illicit drugs scandal. But his urgings were ignored and have been exposed repeatedly by a string of subsequent scandals that engulfed the game.

There was a good reason Gillard's report was kept secret – it had laid bare the fundamental flaw in the AFL's justice system: a complete lack of independence.

An 'internal review' into the league's handling of the Essendon drugs saga released in March 2017 predictably gave the executive and the commission a glowing endorsement of its conduct. 'It sounds like the report was treated like the office birthday card – say something nice and pass it on, thanks champ,' journalist Mark Robinson wrote of its release more than four years after the infamous Bombers tip-off. 'The AFL couldn't even tell us the names of the number of authors of the report, but want us to fully accept its findings.'[19]

Of course, the internal review said nothing about the threats made to club officials, the secret inducements thrown at James

Hird or the cajoling of ASADA to 'take bits out' and prepare an interim report focusing on governance failings in order to support the AFL's prosecution of Essendon and its officials.

As Hird's barrister Julian Burnside declared when the report was announced: 'I'm not at all surprised that they've initiated an internal review that will be controlled entirely by their own interests. I would not be cynical about how meaningful it would be. I would be confident that it will not be meaningful at all.'[20]

The AFL defends its right to do deals with accused parties to resolve disputes but refuses to acknowledge the folly of reaching such outcomes when it plays the roles of investigator, prosecutor, judge, jury and executioner.

Bill Kelty told me he had repeatedly warned his fellow members 'that there was a very good case for the separation of powers. Because when you are the judge and jury at the same time, you get caught out,' he said. 'Montesquieu wrote a book on the separation of powers in the 1700s, which was a great book of history, and I kept reminding them of that. I must have said it on hundreds of occasions.' It fell on deaf ears.

Using the Essendon debacle as an example, the chair of the AFL Commission Mike Fitzpatrick, who was to sit on the body expected to determine charges against the club and its officials, should not have been involved in the secret deal-making that he was so blatantly part of in getting financier John Wylie, on behalf of the AFL, to put extra incentives to Hird in the hope of convincing him to take his medicine.

The fact Fitzpatrick could not see or acknowledge how this action so obviously compromised the integrity of the hearing of the charges was breathtaking.

Demetriou also insisted on sitting on the commission hearing, despite making almost weekly public comments on the Bombers investigation, including claims about being privy to information beyond what had been reported. 'You'd appreciate I've got briefings that are more advanced than what's in the public domain,' he declared in April 2013.[21]

That the AFL Commission seemed not to have a conflict of interest policy and that Fitzpatrick did not demand that Demetriou stand down from the hearing was just as breathtaking.

The so-called 'AFL integrity unit' is the greatest irony in Australian sport. It has proven itself over many years and multiple 'investigations' to in fact be nothing more than a brand-protection operation.

Almost all of the league's rulings on major integrity probes since the West Coast Eagles illicit drugs crisis of 2007 have been reached on the primary basis of protecting the flow of the rivers of gold.

It's a system that has institutionalised mediocrity.

And the AFL machine does not flinch at throwing respected, life-long football servants under the bus of self-interest. The late Dean Bailey, Craig Lambert, Richard Colless, Luke Beveridge, Peter Gordon, James (and Tania) Hird, Danny Corcoran, Mark Thompson, Peter de Rauch, Dale Lewis and Grant Thomas are among those to have been shoved under it.

Journalists such as Chip Le Grand, Tim Lane, Mark Robinson and others, who dared explore dark corners of the league's own processes, were belittled, abused and or punished.

A properly resourced and independent national sports integrity body should be created, forcing sporting bodies like the AFL to surrender control of the most serious integrity investigations. It would allow matters to be dealt with on their merits and without interference.

If that does not occur, at the very least, Gillard's recommendation for an independent body to deal with misconduct allegations should be adopted.

As Browne said: 'If the perception is that you shouldn't be the accuser and ultimately determine the penalty, then that is easily pushed off to another disciplinary body.'[22]

The opportunity for change at the AFL will present itself when McLachlan decides to leave. His replacement should be someone beyond the Melbourne boys' club with a conviction to fix the culture, stamp out cronyism and nepotism and introduce transparency, accountability and independent processes.

But will those who make the appointment be brave enough to do it?

8. *External reform*
It's not just at AFL House where improvements should be made.

Days before his death in December 2019, John Cain lamented the Andrews government's decision to splurge $225 million of taxpayer funds on the renovation of the AFL-owned Docklands Stadium. State and federal governments fall over themselves to spend the public's money on AFL stadiums in a way most rival sporting codes can only dream about. Far too many politicians are unwilling to call out the AFL's poor conduct.

'What about my grand final tickets?' asked one MP half-jokingly when approached for comment.

Governments should better explain their allocation of taxpayer funds.

Wylie, the chairman of the Australian Sports Commission, was not even admonished by the government of the day when it was revealed he had acted as an intermediary when the Essendon matter was before the AFL in August 2013.

Regulators should do their job and properly investigate AFL-related matters. While constructive relationships are appropriate, ASADA's willingness to sing enthusiastically from the AFL's brand-protection hymn book in its interim report blatantly crossed the line. Claims by whistleblowers that the Victorian Commission for Gambling and Liquor Regulation (VCGLR) whitewashed the tanking and Talia incidents (and a betting probe involving Collingwood youngster Jaidyn Stephenson in 2019) because it was beholden to the AFL should be a matter of serious concern.

The VCGLR's incompetence was embarrassingly exposed in late 2020 after its New South Wales counterpart acted swiftly against Crown Resorts when serious money laundering, linked to Asian crime gangs, was uncovered at its casino in Melbourne (where coincidentally Demetriou had been installed as its chairman).

Multiple complaints about the 'goings on' at the Southbank casino had been lodged with the VCGLR in previous years, but it had been asleep behind the wheel. Monash University gambling researcher Dr Charles Livingstone said the rails runs given to the AFL and Crown by the VCGLR over the years were 'classic examples of regulatory capture' or as the state opposition put it, the VCGLR had 'become a lap dog, instead of a watchdog'.

'The three football-betting scandals the whistleblowers refer to are each enough to demand answers, but taken together they reveal a system that relies too much on cooperation with powerful operators, and not enough on the interests of punters and the public,' Dr Livingstone said.[23]

And some senior football journalists, prominent past players, broadcasters, producers and editors should ask themselves if they are aiding and abetting the AFL's media manipulation.

The AFL is comfortably the nation's biggest commercial sporting operation and yet continues to enjoy tax-exempt status.

Why should it be so?

Is it truly a not-for-profit organisation? Clearly not.

A multi-billion-dollar industry that pays its most senior executives undisclosed six- and seven-figure salaries surely cannot seriously argue that it is in effect a charity? Demetriou's monster $3.8 million wage in his final year – four-times the earnings of the highest paid AFL player – was obscene.

The federal government should assess whether or not sporting bodies like the AFL should continue to operate tax-free.

Another issue of contention is the independence of the game's two 'unions': the AFL Players' Association and the AFL Coaches Association.

Both are funded by the AFL. Unions should be funded by their members, not by their master. Imagine if the Construction, Forestry, Maritime, Mining and Energy Union (CFMMEU) was funded by building contractors rather than its members?

The issue was exposed in 2019 when the AFLPA accused some of its own members of having a 'potentially negative impact' on the fledgling AFL Women's competition because they had sought advice from workers' rights law firm Maurice Blackburn over a pay and conditions negotiation with the AFL.

'Never in the history of unions has an employee representative group decided to attack its own members who are asking for better conditions and clarity about their employment rights. It raises real questions about whose interests the AFLPA is acting for,' the law firm said.[24]

\*\*\*

Sporting administrations are inherently unpopular – league boss Ross Oakley was a lightning rod for supporter anger during times of upheaval in the late 1980s and early 1990s – but the current AFL Commission ought to ponder why just 6 per cent of football fans in a 2019 survey said their level of faith in McLachlan's administration was strong. Only 6 per cent.

The custodians of Australian Rules should be better.

At a lavish farewell soiree thrown for Demetriou at the Myer Mural Hall in Melbourne in June 2014, a who's who of the football establishment, including Eddie McGuire, stood up and lauded the man they claimed had led the game to greatness.

But the established national competition was always going to thrive in the professional era because the product is so exhilarating and so entrenched in the Australian psyche. It didn't need a rapacious, win-at-all costs, stuff the rest administration to prosper.

Parallels can be drawn from the findings of the 2019 banking royal commission about the questionable culture of Australian financial institutions and the AFL's own culture. The banks (and the government for a period) strongly resisted the idea that there even should be an inquiry into the industry's culture and governance practices – and yet what did the royal commission find? Rampant cultural and governance issues in an industry that had lost its way.

What the AFL really needs is administrators genuinely dedicated to the advancement of the game instead of a select few members of a boys' club patting themselves on the back and feathering their own nests.

# Epilogue

DAVID FLOOD MET HIS GREAT MATE DEAN BAILEY IN THE
pre-season of 1986.

Both joined the Essendon Football Club that same summer,
training at the team's Windy Hill headquarters, tucked away
in the back streets of Melbourne's inner-north.

Flood hailed from the Victorian Wimmera town of Nhill
and Bailey from North Ringwood in the city's outer east. They
hit it off and forged an enduring friendship under the guidance
of Australian Rules master coach Kevin Sheedy.

'My first impressions of Bails was that he was short, fat
and hairy – and a very funny man,' Flood said. 'He was the
hairiest bloke on the planet. He had hairs on hairs, Bails, but
the thing was, he was very funny and very astute. He had this
warped sense of humour and always had a story or a yarn or a
crank – and he always did it with a smile on his face.'[1]

There was nothing special about either of their playing
careers. Bailey managed just fifty-three games, mainly as a
centreman, and Flood fifty-eight up forward and in defence.

Bailey was cut at the end of 1992, going on to play for Glenelg in the SANFL, while Flood suffered a footballer's greatest heartache, being dropped for the 1993 AFL Grand Final, which the Bombers won.

But Sheedy loved them both and in the 2000 season they shared in the joy of a premiership as development coaches for a powerhouse Bombers team that steamrolled its way to the flag.

'Bails was just a fantastic man to work with,' Flood remembered. 'He loved his scotch finger biscuits first thing in the morning. That was his vice and I think I have carried on that trait ever since.

'He just got along so well with people,' Flood continued. 'He was a very well-rounded man. We dealt primarily with the younger players back then and he was always interested in not only their footy but how they were coping in their lives. In a lot of ways he was twenty years ahead of the game, dealing with players and their welfare – on and off the field. And he was a terrific family man, too, with [wife] Caron and his two boys.

'What you saw was what you got with Bails. He was just an absolute ripper and kept encouraging me to develop my own skills as a coach, and sometimes you still think that he's just around the corner.'

After being removed as coach of Melbourne in July 2011, Bailey was hired by Adelaide as an assistant coach for the 2012 season.

But lung cancer would strike soon after. He died in March 2014, thirteen months after being fingered with the blame, alongside club general manager of football Chris Connolly, for the Melbourne tanking affair.

'To Bails' credit, he didn't say too much,' Flood said of the AFL investigation. 'He'd tell me bits and pieces but I know deep in my heart that whatever decisions he was making for the Demons at that time were always about what was best for the club's future.

'He'd worked under Sheeds for a long time and Sheeds was exactly the same – "How are we going to build a team to win a premiership?" And that's what Bails was always about. He never put himself first, put it that way.

'That was really tough on Dean and Caron. He never used to complain or whinge about stuff like that but he didn't deserve what happened to him. He was a bit of a scapegoat in all of that and it's just disappointing that those sorts of things happen in football today. It was all so contrived, to be seen to be doing the right thing. The top end of town [the AFL] and how they have dealt with some of these issues over the last few years has always been a bit questionable.'

\*\*\*

In the weeks before his death, Bailey confided in another close friend, then-Adelaide high-performance manager Paddy Steinfort, that he believed there was a link between his cancer and the AFL tanking investigation.[2] He recounted to Steinfort the relentless pressure that was applied on him by the AFL.[3]

Those cruel months of torment came to a head in the offices of a Melbourne law firm on the eve of Australia Day in 2013 when McLachlan, determined to tie up the AFL's sham tanking investigation in a neat little bow, leaned in towards Bailey, placed his hand on his shoulder, and warned him point-blank in the presence of his gobsmacked lawyer that if he didn't do a deal and plead guilty to a charge of conduct prejudicial to the game, he'd 'never work in footy again'.

For a man who loved footy and knew of no other way to make a living for his family, it was a dagger through the heart.

But for McLachlan and the AFL machine that had spawned him, it was just business. Our way or the highway, no matter the cost.

And so Bailey, like so many others before and after, surrendered and agreed to be the fall guy.

Everyone knew it stank – a shamefully contrived outcome aimed at covering up the shocking discovery that a conspiracy to lose matches for priority draft picks went right to the top of the Melbourne Football Club.

Yet by pinning a lesser charge on Bailey (and Connolly), the AFL was able to conclude that matches under its watch had not been compromised, and that its obligations as a beneficiary of the lucrative gambling industry had not been breached.

Then, when handing down the verdict, McLachlan declared without a hint of irony that 'I actually don't know what the definition of tanking is'.

Questionable and brutal – a trademark resolution under the leadership of footy's Gang of Three: Fitzpatrick, Demetriou and McLachlan.

Another scandal that threatened the rivers of gold had been defused through blatant manipulation, and the bulk of the industry sat back and accepted it. Like they always do.

Kicked to the kerb went Bailey, a fine football man who would die a year later still perplexed at the audacity of it all.

\*\*\*

As the chairman of the AFL Commission, Ron Evans used to trumpet that the league's administrators were merely the 'custodians' of the game. A group who held the code in trust on behalf of the community and whose job it was to hand it over to the next generation in better shape than they found it.

And on one score, the Demetriou–McLachlan era Evans let loose on Australian Rules football achieved just that. World-class stadia, record TV and commercial deals and sky-high ratings and memberships. The AFL was streets ahead of its nearest rivals.

But the measuring stick cannot be about prosperity alone.

The men who seized control of the Australian Football League had a parallel purpose – the advancement of their own interests. They paid themselves exorbitant salaries, gave preferential treatment to their mates and behaved ruthlessly and without accountability, as if the competition was their personal fiefdom.

They became football's ultimate beneficiaries, selectively distributing wealth and providing a seat at the table only to those who came to heel and abided by the boys' club rules.

Integrity, too, must count for something other than mere brand protection.

Yes, they had succeeded in building a formidable football empire, but the willingness to dispose so clinically of anyone or anything that got in their way, people such as Dean Bailey, tells the other side of the story.

# Endnotes

**Prologue**

1.  'AFL well placed for any coronavirus shock: McLachlan', J. Niall, *The Age*, 1 March 2020. https://www.theage.com.au/sport/afl/afl-well-placed-for-any-coronavirus-shock-mclachlan-20200301-p545su.html
2.  'Footy Classified', E. McGuire, Channel 9, 19 March 2020. https://www.news.com.au/sport/afl/afl-2020-coronavirus-updates-eddie-outlines-financial-doom-round-one-news/news-story/6fa88f62acbc16d02d2a8ef15a7478e7
3.  'Report of the Inquiry under section 143 of the *Casino Control Act* 1992 (NSW)', Volumes 1 and 2, NSW Independent Liquor and Gaming Authority, 1 February 2021. https://www.parliament.nsw.gov.au/la/papers/Pages/tabled-paper-details.aspx?pk=79129
    'Just like the banks, Crown's small bet is now a huge mess', *Australian Financial Review*, 19 October 2020. https://www.afr.com/chanticleer/just-like-the-banks-crown-s-small-bet-is-now-a-huge-mess-20201019-p566er
    'Crown director Andrew Demetriou slammed for taking notes to licence inquiry', ABC Radio, October 2020. https://soundcloud.com/peterryan-3/listen-crown-director-andrew-demetriou-slammed-for-taking-notes-to-licence-inquiry
4.  '"Exist to win", Demetriou worried Crown was too focused on compliance', P. Hatch, *Sydney Morning Herald*, 12 October 2020. https://www.smh.com.au/business/companies/exist-to-win-demetriou-worried-crown-was-too-focused-on-compliance-20201012-p564ax.html

**Chapter 1**

1.  Interview with Ron Joseph, M. Warner, January 2019.
2.  Interview with Grant Thomas, M. Warner, January 2019.
3.  'Demetriou plots his next coup – king of the AFL', Editorial, *The Age*, 3 May 2003. https://www.theage.com.au/sport/afl/demetriou-plots-his-next-coup-king-of-the-afl-20030503-gdvn5m.html
4.  'Denture maker fills gap', R. Robertson, *Australian Financial Review*, 15 October 1996. https://www.afr.com/politics/denture-maker-fills-gap-19961015-k7634
5.  Interview with Ricky Nixon, M. Warner, November 2019.
6.  Interview with James Hird, M. Warner, December 2019.
7.  Interview with Terry O'Connor, M. Warner, January 2020.
8.  'Demetriou breaking the code', M. Gordon, *The Age*, 19 March 2005 (Print Edition).
9.  Interview with Peter Scanlon', M. Warner, January 2020.
10. 'James Hird's wife Tania reveals details of "tip-off" phone call to Essendon over supplements scandal', L. Milligan, ABC 7.30 Report/ABC News, 21 March 2014. https://www.abc.net.au/news/2014-03-20/james-hirds-wife-reveals-details-of-tip-off-phone-call/5335200?nw=0
11. Interview with Graeme Samuel, M. Warner, February 2019.
12. Interview with Jeff Kennett, M. Warner, February 2019.
13. Interview with Richard Colless, M. Warner, February 2019.

**Chapter 2**

1.  'AFL shifts CEO pay goalposts', W. Glasgow and C. Lacy, *The Australian*, 27 March 2018.
2.  Interview with Jeff Kennett, M. Warner, February 2019.

3.   Interview with Terry O'Connor, M. Warner, January 2020.
4.   Hawthorn president Jeff Kennett referred to the AFL payment offer in a *7.30 Report* story by
     Louise Milligan in July 2014, '... And then I was offered a handful of money. Not me personally,
     but the club ... and when they weren't getting their way, in the end, they just turned around
     and said, "We'll try to buy you."' '"James Hird was a scapegoat" for the AFL claims wife',
     L. Milligan, ABC 7.30 Report/ABC News, 14 July 2014. https://www.abc.net.au/7.30/james-
     hird-was-a-scapegoat-for-the-afl-claims-wife/5596164
5.   Interview with Richard Colless, M. Warner, February 2019.
6.   Interview with Professor Ann O'Connell, University of Melbourne, M. Warner, October 2019.
7.   Interview with Peter de Rauch, M. Warner, February 2019.
8.   Interview with David Galbally, M. Warner, November 2019.
9.   Interview with Peter V'Landys, M. Warner, November 2020.
10.  Interview with John Cain, M. Warner, November 2019.
11.  'Top lawyer: AFL investigation into Crows camp a "nonsense" that "does not pass muster",
     M. Warner and R. Homfray, *Herald Sun*, 17 July 2020. https://www.heraldsun.com.au/sport/
     afl/teams/adelaide/top-lawyer-afl-investigation-into-crows-camp-a-nonsense-that-does-not-
     pass-muster/news-story/02132cbad3479cd18333771ae16f735f
12.  'Former Sydney Swans chairman Richard Colless takes swipe at AFL governance', M. Warner,
     *Herald Sun*, 25 February 2015. https://www.heraldsun.com.au/sport/afl/more-news/former-
     sydney-swans-chairman-richard-colless-takes-swipe-at-afl-governance/news-story/a3908f636
     3e5f69bc635da540d850501
13.  'Report of the Review of Australia's Sports Integrity Arrangements', J. Wood AO QC,
     D. Howman CNZM and R. Murrihy, Australian Department of Health, page 271, 3 September
     2018. https://www1.health.gov.au/internet/main/publishing.nsf/Content/the-review-of-
     australias-sports-integrity-arrangements
14.  Interview with Steven Amendola, M. Warner, December 2019.
15.  'Andrew Catterall and the AFL boys' club', C. Wilson, *The Age*, 6 March 2015. https://www.
     google.com.au/amp/s/amp.theage.com.au/sport/afl/andrew-catterall-and-the-afl-boys-club-
     20150305-13wgp3.html
16.  'AFL paid $200,000 settlement to staff member after bullying complaint', M. Warner,
     *Herald Sun*, 4 March 2015. https://www.heraldsun.com.au/news/afl-paid-200000-
     settlement-to-staff-member-after-bullying-complaint/news-story/60e5546076dceafbccbc4
     f45ee725dd5
17.  'AFL's toxic culture: Sleazy "Top 10" list ranked women by looks', S. Drill, *Sunday Herald Sun*,
     15 July 2017. https://www.heraldsun.com.au/sport/afl/afls-toxic-culture-sleazy-top-10-list-
     ranked-women-by-looks/news-story/c3fb9426463b8e1673a553201e3ec467
18.  'AFL faces questions over key appointments, moral issues at league headquarters', M. Warner,
     *Herald Sun*, 9 February 2018. https://www.heraldsun.com.au/sport/afl/more-news/afl-faces-
     questions-over-key-appointments-morale-issues-at-league-headquarters/news-story/8f23b7c2b1
     8cb81750d91cb2611f36f1
19.  Interview with Susan Alberti, M. Warner, October 2019.
20.  'AFL faces questions over key appointments, moral issues at league headquarters', M. Warner,
     *Herald Sun*, 9 February 2018. https://www.heraldsun.com.au/sport/afl/more-news/afl-faces-
     questions-over-key-appointments-morale-issues-at-league-headquarters/news-story/8f23b7c2b1
     8cb81750d91cb2611f36f1
21.  Quotes from G. McLachlan, address to AFL staff, 15 October 2020, provided to author.
22.  'And the big men spy: Andrew Demetriou says bugs a worry at AFL HQ', C. Walsh,
     *The Australian*, 7 June 2013. https://amp.theaustralian.com.au/sport/afl/and-the-big-men-
     spy-andrew-demetriou-says-bugs-a-worry-at-afl-hq/news-story/805f9496523ad5f65c42830d14
     4cc171

Chapter 3
1.   Interview with David Galbally, M. Warner, November 2019.
2.   'Silvio Foschini v. Victorian Football League and South Melbourne Football Club Ltd (1983)
     VSC 126', Supreme Court of Victoria, 15 April 1983. https://www.austlii.edu.au/cgi-bin/
     viewdoc/au/cases/vic/VicSC/1983/126.html
3.   Interview with Ron Joseph, M. Warner, January 2019.
4.   'Report to the VFL Board of Directors', Dr A.J. Aylett O.B.E., VFL Chairman, 1983.
5.   Interview with Dick Seddon, M. Warner, February 2019.
6.   Interview with Graeme Samuel, M. Warner, February 2019.
7.   Interview with Ross Oakley, M. Warner, January 2019.
8.   Interview with Peter Gordon, M. Warner, November 2020.
9.   Interview with Jeff Browne, M. Warner, February 2020.
10.  'You're the Greatest – Oakley tribute to retiring Samuel', M. Sheahan, *Herald Sun*, 20 June 2003
     (Print Edition).
11.  Interview with Richard Colless, M. Warner, February 2019.

12. 'Should Ron Evans wear both hats? Gutnick not only one to object', T. Grant, *Herald Sun*, 22 June 2000 (Print Edition).
13. 'Former Bomber digs up cap past', D. McKenzie, *The Age*, 24 April 2003. https://www.theage. com.au/sport/afl/former-bomber-digs-up-cap-past-20030424-gdvlc9.html
14. AFL chief fatally compromised by his Spotless record', M. McGuire, *The Australian*, 28 April 2000 (Print Edition).

Chapter 4
1. 'Sheedy fuels triple rumble', M. Robinson, *Herald Sun*, 14 September 1999. Print Edition.
2. Big Jack's last stand', A. Rule, *The Age*, 5 October 2002. https://www.theage.com.au/ national/big-jacks-last-stand-20021005-gdunq9.html
3. Interview with Dick Seddon, M. Warner, February 2019.
4. 'Elliott charged over $66m foreign exchange', S. Henry and M. Gunn, *The Australian*, 24 December 1993.
5. Interview with George Varlamos, M. Warner, May 2019.
6. Interview with Peter Kerr, M. Warner, October 2019.
7. Interview with Bill Kelty, M. Warner, February 2020.
8. 'Ex-AFL player agent David Allison comes clean on Carlton salary cap scandal, admitting he received $750,000 in secret cash payments', M. Warner, *Herald Sun*, 27 July 2018. https://www. heraldsun.com.au/sport/afl/teams/carlton/exafl-player-agent-david-allison-comes-clean-on-carlton-salary-cap-scandal-admitting-he-received-750000-in-secret-cash-payments/news-story /6b95e57c1c680ed64f463b8bcc801a89
9. '$.5m tax threat in Blues pay row', D. Timms, *Herald Sun*, 12 December 2000 (Print Edition).

Chapter 5
1. Interview with Graeme Samuel, M. Warner, February 2019.
2. Interview with Richard Colless, M. Warner, February 2019.
3. 'Footy stars' drug shock', M. Robinson, *Herald Sun*, 6 March 2002 (Print Edition).
4. 'AFL outrage over drug claims', Staff Writers, *The Age*, 6 March 2002. https://www.theage. com.au/sport/afl/afl-outrage-over-drug-claims-20020306-gdu0ys.html; Pot Shots, Lewis targeted after blowing whistle', M. Robinson, *Herald Sun*, 7 March 2002 (Print Edition).
5. Interview with Grant Thomas, M. Warner, January 2019.
6. Interview with Brian Waldron, M. Warner, December 2019.
7. Interview with Peter de Rauch, M. Warner, February 2019.
8. Interview with Richard Colless, M. Warner, February 2019.
9. 'All aboard for the Demetriou express', C. Wilson, *The Age*, 31 July 2003. https://www.theage. com.au/sport/afl/all-aboard-for-the-demetriou-express-20030731-gdw501.html
10. 'AFL in Elliott Blue', D. Timms, *Herald Sun*, 7 March 2003 (Print Edition).
11. Interview with Jeff Browne, M. Warner, February 2020.
12. Interview with Graeme Samuel, M. Warner, February 2019.
13. Interview with Bill Kelty, M. Warner, February 2020.
14. Interview with Richard Colless, M. Warner, February 2019.
15. 'Fitzpatrick steps into "big shoes"', G. Denham, *The Australian*, 8 August 2003 (Print Edition).
16. Interview with Dick Seddon, M. Warner, February 2019.
17. Interview with Terry O'Connor, M. Warner, January 2020.

Chapter 6
1. 'Kouta: AFL didn't offer help', J. Wilson, *Perth Now*, 27 October 2007. https://www.perthnow. com.au/news/nsw/kouta-afl-didnt-offer-help-ng-81f6cb9742bf6e7059624e9cba8672a1
2. 'AFL refuse to sign WADA anti-doping code', Staff Writers, ABC News (Online), 30 June 2005. https://www.abc.net.au/news/2005-06-30/afl-refuse-to-sign-wada-anti-doping-code/2049072
3. Interview with Rod Kemp', M. Warner, January 2020.
4. 'Australia Day Speech - Melbourne Convention Centre', A. Demetriou, AFL, January 2005.
5. 'Stick to footy, Andrew – Demetriou's political rant out of bounds', N. Mitchell, *Herald Sun*, January 25, 2005 (Print Edition).
6. 'AFL chief wrong on migrants: Costello', Staff Writers, *The Age*, 26 January 2005. https://www. theage.com.au/national/afl-chief-wrong-on-migrants-costello-20050126-gdzfqw.html
7. 'MP tells AFL chief to stick to sport', Staff Writers, *Sydney Morning Herald*, 10 February 2005. https://www.smh.com.au/sport/mp-tells-afl-chief-to-stick-to-sport-20050210-gdknti.html
8. Interview with Terry O'Connor, M. Warner, January 2020.
9. Interview with Jeff Kennett, M. Warner, February 2019.
10. 'Swimming great slams AFL drug stance', J. Wilson and D. Barrett, *Herald Sun*, 1 July 2005 (Print Edition); In 2005, when Melbourne and Geelong faced off in an elimination final at the MCG, Demetriou had senior journalist Jim Wilson ejected as host of the pre-match function, despite the Channel 7 broadcaster having commenced his duties. Wilson had led the coverage of the AFL-WADA drugs conflict. 'As MC of the function, I had just welcomed guests when

Demetriou lobbed late after flying from Perth,' Wilson said at the time. 'When he was told by an AFL staffer that Jim Wilson would introduce him, he saw red. He demanded my removal, despite his own staff hiring me weeks earlier. "Did you write something nasty about Andrew a couple of months ago?" the AFL employee asked. It then clicked that Demetriou was still smarting at my reporting of the WADA case and the AFL's soft penalties for illicit drug use, in particular cannabis.' 'Atrocious way to get square with me, Andrew', *Herald Sun*, 5 September 2005 (Print Edition).

11. 'AFL cops pounding', J. Wilson, *Herald Sun*, 14 July 2005 (Print Edition).
12. Interview with Jeff Browne, M. Warner, February 2020.
13. 'Demetriou also tested for illicit drugs', Staff Writers, ABC News (Online), 24 June 2011. https://www.abc.net.au/news/2011-06-24/demetriou-also-tested-for-illicit-drugs/2770790
14. 'Bruises and bugbears of AFL boss', M. Davis, *The Australian*, 24 September 2005 (Print Edition).
15. 'Chief's bad call – Demetriou under increasing scrutiny', M. Sheahan, *Herald Sun*, 14 September 2004 (Print Edition).
16. Interview with Peter de Rauch, M. Warner, February 2019.
17. 'Australian football legend Leigh Matthews was an angry man after the 2004 AFL Grand Final', G. McFarlane, *Herald Sun*, 29 July 2013. https://www.heraldsun.com.au/news/national/australian-football-legend-leigh-matthews-was-an-angry-man-after-the-2004-afl-grand-final/news-story/4041bdcd335a78085a5f04ca627f0a04
18. 'Demetriou puts boot into tactics', *Sydney Morning Herald*, 1 May 2005. https://www.smh.com.au/sport/afl/demetriou-puts-boot-into-tactics-20050501-gdl8fb.html
19. Interview with Paul Roos, M. Warner, February 2020.
20. Bruises and bugbears of AFL boss', M. Davis, *The Australian*, 24 September 2005 (Print Edition).
21. 'AFL boss Andrew Demetriou revisits playing days', M. Robinson, *Herald Sun/Adelaide Now*, 29 March 2012. https://www.adelaidenow.com.au/ipad/afl-boss-andrew-demetriou-revisits-playing-days/news-story/c0e53609f666a36dfa3f5d9f7623d6ef
22. Interview with Jeff Kennett, M. Warner, February 2019.
23. Interview with Peter de Rauch, M. Warner, February 2019. Note: De Rauch's account of the board meeting was backed by fellow Kangaroos director John Nicholson, who confirmed to me on 21 March 2021 that Demetriou had 'strongly encouraged' the appointment of Mark Brayshaw.
24. 'Carlton its own worst enemy badly in need of class, sophistication', P. Smith, *The Australian*, 23 September 2006 (Print Edition).
25. 'A league of his own', R. Sexton, *Sunday Age*, 8 July 2007 (Print Edition).
26. Interview with Grant Thomas, M. Warner, January 2019.
27. Interview with Mark Parker, M. Warner, January 2019.

Chapter 7
1. 'Julie's in trim for the Royal Battle of Waterloo', G. Kenihan, *The Advertiser*, 28 January 1988.
2. 'The extraordinary link between AFL boss and the Melbourne Cup', B. Collins, AFL.com.au, 6 November 2018. https://www.afl.com.au/news/66539/the-extraordinary-link-between-afl-boss-and-the-melbourne-cup
3. 'McLachlan releases PM leadership note', *Sydney Morning Herald*, 11 July 2006. https://www.smh.com.au/national/mclachlan-releases-pm-leadership-note-20060711-gdnxpd.html
4. 'How the move to Adelaide Oval happened', A. Browne, Port Adelaide FC/AFL.com.au, 27 March 2014. https://www.portadelaidefc.com.au/news/75783/how-the-move-to-adelaide-oval-happened
5. 'CAS Hawker Scholars – 1992 – Mr Gillon McLachlan', G. McLachlan, Hawker Scholarship, April 2016. https://www.hawkerscholarship.org/scholars/mr-gillon-mclachlan/
6. Interview with Chris Pollard, M. Warner, January 2020.

Chapter 8
1. 'Footy's finest - young, rich and out of it', A. Rule, *The Age*, 11 March 2007. https://www.theage.com.au/national/footys-finest-young-rich-and-out-of-it-20070311-ge4ebo.html
2. Interview with Andrew Rule, M. Warner, January 2019.
3. 'Tributes flow for former AFL chairman, Ron Evans', A. Caldwell, PM/ABC Radio Current Affairs, 9 March 2007. https://www.abc.net.au/pm/content/2007/s1868225.htm
4. 'Chris Mainwaring had "plate of cocaine the night he died"', Staff Writers, *Perth Now*, 20 March 2010. https://www.perthnow.com.au/news/chris-mainwaring-had-plate-of-cocaine-the-night-he-died-ng-0812641e6fd3f028dab3c4390b86bf5d
5. In March 2017, Melbourne's *Herald Sun* newspaper obtained the full 87-page report into illicit drug use at the West Coast Eagles Football Club compiled by retired Victorian Supreme Court Judge William Gillard, QC. Edited extracts published by the newspaper have been relied on for the writing of this book. Gillard completed his secret report into the West Coast Eagles in

February 2008, handing it to the AFL Commission. The Commission determined the following month not to release the document. Gillard had been appointed as a special investigator by the Commission in November 2007, a month after the Eagles sacked star midfielder Ben Cousins. Gillard completed his probe in three months, having interviewed 47 people.

6.      'Report to AFL Commission of Investigation of West Coast Eagles' by Mr E. William Gillard, QC, February 2008.
7.      'West Coast secret report: AFL restricted author on probe', M. Warner, *Herald Sun*, 24 March 2017. https://www.heraldsun.com.au/sport/afl/teams/west-coast/west-coast-secret-report-afl-restricted-author-on-sanctions/news-story/85df7716af8b5ff468e4dc0e9acd48c1
8.      Interview with Bill Kelty, M. Warner, February 2020.
9.      'Current and Historic Dynamic Company Report for Ruthinium Group Pty Ltd', Australian Securities and Investments Commission (via SAI Global Property).
10.     Interview with Dalton Gooding, M. Warner, January 2020.
11.     'Demetriou proves his versatility around the business field', S. Dabkowski, *The Age*, 15 May 2004, p. 5 (Print Edition).
12.     'AFL lobbies state government over bosses' private company', R. Baker and N. McKenzie, *The Age*, 17 September 2014. https://www.theage.com.au/national/victoria/afl-lobbies-state-government-over-bosses-private-company-20140916-10hmzn.html

Chapter 9
1.      'On the Couch – 30 July, 2012', Brock McLean, Fox Footy, 30 July 2012.
        'Carlton midfielder Brock McLean reveals he left Melbourne Demons because the club was tanking', Staff Writers, Fox Sports, 31 July 2012. https://coupler.foxsports.com.au/api/v1/article/amp/afl/afl-premiership/carlton-midfielder-brock-mclean-reveals-he-left-melbourne-demons-because-the-club-was-tanking/news-story/92b6ab1b989252e4f7b45d3d0095073e
2.      'Boss's head in sand', M. Sheahan, *Herald Sun*, 19 June 2013 (Print Edition).
3.      'AFL convinced Dees didn't tank', M. Stevens and G. Baker, *Herald Sun*, 2 August 2011. https://amp.heraldsun.com.au/sport/afl/afl-quiz-dean-bailey-about-tanking/news-story/2f4378bc30a30f2b27529bc36e04adf9
4.      'Eight changes, we'll be right', M. Robinson and M. Warner, *Herald Sun*, 17 August 2012. https://amp.heraldsun.com.au/sport/afl/eight-changes-well-be-right/news-story/84451fd384fa6f17ca68482b27bdf9c0
5.      Melbourne Football Club tanking investigation: In April 2019, Melbourne's *Herald Sun* newspaper obtained more than 80 pages of secret AFL integrity department transcripts from interviews conducted with Melbourne Football Club players and officials in 2012 as part of the league's probe into allegations of 'tanking' at the club in 2009. Interviews were conducted with 58 MFC figures as part of a report submitted to the AFL Commission in early 2013. The documents revealed eight senior club figures admitted to the AFL's investigators that they had been directed not to win more than four games in 2009 in order to secure a 'priority draft pick'. The AFL announced the findings of its tanking probe in February 2013, declaring Melbourne did not deliberately set out to lose games.
6.      'Melbourne tanking scandal: David Schwarz blasts "disgraceful" period in Demons history after explosive revelations', *Herald Sun*, 5 April 2019. https://www.heraldsun.com.au/sport/afl/teams/melbourne/melbourne-tanking-scandal-david-schwarz-blasts-disgraceful-period-in-demons-history-after-explosive-revelations/news-story/23ed44760c4e14d804a0443828 1e1c2b
7.      ibid.
8.      'Two suspensions and $500,000 fine, but not for tanking', G. Denham, *The Australian*, 20 February 2013. https://www.theaustralian.com.au/sport/afl/two-suspensions-and-500000-fine-but-not-for-tanking/news-story/b64f96ba348c3bb592cd3b80ad386293
9.      Interview with Dr Charles Livingstone, M. Warner, December 2019.
10.     Interview with Chris Pollard, M. Warner, January 2020.
11.     *Breakfast with Bails, What a dying coach taught me about life, learning and leadership*, P. Steinfort, Allure Publishers, Melbourne, 2015, p. 161.
12.     'No action taken against AFL over 2009 Melbourne tanking scandal', M. Warner, *Herald Sun*, 30 August 2019. https://www.heraldsun.com.au/sport/afl/more-news/no-action-taken-against-afl-over-2009-melbourne-tanking-scandal/news-story/d1282085fc6dd94c27dcdd41cdb5f5ca
13.     Interview with David Galbally, M. Warner, November 2019.
14.     'Gambling watchdog referred to IBAC over claims of corruption', M. Warner, *Herald Sun*, 18 September 2019. https://www.heraldsun.com.au/news/victoria/gambling-watchdog-referred-to-ibac-over-claims-of-corruption/news-story/69cc67720c62f50702ef674281721cab
15.     Interview with Richard Colless, M. Warner, February 2019.

Chapter 10
1.      'Transcript of Federal Court proceedings, VID 327 of 2014, 11 August 2014, p. 84', Presiding Officer: Justice J. Middleton.

2. 'James Hird, interview with ASADA and the AFL', 16 April 2013.

3. 'Essendon board was divided, David Evans was impatient: ex-director', S. Lane, *The Age*, 5 May 2016. https://www.theage.com.au/sport/afl/essendon-board-was-divided-evans-was-impatient-exdirector-20160505-gong0a.html

4. 'Review of Essendon Football Club governance – publicly released executive summary', Dr. Z. Switkowski, 6 May 2013. https://www.essendonfc.com.au/news/729418/dr-ziggy-switkowski-report

5. 'James Hird v AFL', Supreme Court of Victoria writ, filed 22 August 2013, SC201304370.

6. 'Ex-Bomber McVeigh slams drug allegations', Staff Writers, ABC News (Online), 6 February 2013. https://www.abc.net.au/news/2013-02-06/ex-bomber-mcveigh-slams-drug-allegations/4504638

7. 'Aurora Andruska, hand-written notes from Australian Crime Commission briefing, January 31, 2013', Federal Court of Australia, VID327.

8. 'Hird injected drugs', N. McKenzie and R. Baker, *The Age*, 11 April 2013. https://www.theage.com.au/sport/afl/hird-injected-drugs-20130410-2hlvx.html

9. 'Hird under huge pressure to step aside', G. Hand and R. Vaughn, *The Age*, 12 April 2013. https://www.smh.com.au/sport/hird-under-huge-pressure-to-step-aside-20130412-2howw.html

10. 'Essendon legend James Hird has no choice but to walk away, writes *The Australian*'s Patrick Smith', P. Smith, *The Australian* / Fox Sports, 11 April 2013. https://www.foxsports.com.au/afl/essendon-legend-james-hird-has-no-choice-but-to-walk-away-writes-the-australians-patrick-smith/news-story/9fedd3f6018541c208d838b3e2c024da

11. 'James stays strong in face of growing storm', M. Warner and M. Robinson, *Herald Sun*, 6 August 2013 (Print Edition).

12. 'Dispute over what James Hird told ASADA', C. Le Grand, *The Australian*, 4 December 2013. https://www.theaustralian.com.au/sport/afl/dispute-over-what-james-hird-told-asada/news-story/dd1e1a318ae3cb509607aaff34e27a0a

13. Interview with Andrew Demetriou', N. Mitchell, 3AW Mornings, 25 July 2013.
    Note: Demetriou repeatedly denied tipping off David Evans. On 26 July 2013 he told ABC Radio 774: 'Being accused of tipping off Essendon and breaking the law because I signed a confidentiality agreement with the ACC – not withstanding that they didn't actually disclose to me this club – I take those matters seriously. I will defend my reputation and clear the air to make sure the truth is told. In my world it is very easy to sell the truth. I learned that a long time ago.' The same day, Australian Crime Commission chief executive John Lawler issued a statement, which read: 'The ACC does not have any information to support the assertion that representatives of the AFL failed to honour their written undertakings given to the ACC in accordance with the Australian *Crime Commission Act* 2002, to protect the content of the confidential briefing they received. The ACC will not disclose the details of these classified briefings, as to do so would cause the ACC to be in breach of its' own Act. Importantly, the ACC has never confirmed publicly which clubs are involved in Project Aperio. The ACC has been very careful to ensure, in accordance with the Act, that no information was disclosed that could affect the safety, reputation or fair trial of any person.' In another interview with sports broadcaster Gerard Whateley on ABC Radio 774 on 20 September 2013, Demetriou said: 'There have been two or three journalists ... who have been inferring for quite a while that myself and Gillon McLachlan were party to providing information to David Evans, a consequence of which would have seen us in jail. Despite the fact that we denied it, despite the fact that also David Evans denied it, the ACC clarified that it was not true and so did ASADA. So, Gerard, if you think that having your reputation impugned, a consequence of which is going to jail, goes just past the wicket keeper, you are mistaken.'

14. 'AFL warned Hird against peptides', C. Wilson, *The Age*, 17 July 2013. https://www.theage.com.au/sport/afl/afl-warned-hird-against-peptides-20130716-2q2ih.html

15. 'James Hird's lawyers in war of words with AFL', M. Warner, *Herald Sun*, 29 July 2013. https://www.heraldsun.com.au/sport/afl/james-hirds-lawyers-in-war-of-words-with-afl/news-story/77800ff1586feca343a7db97db774ea6

16. ibid.

17. 'Essendon punishment claim "just offensive", says AFL boss Andrew Demetriou', M. Warner and M. Robinson, *Herald Sun*, 7 August 2013. https://www.heraldsun.com.au/sport/afl/james-hird-will-finally-get-to-see-the-drugs-report-that-threatens-to-derail-his-coaching-career/news-story/a21a02a715f9111883e4021106bf48c6

18. 'Former Essendon spin doctor Elizabeth Lukin appointed AFL head of corporate affairs', S. Gullan, *Herald Sun/Perth Now*, 10 December 2014. https://www.perthnow.com.au/sport/afl/former-essendon-spin-doctor-elizabeth-lukin-appointed-afl-head-of-corporate-affairs-ng-adfc5393b4354b1d637443f3e63b7686

19. 'Essendon will be given the chance to respond to the charges against them, says AFL's Andrew Demetriou', Staff Writers, ABC News (Online), 21 August 2013. https://www.abc.net.au/news/2013-08-21/afl-issues-statement-on-grounds-for-essendon-charges/4902472

20. Note: In February 2017, Melbourne's *Herald Sun* newspaper obtained a secret tape recording of a crisis meeting attended by senior Essendon Football Club figures Paul Little, James Hird, Mark Thompson and Danny Corcoran at the height of the club's drugs war with the AFL. The meeting took place at Essendon's then Windy Hill headquarters on 8 August 2013. The tape exposed how the Bombers felt the AFL was threatening them to either accept penalties or be 'stood down' as a club. The league has always maintained that the AFL Commission 'hearing' to decide the fate of Essendon and its officials – held two weeks after the recorded crisis meeting – was not compromised by backroom deals and negotiations.
21. 'Essendon player's mother Sarah, interviewed by Triple M host Eddie McGuire, remains a mystery', M. Robinson, *Herald Sun*, 24 June 2014. https://www.heraldsun.com.au/sport/afl/teams/essendon/essendon-players-mother-sarah-interviewed-by-triple-m-host-eddie-mcguire-remains-a-mystery/news-story/287406b5bf3e12bd539b89161fd4f7de
22. Interview with Bill Kelty, M. Warner, February 2020.
23. 'Private deals for a public scapegoat', C. Le Grand, *The Australian*, 3 December 2013. https://www.theaustralian.com.au/sport/afl/private-deals-for-a-public-scapegoat/news-story/010652663ea0c28951a572ba08f6fceb
24. 'AFL Commission hearing transcript – Mike Fitzpatrick', August 2013.
25. Interview with Steven Amendola, M. Warner, December 2019.
26. 'Lawyers at odds over Hird apology', J. Niall and W. Brodie, *The Age*, 29 August 2013. https://www.theage.com.au/sport/afl/lawyers-at-odds-over-hird-apology-20130828-2sqxc.html
27. Interview with Julian Burnside, M. Warner, November 2019.
28. 'AFL's behind-the-scenes tactics in Essendon punishment talks exposed', M. Warner and M. Robinson, *Herald Sun*, 4 December 2013. https://www.heraldsun.com.au/sport/afl/afls-behindthescenes-tactics-in-essendon-punishment-talks-exposed/news-story/46ef54b634c58577c826d4b9c3270fd8
29. 'Revealed: the secret offer to James Hird to end the AFL's drugs shame', C. Le Grand, *The Australian*, 4 December 2013. https://www.theaustralian.com.au/sport/afl/revealed-the-secret-offer-to-james-hird-to-end-the-afls-drugs-shame/news-story/0e9f023db272e8245baa7b7d0efb31ab
30. 'Mike Fitzpatrick – Open Mike interview', Fox Footy, 16 May 2018. https://www.youtube.com/watch?v=raez19un1Mk
31. Interview with Andrew Demetriou', N. Mitchell, 3AW Mornings, 4 December 2013.
32. *The Straight Dope: The inside story of sport's biggest drug scandal*, C. Le Grand, Melbourne University Press, 2015, p. 226
33. 'James Hird's wife Tania says Andrew Demetriou knew about payments to suspended coach', M. Warner and A. Argoon, *Herald Sun*, 12 December 2013. https://www.heraldsun.com.au/james-hirds-wife-tania-says-andrew-demetriou-knew-about-payments-to-suspended-coach/news-story/1f1ec29d5b78f94dd86ddfe35d73b16d
34. 'Retiring AFL boss Andrew Demetriou came to mistake competence for omnipotence', R. Hinds, *Daily Telegraph*, 4 March 2014. https://www.heraldsun.com.au/retiring-afl-boss-andrew-demetriou-came-to-mistake-competence-for-omnipotence-writes-richard-hinds/news-story/c403de762782c40b0e0c4665fd20a786
35. 'New ASADA chief Ben McDevitt wants quick completion to ongoing supplements investigation', M. Warner, *Herald Sun*, 1 June 2014. https://www.heraldsun.com.au/sport/afl/teams/essendon/new-asada-chief-ben-mcdevitt-wants-quick-completion-to-ongoing-supplements-investigation/news-story/48edfd1268f1506d19f5ea11a4def30a
36. 'Essendon Football Club opening submission', Federal Court of Australia, 4 August 2014, (VID327).
37. 'Transcript of Federal Court proceedings,' Federal Court of Australia, VID327 of 2014, P. 147, Justice J. Middleton presiding.
38. 'Essendon Football Club opening submission', Federal Court of Australia, 4 August 2014, (VID327).
39. 'Political fix was in for Hird and Bombers', C. Le Grand, *The Australian*, 8 August 2014.
40. 'Bastion Group adds senior executives, new divisions', L. Sinclair, *The Australian*, 4 May, 2015 (Print Edition).
41. 'Hird tells judge: I was threatened over supplements controversy', M. Warner, G. Baker and J. Dowling, *Herald Sun*, 11 August 2014. https://www.heraldsun.com.au/sport/afl/more-news/hird-tells-judge-i-was-threatened-over-supplements-controversy/news-story/5c7ea0cbd7052d015965ae0790477572
42. 'Essendon blasts former ASADA chief Aurora Andruska following Federal Court trial', M. Warner, *Herald Sun*, 27 August 2014. https://www.heraldsun.com.au/sport/afl/teams/essendon/essendon-blasts-former-asada-chief-aurora-andruska-following-federal-court-trial/news-story/f079fbe3ef75bc7522a1b08da660bcb0
43. *The Straight Dope: The inside story of sport's biggest drug scandal*, C. Le Grand, Melbourne University Press, 2015, p. 226.

44.	'Ex-Essendon football boss breaks four-year silence', M. Warner, *Herald Sun*, 13 January 2017. https://www.heraldsun.com.au/sport/afl/more-news/exessendon-football-boss-breaks-fouryear-silence/news-story/ca8a7899af5762f6e658107dd4e459d3
45.	'AFL boss ruled out fallen Bomber's return, claims ex-Essendon football manager, M. Warner, *Herald Sun*, 13 January 2017. https://www.heraldsun.com.au/sport/afl/more-news/afl-boss-ruled-out-fallen-bombers-return-claims-exessendon-football-manager/news-story/2bffa3586827 6e96e31cf0cd8d35b47d
46.	'Essendon great James Hird "bullied, hounded, verbally assaulted"', M. Warner, *Herald Sun*, 6 January 2017. https://www.heraldsun.com.au/news/essendon-great-james-hird-bullied-hounded-verbally-assaulted/news-story/28bf6dbff21d7bfbd823db9d9c8fd5a9
47.	'The Bomber interviews: The depths of my drug abuse, the police raid that saved me and how I pulled through', M. Warner, *Herald Sun*, 18 August 2020. https://www.heraldsun.com.au/sport/afl/the-bomber-interviews-the-depths-of-my-drug-abuse-the-police-raid-that-saved-me-and-how-i-pulled-through/news-story/7e69dca2c83aee208b4c566861e313a6
48.	Interview with Peter Scanlon, M. Warner, January 2020.

Chapter 11
1.	'Series of text messages between Stephen Dank and Dan Bates', tendered to AFL Anti-Doping Tribunal by Australian Sports Anti-Doping Authority, December 2014
2.	'Text messages reveal Dank involved with Demons', C. Meldrum-Hanna, ABC 7.30/ABC News, 18 April 2013. https://www.abc.net.au/news/2013-04-18/text-messages-reveal-danks-demons-involvement/4637954
3.	'Transcript, David Thurin ASADA interview, May 1, 2013', tendered to AFL Anti-Doping Tribunal, December 2014.
4.	'Stephen Dank says he supplied Nathan Bock with WADA-banned drug CJC-1295', M. Warner, *Herald Sun*, 13 April 2013. https://www.heraldsun.com.au/sport/afl/stephen-dank-says-he-supplied-nathan-bock-with-wadabanned-drug-cjc1295/news-story/3a4b3b1e82806ad72a3b3 cb56921be5b
5.	'Neil Balme says Geelong did not employ Stephen Dank', D. Cherny, *The Age*, 10 August 2015. https://www.theage.com.au/sport/afl/neil-balme-says-geelong-did-not-employ-stephen-dank-20150810-givhv8.html
6.	'Geelong admits sourcing drug from Stephen Dank in 2009', C. Crawford, M. Warner and G. Baker, *Herald Sun*, 11 August 2015. https://www.heraldsun.com.au/news/victoria/geelong-admits-sourcing-drug-from-stephen-dank-in-2009/news-story/32deaa6e15dcb1984fb587397 f6d615a
7.	'Email sent from Steve Hocking to Geelong Football Club staff, June 30, 2008', tendered to AFL Anti-Doping Tribunal, December 2014.
8.	'Email sent from Dean Robinson to Geelong Football Club staff, July 30, 2007', tendered to AFL Anti-Doping Tribunal, December 2014.
9.	'Australian Football League Notice of Charge Rule 1.6', Essendon Football Club, 13 August 2013. http://images.theage.com.au/file/2013/08/21/4679457/EssendonFCnoticeofcharge.pdf
10.	'World Anti-Doping Agency appeal brief', Court of Arbitration for Sport, July 2015, Arbitration Number CAS2015/A/4059.
11.	'Injury Care Pty Ltd invoices to Geelong Football Club', tendered to AFL Anti-Doping Tribunal, December 2014.

Chapter 12
1.	Interview with Jason McCartney, M. Warner, October 2019.
2.	Interview with Peter de Rauch, M. Warner, February 2019.
3.	'How cuppa with AFL boss sealed Karmichael Hunt's deal', J. Phelps, *Daily Telegraph/Herald Sun*, 30 July 2009. https://amp.heraldsun.com.au/sport/nrl/how-cuppa-with-afl-boss-sealed-karmichael-hunts-deal/news-story/e7a8f16050a687271dae1bd954165ff3
4.	'The Putting President', M. Warner, *Herald Sun*, 16 June 2012.
5.	'AFL paid $200,000 settlement to staff member after bullying complaint', M. Warner, *Herald Sun*, 4 March 2015. https://www.heraldsun.com.au/news/afl-paid-200000-settlement-to-staff-member-after-bullying-complaint/news-story/60e5546076dceafbccbc4f45ee725dd5
6.	'Andrew Demetriou gave Andrew Catterall positive reference amid bullying allegations', M. Warner, *Herald Sun*, 6 March 2015. https://www.heraldsun.com.au/sport/afl/more-news/andrew-demetriou-gave-andrew-catterall-positive-reference-amid-bullying-allegations/news-story/feddad3caeebcc5e972b6c24561bede3
7.	'AFL paid $200,000 settlement to staff member after bullying complaint', M. Warner, *Herald Sun*, 4 March 2015. https://www.heraldsun.com.au/news/afl-paid-200000-settlement-to-staff-member-after-bullying-complaint/news-story/60e5546076dceafbccbc4f 45ee725dd5
8.	'Cocaine confession: Karmichael Hunt reveals footy party boy lifestyle', P. Rothfield, *The Sunday Telegraph*, 28 June 2015. https://www.dailytelegraph.com.au/news/nsw/cocaine-

confession-karmichael-hunt-reveals-footy-party-boy-lifestyle/news-story/50c16ae894050614e
76dd8e82aad15d9

9. 'Gold Coast coach Rodney Eade has accused the AFL of failing to properly support the Suns',
J. Ralph, *Herald Sun*, 19 February 2017. https://www.heraldsun.com.au/sport/afl/teams/gold-
coast/gold-coast-coach-rodney-eade-has-accused-the-afl-of-failing-to-properly-support-the-
suns/news-story/45e44c816013bcf82369505c6397e4a7

**Chapter 13**

1. 'AFL 2015: Richard Colless tells of expletive laden tirade from AFL commission chairman',
M. Warner, *Herald Sun*, 4 August 2015. https://www.heraldsun.com.au/sport/afl/afl-2015-
richard-colless-tells-of-expletive-laden-tirade-from-afl-commission-chairman/news-story/11ab
c847e7628596639ec160d0e86334

2. 'AFL Statement – Move of Lance Franklin from Hawthorn to Sydney Swans', AFL Commission,
4 August 2015. https://www.afl.com.au/news/197971/afl-statement-move-of-lance-franklin-
from-hawthorn-to-sydney-swans

3. 'Triple M Hot Breakfast, 5 August 2015', E. McGuire, Triple M, 5 August 2015.

4. Interview with Ron Joseph', M. Warner, January 2019.

5. 'Eddie McGuire apologises to Adam Goodes for King Kong comment but will not resign', Staff
Writers, ABC News (Online), 29 May 2013. https://www.abc.net.au/news/2013-05-29/eddie-
mcguire-apologises-for-adam-goodes-king-kong-comment/4720152

6. Interview with Peter Jess, M. Warner, December 2019.

7. 'Olympic Park grab for Pies', M. Warner, *Herald Sun*, 2 July 2013 (Print Edition).

8. 'Is Eddie McGuire the most powerful man in football?', C. Wilson, *The Age*, 28 April 2014.
https://www.theage.com.au/sport/afl/is-eddie-mcguire-the-most-powerful-man-in-football-
20140428-zr0x0.html

9. 'Andrew Demetriou defends Eddie McGuire, says racism report lacked detail', R. Williams, *The
Australian*, 10 February 2021. https://www.theaustralian.com.au/sport/afl/demetriou-defends-
eddie-says-racism-report-lacked-detail/news-story/c1d217411f05f98eb88377da8b7bdadd

10. 'Mike Fitzpatrick – Open Mike interview', Fox Footy, May 2018.

11. Interview with Terry O'Connor, M. Warner, January 2020.

12. Interview with Richard Colless, M. Warner, February 2019.

**Chapter 14**

1. Nat Edwards, 3AW Football, 2019. https://www.3aw.com.au/nat-edwards-opens-up-on-weird-
and-odd-experience-at-marvel-stadium-on-friday-night/

2. 'AFL says Carlton fan was evicted for "spooking" umpire by running, screaming, waving his
arms', M. Gleeson, Z. Hope and R. Eddie, *The Age*, 11 June 2019. https://www.theage.com.
au/national/victoria/afl-says-carlton-fan-was-evicted-for-spooking-umpire-by-running-
screaming-waving-his-arms-20190611-p51woc.html

3. 'AFL concedes Blues supporter did not run across two bays of seats to abuse umpire Mathew
Nicholls', M. Warner, *Herald Sun*, 2 August 2019. https://www.heraldsun.com.au/sport/afl/
more-news/afl-concedes-blues-supporter-did-not-run-across-two-bays-of-seats-to-abuse-
umpire-mathew-nicholls/news-story/ae2302552e6db5a1201884d5a145b5ea

4. 'Security presence to change after Marvel, AFL officials meet', S. McClure, *The Age*, 17 June
2019. https://www.theage.com.au/sport/afl/security-presence-to-change-after-marvel-stadium-
afl-officials-meet-20190617-p51yg9.html

5. 'Walsh, Demetriou unite', W. Glasgow, *Australian Financial Review*, 6 November 2014.

6. Interview with Ben Hart, M. Warner, February 2020.

7. Interview with Tim Lane, M. Warner, February 2019.

8. 'Investigated, whitewashed?' T. Lane, *The Age*, 11 December 2011. https://www.theage.com.
au/sport/afl/investigated-whitewashed-20111210-1oovx.html
'Doubts raised over Jack's draft', T. Lane, *The Age*, 11 December 2011. https://www.theage.
com.au/sport/afl/doubts-raised-over-jacks-draft-20111210-1ool4.html
'All-clear on Jack deal can't be taken seriously', T. Lane, *The Age*, 24 December 2011. https://
www.theage.com.au/sport/afl/allclear-on-jack-deal-cant-be-taken-seriously-20111223-
1p8n9.html

9. Interview with David Galbally, M. Warner, November 2019.

10. 'Demetriou admits time has come for AFL to air its dirty laundry', P. Smith, *The Australian*,
5 December 2012. https://www.theaustralian.com.au/sport/opinion/demetriou-admits-time-
has-come-for-afl-to-air-its-dirty-laundry/news-story/c6c8be7663257e5e31a493f73c4d4c1c

11. 'Whateley calls out AFL for "betrayal of journalism"', Staff Writers, SEN 1116, 3 August 2020.
https://www.sen.com.au/news/2020/08/03/whateley-calls-out-afl-for-betrayal-of-journalism/

12. Interview with Grant Thomas, M. Warner, January 2019.

13. Note: The AFL strongly denied having an involvement in Thomas's SEN sacking. In an
interview with Neil Mitchell on 3AW radio on 12 May 2009, Demetriou described a story
written by journalists Mark Robinson and Daryl Timms ('SEN sacks AFL's nagging critic',

*Herald Sun*, 12 May 2009) as 'self-indulgent, self-righteous, nonsense, drivel'. He warned media outlets claiming the AFL was trying to influence editorial content to be careful. 'They should have a good look at themselves because it's completely untrue,' Demetriou said. 'Unless people are going to start calling me a liar or call the AFL a liar – and I encourage them to because I need a new pool – but I mean it's just nonsense. We don't do that. Grant Thomas has been sacked from many organisations and we've had nothing to do with that. I had nothing to do with Grant Thomas's sacking. We never pick up the phone and ring a boss, an editor, anyone to complain about a journalist or try to get something not written pulled. It's one of my big no-nos.' Thomas expanded on his sacking from SEN and resignation from Footy Classified in the *Herald Sun*'s Sacked podcast in July 2019. 'They [SEN management] would say, "Do you have to ridicule the AFL and ridicule the umpires?" I would say, "If they do a s--- job, what do you want me to do?" They said, "They have threatened that we won't get the AFL rights if we do." I told them I am completely useless if I can't say what I think.' https://www.heraldsun.com.au/sport/afl/more-news/sacked-podcast-grant-thomas-tells-all-on-sen-the-age-sackings-and-why-he-quit-footy-classified/news-story/7544079278c42afa92521ee8bfec9ab3

14. 'Demetriou taunts reporter on air', N. Leys, *The Australian*, 13 September 2013. https://www.theaustralian.com.au/news/demetriou-taunts-reporter-on-air/news-story/63efe0f59cc1ac5c7d7f65aa910b527a
15. 'Craig Kelly – Open Mike interview', Fox Footy, May 2011.
16. 'Transcript of phone conversation between Michael Warner and Eddie McGuire', M. Warner, July 2010.
17. 'AFL boss says journo shared tape of expletive-riddled tirade', N. Leys, *The Australian*, 2 November 2013. https://www.google.com.au/amp/s/amp.theaustralian.com.au/business/media/afl-boss-says-journo-shared-tape-of-expletive-riddled-tirade/news-story/184ee472aab6a2c9b19824e67cbe6334

### Chapter 15
1. Note: In October 2016, Melbourne's *Herald Sun* newspaper obtained a cache of secret Western Bulldogs Football Club documents detailing previously undisclosed claims about the leaking of inside information to the Adelaide Crows Football Club before the two teams faced off in an elimination final at the MCG in September 2015. The documents revealed that the Bulldogs had informed the AFL they had obtained 'independent corroboration' of allegations that disaffected Dogs defender Michael Talia had leaked parts of the team's game plan to his brother, star Adelaide backman Daniel Talia, in the days before the match. The Talias, who have always maintained their innocence, were cleared by the AFL in late 2015 after a 63-day integrity unit investigation, but the documents exposed the Bulldogs' fury at the AFL's handling of the probe and its exoneration of the Talia brothers.
2. 'Liam Pickering certain Michael Talia will be cleared of leak claims and will find new AFL home', W. Green, Fox Sports/*Herald Sun*, 8 October 2015. https://www.foxsports.com.au/news/liam-pickering-certain-michael-talia-will-be-cleared-of-leak-claims-and-will-find-new-afl-home/news-story/783ceda7e3eafa5753c32c951e914ea2
3. Interview with Peter Gordon, M. Warner, November 2020.
4. Interview with Richard Colless, M. Warner, February 2019.

### Chapter 16
1. 'Handshake deal – Scully Sr offered $680k job in November 2010', M. Warner, *Herald Sun*, 15 November 2011 (Print Edition).
2. 'A Giant miscue lost in the crowd', C. Wilson, *The Age*, 26 November 2011. https://www.theage.com.au/sport/afl/a-giant-miscue-lost-in-the-crowd-20111125-1nz8u.html
3. 'Graeme Allan will spend part of his 12-month ban working and studying in New York', M. Warner, *Herald Sun*, 6 March 2017. https://www.heraldsun.com.au/sport/afl/more-news/graeme-allan-will-spend-part-of-his-12month-ban-working-and-studying-in-new-york/news-story/f51cefe83e4c0253f8a4a8a70b32e986
4. Interview with Jeff Browne, M. Warner, February 2020.
5. 'Emails reveal rapport between Gillon McLachlan and Craig Kelly', M. Warner, *Herald Sun*, 14 September 2018. https://www.heraldsun.com.au/sport/afl/more-news/emails-reveal-rapport-between-gillon-mclachlan-and-craig-kelly/news-story/e57fd3f06f060984bd15f8110454cda0
6. Mentha, in the matter of Spyglass Management Group Pty Ltd (Administrators Appointed), 2004 FCA 1469, Federal Court of Australia.
7. 'AFL funds home for its hall of fame', C. Wilson, *The Age*, 24 May 2003 (Print Edition).
8. 'AFL man had links to ailing Hall of Fame', C. Wilson, *The Age*, 18 November 2004 (Print Edition).
9. 'Leading AFL player agent Craig Kelly splits from ranks on whether players should strike', M. Warner, *Herald Sun*, 29 March 2016. https://www.heraldsun.com.au/sport/afl/more-news/

leading-afl-player-agent-craig-kelly-splits-from-ranks-on-whether-players-should-strike/news-story/a3aa4aa6f9bf1a9aee92cc78e346c08b

10. Interview with Bill Kelty, M. Warner, February 2020.
11. Interview with Peter Jess, M. Warner, December 2019.
12. 'Craig Kelly: Pin-up pie to AFL man of influence', M. Warner, *Herald Sun*, 14 September 2018. https://www.heraldsun.com.au/sport/afl/more-news/craig-kelly-pinup-pie-to-afl-man-of-influence/news-story/b010f9925f793dd8a61203dc15c04a9b

Chapter 17

1. 'AFL faces questions over key appointments, moral issues at league headquarters', M. Warner, *Herald Sun*, 9 February 2018.
2. 'AFL must "toughen up": "People have affairs, that's life", says Josh Bornstein', M. Bailey, *Australian Financial Review*, 17 July 2017. https://www.afr.com/work-and-careers/workplace/afl-must-toughen-up-people-have-affairs-thats-life-says-josh-bornstein-20170716-gxcamw
3. 'AFL sex scandal: Inquiries made with senior league figures months before Simon Lethlean resigned', M. Warner, *Herald Sun*, 9 November 2017. https://www.heraldsun.com.au/sport/afl/more-news/afl-sex-scandal-inquiries-made-with-senior-league-figures-months-before-simon-lethlean-resigned/news-story/9681a0db195b2b84fc05869e73763f81
4. 'AFL affair ruckus', S. Drill, *Herald Sun*, 10 July 2017, P.3.
5. 'Human rights commissioner Kate Jenkins names AFL chief Gill McLachlan among 19 male champions of women in the workplace', S. Green, *The Age*, 15 April 2015. https://www.theage.com.au/national/victoria/human-rights-commissioner-kate-jenkins-names-afl-chief-gill-mclachlan-among-19-male-champions-of-women-in-the-workplace-20150414-1mkltk.html
6. Quotes from G. McLachlan, address to AFL staff, 15 October 2020, provided to author.
7. 'Annual Reports – 2015 Annual Report', AFL.com.au, AFL. https://www.afl.com.au/annual-reports
8. 'AFL's fans must lead game out of Adam Goodes booing controversy, says Gillon McLachlan', Staff Writers, ABC News (Online), 31 July 2015. https://www.abc.net.au/news/2015-07-31/afl-boss-mclachlan-calls-on-fans-to-show-leadership-over-goodes/6662566
9. 'Top Indigenous figure Mick Gooda slams Gill McLachlan's leadership during Adam Goodes racism row', M. Warner, *Herald Sun*, 12 June 2019. https://www.heraldsun.com.au/sport/afl/more-news/top-indigenous-figure-mick-gooda-slams-gill-mclachlans-leadership-during-adam-goodes-racism-row/news-story/f290faf12aebaea02a9ad07260bb1bbc
10. 'Footy's indigenous radio service on brink of collapse despite reaching over 700,000 Australians', M. Warner, *Herald Sun*, 19 November 2018. https://www.heraldsun.com.au/sport/afl/more-news/footys-indigenous-radio-service-on-brink-of-collapse-despite-reaching-over-700000-australians/news-story/29270e6e03c31f2f4bebd7af1b83c602
11. 'Aboriginal leaders left "gobsmacked" by AFL operating without a Reconciliation Action Plan', M. Warner, *Herald Sun*, 18 June 2020. https://www.heraldsun.com.au/sport/afl/more-news/aboriginal-leaders-left-gobsmacked-by-afl-operating-without-a-reconciliation-action-plan/news-story/63879c2e5b6bdfffa4c014f4bb1e4830
12. 'Western Bulldogs president Peter Gordon on Good Friday footy, AFLX overlapping AFLW and more', M. Warner, *Herald Sun*, 19 March 2019. https://www.heraldsun.com.au/sport/afl/teams/western-bulldogs/western-bulldogs-president-peter-gordon-on-good-friday-footy-aflx-overlapping-aflw-and-more/news-story/09e9fe0d6fd37a3cb86bf2bd2f9b7b72
13. Interview with Dick Seddon, M. Warner, February 2019.
14. 'Fresh claims over Ross Lyon sex slur scandal set to rock AFL', S. Drill and M. Warner, *Herald Sun*, 4 May 2018. https://www.heraldsun.com.au/sport/afl/more-news/fresh-claims-over-ross-lyon-sex-slur-scandal-set-to-rock-afl/news-story/eca41724f89596d5a1a5c58ecdf2f8c8
15. 'Ross Lyon at centre of Fremantle payout over harassment claim', J. Pierik and C. Houston, *The Age*, 30 April 2018. https://www.theage.com.au/sport/afl/ross-lyon-at-centre-of-fremantle-payout-over-harassment-claim-20180429-p4zcbi.html
16. 'Fremantle Dockers sponsors issue please explain notice over Ross Lyon club culture scandal', T. Wildie, ABC News (Online), 10 May 2018. https://www.abc.net.au/news/2018-05-10/fremantle-dockers-sponsors-issue-please-explain-notice/9748878
17. 'Top lawyer: AFL investigation into Crows camp a "nonsense" that "does not pass muster"', M. Warner and R. Homfray, *Herald Sun*, 17 July 2020. https://www.heraldsun.com.au/sport/afl/teams/adelaide/top-lawyer-afl-investigation-into-crows-camp-a-nonsense-that-does-not-pass-muster/news-story/02132cbad3479cd18333771ae16f735f
18. 'Master Chef', J. Anderson, *Herald Sun*, 16 June 2018 (Print Edition).
19. 'Peter Dutton intervened in au pair visa case for AFL boss Gillon McLachlan's relative', L. Martin, *Guardian Australia*, 28 August 2018. https://www.theguardian.com/australia-news/2018/aug/28/peter-dutton-intervened-in-third-au-pair-visa-case-for-afl-bosss-relatives
20. 'McLachlan defends au pair intervention as "fair and appropriate"', R. Lewis and R. Varga, *The Australian*, 31 August 2018. https://www.theaustralian.com.au/nation/politics/peter-dutton-au-pair-saga-payback-for-wrecking-liberals/news-story/e8fbc564850678bb3da3cf24e1e7a7ce

21.    'Mark Duffield: The MCG grand final deal is nothing but a VFL relic', M. Duffield, *The West Australian*, 13 April 2018. https://thewest.com.au/sport/mark-duffield/mark-duffield-the-mcg-grand-final-deal-is-nothing-but-a-vfl-relic-ng-b88805842z
22.    Interview with Terry O'Connor, M. Warner, January 2020.
23.    'Crown Resorts 2019 Annual General Meeting', A. Demetriou, October 2019.
24.    Interview with Tim Costello, M. Warner, January 2020.
25.    'Demetriou switches from football to legal blood sport', S. Danckert, *Sydney Morning Herald*, 17 October 2020. https://www.smh.com.au/business/companies/demetriou-switches-from-football-to-legal-blood-sport-20201016-p565nf.html
26.    'Acquire Learning fined $4.5m', P. Durkin, *Australian Financial Review*, 30 May 2017. https://www.afr.com/policy/health-and-education/andrew-demetrious-acquire-learning-fined-45m-20170530-gwg1yh
27.    'Report of the Inquiry under section 143 of the *Casino Control Act* 1992 (NSW)', Volumes 1 and 2, NSW Independent Liquor and Gaming Authority, 1 February 2021. https://www.parliament.nsw.gov.au/la/papers/Pages/tabled-paper-details.aspx?pk=79129
28.    'Andrew Demetriou has only himself to blame', M. Robin, *Australian Financial Review*, 14 February 2021. https://www.afr.com/rear-window/andrew-demetriou-has-only-himself-to-blame-20210214-p572dh
29.    Interview with Bruce Mathieson, M. Warner, January 2019.

Chapter 18
1.    Interview with Peter Gordon, M. Warner, November 2020.
2.    'AFL chief medical officer Peter Harcourt cancels overseas trip as league deals with coronavirus threat', S. Landsberger and M. Warner, *Herald Sun*, 12 March 2020. https://www.heraldsun.com.au/sport/afl/more-news/afl-chief-medical-officer-peter-harcourt-headed-overseas-as-league-deals-with-coronavirus-threat/news-story/009e2d2d4bddbd9d290f248be09536f3
3.    'Inside the AFL's "war cabinet": Peter Gordon breaks down key meetings and lays out the challenges ahead', M. Warner, *Herald Sun*, 27 May 2020. https://www.heraldsun.com.au/sport/afl/news/inside-the-afls-war-cabinet-peter-gordon-breaks-down-key-meetings-and-lays-out-the-challenges-ahead/news-story/c4470fb78471e2ddbfe5f2f41b7aea32
4.    'Footy Classified', E. McGuire, Channel 9, 19 March 2020. (Video courtesy of News.com.au) https://www.news.com.au/sport/afl/afl-2020-coronavirus-updates-eddie-outlines-financial-doom-round-one-news/news-story/6fa88f62acbc16d02d2a8ef15a7478e7
5.    'AFL boss Gillon McLachlan vows AFL executive will match any pay cut the players agree to', M. Warner, *Herald Sun*, 25 March 2020. https://www.heraldsun.com.au/sport/afl/veteran-player-agent-peter-jess-believes-afl-executives-must-match-80-per-pay-cut-forced-on-players/news-story/05d3273d03fd57c06ea5a38b28b05d16
6.    'Players demand AFL opens up its financial records before agreeing to further pay changes', M. Warner, *Herald Sun*, 2 June 2020. https://www.heraldsun.com.au/sport/afl/news/players-demand-afl-opens-up-its-financial-records-before-agreeing-to-further-pay-changes/news-story/de57a10282d06635e4d0d05252805696
7.    'AFL restart plans in chaos after South Australian health chiefs reject request and extend contact training ban', M. Warner and J. Clark, *Herald Sun*, 14 May 2020. https://www.heraldsun.com.au/sport/afl/teams/west-coast/wa-clubs-have-voiced-concerns-over-relocating-to-eastern-hub-gold-coast-in-the-frame/news-story/5e74a905683c71e81438133963f041e7
8.    'AFLPA boss Paul Marsh fires back at Eddie McGuire over union attack', M. Warner, *Herald Sun*, 30 April 2020. (Video courtesy of the *Herald Sun*) https://www.heraldsun.com.au/sport/afl/news/aflpa-boss-paul-marsh-fires-back-at-eddie-mcguire-over-union-attack/news-story/b5751e1f3ab32570bfd8a538c65ce4fe
9.    'AFL find Tasmanian Government blocking their plans', R. Shaw, *The Launceston Examiner*, 27 July 2020. https://www.examiner.com.au/story/6847768/afl-display-an-asterisk-and-gall/
10.    'Eddie McGuire explains why he was partying at Gold Coast nightclub', P. Rolfe and Staff Writers, *Herald Sun*, 21 September 2020. https://www.heraldsun.com.au/news/jeff-kennet-slams-eddie-mcguire-for-partying-at-gold-coast-nightclub/news-story/25ecf960a89e49a648e9536992e998c2
11.    'Scheme for AFL fans to claim club membership fees as tax deduction labelled a "rort"', M. Warner, *Herald Sun*, 2 June 2020. https://www.heraldsun.com.au/news/victoria/scheme-for-afl-fans-to-claim-club-membership-fees-as-tax-deduction-labelled-a-rort/news-story/9ece38d9f541d8b09bca6a017f3b42fe
12.    'How a bloated AFL plans to streamline itself and shed hundreds of staff', M. Warner, *Herald Sun*, 2 July 2020. https://www.heraldsun.com.au/sport/afl/more-news/how-a-bloated-afl-plans-to-streamline-itself-and-shed-hundreds-of-staff/news-story/9c923a835f7520b547f21e400eb6d8eb
13.    'Andrew Pridham believes timing is ripe for AFL's first review in 30 years', C. Walsh, *The Australian*, 15 October 2020. https://www.theaustralian.com.au/sport/afl/andrew-pridham-believes-timing-is-ripe-for-afls-first-review-in-30-years/news-story/d52407b1f41d49bcbae026ad36a4409e

14. 'How Gillon McLachlan saved footy from coronavirus pandemic while working 18-hour days', M. Robinson, *Herald Sun*, 6 June 2020. https://www.heraldsun.com.au/sport/afl/expert-opinion/mark-robinson/how-gillon-mclachlan-saved-footy-from-coronavirus-pandemic-while-working-18hour-days/news-story/6369aacffd95613dd4d85d0c1bbde9d8

15. Interview with Bill Kelty, M. Warner, October 2020.

**Chapter 19**
1. 'Ivor Warne-Smith – Australian Football', Sport Australia Hall of Fame, Inducted on 9 December 1986. https://sahof.org.au/hall-of-fame-member/ivor-warne-smith/
2. Interview with Colin McLeod, M. Warner, December 2019.
3. Interview with Jeff Kennett, M. Warner, February 2019.
4. Interview with Richard Colless, M. Warner, February 2019.
5. Interview with Terry O'Connor, M. Warner, January 2019.
6. Interview with Graeme Samuel, M. Warner, February 2019.
7. Interview with Dick Seddon, M. Warner, February 2019.
8. Interview with Peter Scanlon, M. Warner, January 2020.
9. Interview with John Cain, M. Warner, November 2019.
10. Interview with Ron Joseph, M. Warner, January 2019.
11. Interview with David Galbally, M. Warner, November 2019.
12. Interview with Grant Thomas, M. Warner, January 2019.
13. Interview with Jeff Browne, M. Warner, February 2020.
14. Interview with Peter Gordon, M. Warner, November 2020.
15. Interview with Bill Kelty, M. Warner, February 2020.
16. 'AFL Administrative Structure Review – Findings, March 1993', D.A Crawford, AFL, March 1993. http://footyindustry.com/files/afl/Documents/AFL%20Administrative%20Structure%20Findings%20-%20The%20Crawford%20Report%20%281993%29.pdf
17. Interview with Richard Colless, M. Warner, February 2019.
18. In March 2021, under pressure from a block of presidents led by Swans boss Andrew Pridham, the AFL agreed that five club presidents (David Koch, Dale Alcock, Mark LoGiudice, Andrew Wellington and Pridham) could help select candidates to replace retiring commissioners Kim Williams and Jason Ball, however the push for an independent review of the game's governance and operations was still being resisted.
19. 'AFL internal review into Essendon investigation leaves biggest questions unanswered', M. Robinson, *Herald Sun*, 28 March 2017. https://www.heraldsun.com.au/sport/afl/expert-opinion/mark-robinson/afl-internal-review-into-essendon-investigation-leaves-biggest-questions-unanswered-says-mark-robinson/news-story/6ab5a500df7ef91bf11a1b0d352fb8df
20. 'Lawyers mock AFL Commission-led review of Essendon doping probe', S. Lane, *The Age*, 22 February 2014. https://www.theage.com.au/sport/afl/lawyers-mock-afl-commissionled-review-of-essendon-doping-probe-20140221-337pg.html
21. 'Hird refuses to stand aside', Staff Writers, ABC News (Online), 12 April 2013. https://www.abc.net.au/news/2013-04-12/i-won27t-stand-aside3a-hird/4625848
22. Interview with Jeff Browne, M. Warner, February 2020.
23. Interview with Dr Charles Livingstone, M. Warner, December 2019.
24. 'AFLPA says AFLW players who have engaged lawyers in pay dispute could have negative impact on competition', M. Warner, *Herald Sun*, 3 October 2019. https://www.heraldsun.com.au/sport/swoop/aflpa-says-aflw-players-who-have-engaged-lawyers-in-pay-dispute-could-have-negative-impact-on-competition/news-story/8c81f5743db0803c3369489de6266a1f

**Epilogue**
1. Interview with David Flood, M. Warner, January 2020.
2. 'Dean Bailey had every right to hold onto anger but capacity to forgive captured in new book', J. Ralph, *Herald Sun*, 7 December 2015. https://www.heraldsun.com.au/sport/afl/dean-bailey-had-every-right-to-hold-onto-anger-but-capacity-to-forgive-captured-in-new-book/news-story/478a89d8072213d2bca5003af2cf104d
3. *Breakfast with Bails, What a dying coach taught me about life, learning and leadership*, P. Steinfort, Melbourne, Allure Publishing, 2015, p. 159–162.

# Acknowledgements

I AM INDEBTED TO MANY PEOPLE FOR THEIR ASSISTANCE, none more than Lucy and our two boys, William and Charlie. For the sacrifice of (several) family holidays and precious weekends lost, I promise I'll pay you back. In no particular order I also want to thank Louise Adler, Sally Heath, Jacquie Brown, Vanessa Radnidge, Nic Pullen, Kate Doak, Meaghan Amor, Deonie Fiford, the team at Hachette, Steven Amendola, Drew Warne-Smith, Chris Matthews, the Class of '92, Mum, Dad, Daryl, Fiona, Gai and Rowley, Chris Tinkler, Matt Kitchin and my *Herald Sun* and 3AW colleagues. And to the countless victims, whistleblowers, industry officials and on-the-record interviewees (sadly some who have departed), thank-you for trusting me.

# Index